Praise for *Bargain Witch*

"Eager to forge a new reality, or recover an old one, with better metaphysics than the modern West? *Bargain Witch* can guide your self-initiation. It's magic, through and through."

—Susan Stryker, author of *Transgender History* and *When Monsters Speak*.

"I love this book. My only critique is that it wasn't long enough. I never wanted it to end! Reading this book is like doing a ritual with your coolest, smartest, queerest friend—it feels sexy, dangerous, and ecstatic all at once. Honestly, if you only get one book this year, get this one. Just reading it is like lobbing a molotov through the window of patriarchy: it's fun, it's educational, it's good for the world. Read it! Then go be gay and do witchcraft."

—Amanda Yates Garcia, author of *Initiated: Memoir of a Witch* and host of the *Between the Worlds* podcast

"Impeccably researched, passionately political, vast in scope, yet unfailingly intimate, *Bargain Witch* is far more than an exploration of witchcraft—it is an autobiography of consciousness. Standing with Brooke Palmieri beneath the stars at midnight, invoking the primaeval, is utterly thrilling. I loved this book."

—Dodie Bellamy, author of *Bee Reaved* and *When the Sick Rule the World*

"Reading *Bargain Witch* is like taking home a thrifted mystery box and cracking it open to discover a trove of letters from wild mages, keys to lost archives, and strange objects that combine to form the perfect spell. This book brought me into communion with writers and wizards from centuries past while offering a new way forward, a way to live a life formed from communion and collection, from being with dead writers and the living earth, from finding teachers and kin everywhere. Palmieri's debut has left me feeling enchanted and alive—a gift to witches and queers (and nerds and freaks) everywhere."

—Sam Cohen, author of *Sarahland*

Praise for *Bargain Witch*

"This book is going to become very important in some people's lives, a blueprint for the romantic life of future libertine queer witches."
—Morgan M. Page, co-author of *Boys Don't Cry* and *Framing Agnes*

"Brooke Palmieri's *Bargain Witch* is an idiosyncratic, syncretic delight. It is a deep dive into what it means to be a witch in the modern world, conjured with love, rigor, and a generosity of spirit. It draws equally on Palmieri's extensive Oxford education in literature and his time working at Treadwells, one of London's premiere magic bookshops. But Palmieri makes equal space in his theology for the Teenage Mutant Ninja Turtles and the Goosebumps books, creating a quick moving, far-ranging text that shows a witch practice that is both modern and ancient; accessible and esoteric. Palmieri never shies away from the grift, the acts of self-creation, and the always-already lost history of witchcraft. Each possible negative is explored as a positive, embracing a queer methodology and spirituality that thrums through every part of this unique collection."
—Hugh Ryan, author of *The Women's House of Detention: A Forgotten Queer History*, and *When Brooklyn Was Queer*

"*Bargain Witch* is a spellbinding triumph! Brooke Palmieri doesn't just write about magic, he channels it. With wit, wisdom, and a reverence for the fabulously freaky lineage of queer mystics, this book conjures an occult history that feels as lived-in as a dusty spellbook behind the counter of your favorite witchy thrift store. It's hilarious, heartfelt, and haunting in the best way, like a séance with your smartest, sassiest coven."
—Peaches Christ

BARGAIN WITCH

ESSAYS IN SELF-INITIATION

BROOKE PALMIERI

Published by DOPAMINE
301 N. Kenwood St, Glendale, CA 91206
www.dopaminepress.org

Covert Art: *Pony in Meditation* (1985), Steven Arnold.
Courtesy of the Steven Arnold Museum and Archives.
Layout & Design: Brooke Palmieri

ISBN: 978-1-63590-265-5
Distributed by the MIT Press, Cambridge, Mass., and London, England.
Printed in the United States of America

10 9 8 7 6 5 4 3 2

To Hekate, in all her glory.

To Beth, in all her beauty.

To you, in all your sorcery.

CONTENTS

SELF-INITIATIONS

Throughout my life I have initiated myself into the worship of witches. These self initiations have come from books, from dreams, from chance encounters; from surrender to my intuition and to the unknown. Despite the fragmentary history of witchcraft, my attraction to witches is all about continuity; it's the major continuity I've had in a life of denial and dissociation. I call myself a witch, I write of witches, I read about witches, to honor and connect with the fact that I've called myself a witch, written about witches, and read about witches, dating back to my earliest memories. Again and again, I have initiated myself into their companionship, used their wisdom to nourish my spirituality and move beyond survival to enjoyment and appreciation of the world as I have been born into it.

Amidst all of the disruptions of my life, the intuitions I have had about myself from a young age, the ways I have been stripped of or punished for them, the witch is there. My strangeness from childhood, the awareness of estrangement from everyone around me as a matter of my feminism and my queerness and my transsexuality, the grief, the loss, the loneliness and isolation, the brushes with death, the witch is there.

When I was a kid, reading about witches made me a little afraid, inviting contemplation of the dark, the dangerous, the supernatural. When I was an adolescent, reading about witches and books of magic sparked my imagination: *I want to be a witch*. As a teenager, reading about witches made me think:

That's me. My first self-initiation to Hekate, the Triple Moon Goddess of the Witches, was a low-budget but earnest ritual informed by pagan websites on the early internet. Encouraged by a girl at school, I took the craft name "Phoenix." I waited until the house was empty. It was around Halloween, by design. I lit a red candle that reeked of apple pie from Bath and Body Works, dressed in red and black, and read the Charge of the Goddess printed out from witchs-brew.com: *For behold: I have been with thee from the beginning, and I am that which is attained at the end of desire.* I asked Hekate to protect and watch over me, I asked for her love and her wisdom and felt so nervous and so ridiculous, more vulnerable than I had ever felt, the feeling of talking to a pretty girl times one thousand. That's how I know I was onto something: how could I feel so vulnerable if I was truly alone? She must have been there.

The years passed and the witch stayed with me in pop culture and in scholarship, in the friends I made and in the histories I studied, the books I read and the places I travelled. My pursuit of witchcraft and magic led me to London, an epicenter of esoteric spiritual pursuits for centuries. Then in the summer of 2016, the next level of initiation presented itself to me in the form of a job at an occult bookshop there named Treadwell's. The door to my job at the bookshop was opened in dreams; I'd first visited Treadwell's in 2007, then I started going to the shop more in 2013 when I was enrolled in grad school just around the corner, but it was only in 2016 that I started dreaming of being there. In the dream I'd walk into the shop, down the steps into the basement to the far door that lead to the storage closet, and when I opened the door, the world would unfold into a vast, painted desert at sunset— the kind of otherworldly orange that you see only in the sky and certain flowers; a dusty-rose gradient that cools into the impending indigo of evening. In the sky of this desert I could see two stars, one bright and one much fainter. "Jupiter and Saturn," I'd say, and wake up.

In my waking life I was in trouble, and in need of sanctuary; it was my Saturn return and within a month of these dreams the owner of the bookshop, a Witch Queen in her own right, said to me: *Why don't you come work here? We need the help and you've read enough about witches to do a good job.* We met in the basement to talk about it, and to my surprise I was handed a photocopied sheaf of paper. *Fill this out to the best of your ability, just write what you know about everyone here.* It was mostly blank, with names upon on it: *John Dee, Éliphas Lévi, Joseph Campbell, Samuel Liddell MacGregor Mathers, A.E. Waite, Florence Farr, Pamela Colman Smith, Margaret Murray, Dion Fortune, Robert Graves, Austin Osman Spare, Aleister Crowley, Jack Parsons, Gerald Gardner, Patricia Crowther, Doreen Valiente, Alex Sanders.* I've always been a good test taker, even pop quizzes, and here was a many-branched family tree whose members I had chosen or rejected, but in some way had learned from over the years and would continue to learn from.

Throughout my life, the wide-ranging language of witchcraft as I have encountered it—from social pariah and servant of the Devil to mystic and magician and lover of nature and animals—has been the lexicon from which I had always been able to find the words to describe something of my own experiences and desires. The witch—alive in all cultures and times, a source of infinite learning and revelation—has provided a spiritual archetype vast enough, flexible enough, to accompany me through all trials and transformations. Bringing together disparate histories of witchcraft and pagan spirituality has brought hilarity and hijinks, friendship and fullness to my life. What is a witch? What do witches do? The witch is elusive but cuts a clearer figure in the present as a syncretic spiritual seeker who desires to encounter the divine and harm none in the process. To be a witch in the present is to stitch together a spirituality from many sources: some of them about witches, some about cunning folk and wise men and women who made a living offering healing and spells, some of them ceremonial magicians influenced by other religions, Christianity, Judaism, Islam, some from archaeological records of ancient cultures engaging in pagan worship. There are many ways of being a witch, of relating to the world in its beauty and its brutality, of seeking out ecstatic communion with the divine.

To the people who visited Treadwell's day after day, asking me if I were a witch because they wanted to know if they could be one too, I'd offer one step toward self-initiation: *Have you ever lit a candle for yourself or for a loved one? Well, that's a start, you're halfway there. When you go home tonight, turn out all the lights, and light a candle for yourself. Trust that how you feel by candlelight will tell you everything you need to know. All you have to do to be a witch is want it, and however badly you want it will be badly enough.*

DIONYSUS AS A GIRL

Madness, wildness, and wandering are consistent elements of the many myths of Dionysus, also known as Bacchus, the god of ecstasy and insanity, drunkenness, dance, and drama. Dionysus is cursed from the beginning: the son of Zeus and the mortal Semele, an enraged Hera tricks young Semele when she finds out of their affair. Zeus had promised to fulfill any of Semele's desires; so, Hera encourages Semele to ask Zeus to appear as he had appeared to *her*, his wife, "that you may know, what pleasure it is to lie with a god." As if Semele could be her equal. Oathbound, Zeus indulges Semele's horny request to fuck like gods, although it seals her doom. He appears to her in all his thunderous glory, and Semele is stricken with a lightning bolt, and is either killed instantly by the electricity or by the fear of it.

Mourning her loss but desiring their offspring, Zeus grabs the unborn Dionysus and sews him up into his thigh—he calls it his man-womb—to continue gestating. After the child is born, Zeus entrusts him to Hermes to escape Hera's wrath. To disguise Dionysus, he is brought up as a girl, in girl's clothes. But forced feminization is not enough to protect him.

Hera finds out everything and continues to take her revenge by driving the infant Dionysus's caretakers Athamas and Ino out of their minds, before turning her focus on Dionysus himself. This version comes from a second century A.D. telling, but there are many more that date back centuries, with variations of anger, deception, madness, and eventually, ecstatic revels.

These revels are born alongside Dionysus himself and seem to follow him through his life: from the clashing cymbals and wild dancing baby Dionysus's caretakers use to muffle the sound of his crying so Hera won't hear, or from the vines of grapes that become wine that kid Dionysus miraculously creates while fleeing Hera's wrath by sea, or the liquor that Dionysus draws from bashing rocks with a fennel stalk to impress the other kids. Dionysus has the powers of a god, and they draw followers. His powers are no match for Hera; he must keep on the move, managing the insanity she inflicts to torment him, a punishment for his father's transgressions he can never live down. As he travels, his followers grow in number, drunk and divinely enthralled, so do the violent outbursts and outrageousness of his parties.

I was a follower of Dionysus and I believed in this road to frenzied, ecstatic spiritual understanding. I sought revelation and knowledge through overindulgence in drink and drugs, drunk with wine and song on a dancefloor with hundreds of other bodies night after night, or locked away with the good stuff to stay awake for days to laugh and flirt and come up with new embodied philosophies about why we exist with my friends. These voracious pursuits of expanded consciousness broadened my horizons and my ambitions, pushed me to new limits, but there came a point where they began to betray me into madness. And there came a point when I realized that, as a lesser Dionysus raised against my will as a girl and out of my mind with the grief of it, I was using these substances under a false pretense, ultimately to close off and numb out my spirit. Intoxicated, I had wandered into dangerous territory and realized it was time to turn back, to seek more sustainable thrills, pleasure and spiritual enrapturement through simpler means, through focusing on what I loved most about living, through pursuing it in total sobriety and letting the giddiness and psychedelic downloads come in their own time and at their own pace, borne on waves of my own breathing and body chemicals and the powerful hormones I took by the grace of the gods.

Of course, this desire to get drunk on language alone had been there for me all along, no need for intoxicants. In choosing to write of a sober magic, I still have almost too much to share in this book, whose subject is love and ecstatic communion.

BIBLIOMANCY

In August 2023 my fourteen-year period of living in London was coming to an end almost too quickly for me to keep up with, and I felt like a walking nerve ending, hypersensitive to everything I was encountering "for the last time." An old friend was passing through town and we met up for pizza. I'd known Thomas since I was nineteen and he was a grad student, and we'd kept in touch ever since when he took trips to London for research. Thomas has seen me in all my incarnations. We were reminiscing about that, how long we've known each other, how our early friendship had a fated quality that felt cinematic. It began when we passed each other as strangers on street and both turned back and looked at one another and smiled, then kept seeing each other around town, then were both cast in a play opposite one another. One day Thomas walked into the library where I worked and signed into the guest book. When I saw his name I said: "*YOU'RE THOMAS?*" He responded: "I've always wanted someone to ask me my name that dramatically!" I'm shocked because I know we've been cast together in a play, and I told him so. We're instantly friends, pouring over books together in the library, stealing away for coffee breaks. There is bibliomancy at work in our lives: we share an interest in sixteenth and seventeenth century English literature, Shakespeare and Marlowe and Milton, and we like to tell everyone about the chance encounters that lead to our meeting and pace it like a Romantic Comedy: "*Except we're GAY so like the twist is that we're into the romance of our meeting but we're not, like, romantically into each other!!!!*" Thomas, in fact, initiated me into a world of flaming homosexual erudition and camaraderie I had until that time only observed with awe and yearning.

Bibliomancy is the use of books for divination: open a book at random, to a page at random, and put your finger on a line at random, then interpret its meaning. Its "western" origins (there's also an Islamic tradition) are rooted in using only one book, the bible, for such a purpose, but the practice goes back further, before the shape of books had replaced scrolls, to ancient Rome and the *Sortes* tradition of drawing lines of text from the poetry of Virgil, and further still, back to Homer.

Sors, Sortes is Latin for "lot" as in lots cast in divination or random decision-making. As one of the characters in Lambertus Daneau's *A Dialogue of Witches* (translated into English in 1575) defines it:

> This word Sortiarius, a sorcerer, doubtlesse is derived from the more frequented Latine word Sortilegus . . . that is to say, casters of lots or tellers of fortunes . . . those who through divelish artes foretell things to come . . . The Frenchmen following the accustomable proprietie of theyre toongue, and by clipping shorter the word, out of the latin Sortilegus, have made it Sorcier . . . that among the manifolde causes wherupon men joyne & binde themselves to the divel, this hath bin the chiefest and most auncient, namely (such being the vanitie & curiositie of us al, even of nature,) to know things to come, and to foretel them also to [an]other.[1]

1 Lambertus Danes, *A Dialogue of Witches, in the Forename Named Lot-Tellers and Now Commonly Called Sorcerers* (London: R.W., 1575) sig. B7v.

The origins of the word sorcerer are tied up in this sordid divination through lot-casting—guts, bones, dice, murmurations of birds, cards, lines of poetry, pages of books.

Adjusting my perception to the divinatory power of signs and symbols in the world around me has been a lifelong, cheap and abundant source of magic. Bibliomancy has loomed large; my local library as a child, the used bookstore near my high school, and then, as an undergraduate, totally overwhelmed by the size and scope of the university library, I'd allow myself the luxury of wandering around until I felt lost, then grabbing a book off the shelves and reading it. Working at the rare book library and archive where I met Thomas only increased the spookiness of fated exposure to a random assortment of scholars and students who walked through the glass doors of the reading room to request books and papers that I wouldn't have known existed otherwise. It was a generous, expansive environment to learn whatever the gods had in store for me that day.

"But here's the thing . . . " Thomas was telling me sixteen years later, "My argument is, like, all reading is bibliomancy!"

He was right. My reading life had, in its way, been a continuous source of prophecy.

Alongside books, the pace of my life has long been impacted by the stars. Pay attention to something long enough and patterns emerge. I look to astrological information because, quite simply, the sky is the first book people tried to read and make sense of, it connects me to my most deeply rooted humanity. And using astrological timing to plan reading certain books? Even better. Ever Mercury retrograde I indulge in looking backward and re-reading at least one book I think I love. But it goes farther than that. January 21, 2023: timed with the new moon in Aquarius, I lit some candles, burned some incense, meditated for a half hour, and among other aspects of the ritual, fired off an email to a private archive through a website contact form. That felt very Aquarian, in the sense that writing lovingly to an unknown recipient through a public, open-letter digital format feels both impersonal and communal. What were the chances it would be received and read? Still, the astrological timing was harmonious: Aquarius rules my third house, which is all about communication. The dates I had proposed to visit the archive fell within Taurus season, in my sixth house of work, around the time Jupiter would be moving into Taurus, the great benefic. And maybe most importantly, the artist whose archive I was hoping to visit was Steven Arnold, a visionary queer Taurus, and I wanted to read through his writing.

My email to the privately housed Steven Arnold Archive took the form of 1) a fan letter, 2) a celebration of *Heavenly Bodies*, the documentary about Arnold I'd just seen at its London premiere in December, and 3) a description of a history book I'd been working on about queer pagan spirituality, Arnold's place in its cosmos, the long line of queer and trans witches whose spiritual path had altered my own. I didn't get a response.

Months later, by the time of the new moon in Scorpio, I was living in LA, where the archive was held, and had the idea to revive the spell. I sent another email, this time with the smirking new moon emoji and a scorpion on the subject line. I wondered what it would be like if the email made it through, since I sent it while the sun moved through my twelfth house—the house of the deep subconscious, the place of trawling up hidden beliefs and emotions and working through them behind-the-scenes, in solitude. At that time I was the writer in residence at the Huntington Library and Botanical Gardens, using the library as much as the gardens to engage in pagan worship. After sending the email, I wandered my way through the gardens to an antique statue of Abundance personified to pray that my writing and my work would increase and multiply and for my admittance into the Steven Arnold Archive to be granted to that end.

Three weeks later I got a response, after the sun had moved into my ascendant, Sagittarius. Who knows why communication spells work at the rate that they do? All I could think of at the time was that I had underestimated the spirit I wanted to cultivate in my life called Steven Arnold. I had mistakenly thought to confine him to my sixth house, when in reality it went deeper than that, having implications for my first house, my whole self. Steven Arnold didn't want to be confined to a house in which I had no planetary placements—he wanted my full attention. Sometimes you tap into the Universe, and it responds by escalating the situation.

A 1984 *Los Angeles Reader* describes Steven Arnold (1943-1994) as "one of Los Angeles' most iconiconoclastic [sic] forces." This was in a review of his ballet, *Gomorrah Borealis*, which gives a sense of both his sprawling visions and artistic capabilities, working across painting, photography, film, set, costume design, furniture building, and his friend group:

> The theatrically choreographed fashion extravaganza, billed as *Gomorrah Borealis*, was written and directed by Arnold, whose cosmic other-worldliness alluded to ancient rituals and mythical dream states. His tribal masks, pyramid-shaped headpieces, and Cocteau-like set underscored a sense of the mystical, the rites of passage that transcend temporary cultural moorings. *Gomorrah Borealis* was populated by the disciplined troops of the Los Angeles Ballet, who responded with brio to Jennifer Narin-Smith's hypnotic choreography. The entire event pivoted around a musical score culled from epic chariot films of the fifties and sixties, including *The Ten Commandments* and *Ben Hur*. The SRO crowd ranged from colorful paste-and bauble glam queens to handsome Capri-panted young men sporting tuxedo

> shirts and Egyptian eye makeup. By comparison, Parachute's fall line of simple cotton coordinates faded into the background, eclipsed by Arnold's innovative theatrics and a fascinating collection of the city's most fashionable cognoscenti.[2]

Arnold had grown up in Oakland, travelled Europe in the early sixties taking LSD regularly, then returned to live in San Francisco in 1964. In 1969, he started holding Nocturnal Dream Shows, midnight movie screenings of his own work alongside other experimental and underground films, many of them steeped in occult and esoteric imagery. The Nocturnal Dream Shows also served as a petri dish for the Cockettes' first drag shows—these were wild, witchy, gender anarchists. This wasn't the tame, toothless and peaceable kingdom of New Age hippies, but my kind of magic: drug-fueled, rabid punk ritual with intent to destroy polite society as we know it.The Nocturnal Dream Shows were how I first learned about Arnold: I saw a poster Arnold had drawn describing the program he had put together and it included a lot of my favorite artists—references to Kenneth Anger, Jack Smith, *The Passion of Joan of Arc*, Felix the Cat cartoons—who was this mysterious artist I'd never met and how did he know what I liked? Or, how had I come to like the same things without his Nocturnal Dream Shows to go to? He had this way of drawing that was both psychedelic and incredibly clean and precise, like Aubrey Beardsley writing for the *San Francisco Oracle*. Little glimpses of heaven grounded in plain black ink and crisp lines. I would soon get to see drafts of these posters in his sketchbooks.

Steven Arnold achieved a kind of cult status by the early seventies, with his films *Messages Messages* and *Luminous Procuress*. He was invited by Salvador Dalí to live and work in Spain where he rubbed shoulders with other darlings of the

2 William Franklin, "'Gomorrah Borealis Lights Up the Palace,'" *The Los Angeles Reader*, July 6, 1984.

counterculture: Ultra Violet, Amanda Lear, David Bowie, Mick Jagger. His art—whether in film, photography, sculpture, or interior decoration in his various houses and studios—embodies a trippy maximalism that channels occult iconography through low camp materiality and elevates it to high camp surrealism. Picture it: a bulk lot of cheap rubber seahorses painted gold and nailed onto the sumptuous cosmic assemblage for the background, thrifted fabrics and costume jewelry on the model in the foreground of one of his tableau vivant. Like me, Steven Arnold was a total bargain witch, making magic from whatever he could get his hands on, enjoying the entire worlds made from scratch and on a budget.

Arnold's transformation of trash to treasure manifests the same kind of alchemy I try to bring about in my daily life. Beyond that, I'm spellbound by Arnold's knack for cultivating a forest from trees, moving from little, meticulous assemblages to build big, unified visions that feel like they bleed off the edges of whatever scene or set and extend his reality into everyone else's. I accept people who want change from within, who want to reform things, like lawyers and public servants. But it could never be me, I'll always choose the weirdos who do everything they can to make their own scene. Or at least open a door for you to enter, if you want, into someplace else. If you get it. As Arnold wrote of his own practice around 1989:

> I honestly think that many of my pictures are so brilliant that 99% of the folks just don't get it—It's why I am just forgetting about doing an opera or a film because they won't get it—So do it in Tableaux—Some still get it and I get it doing them! I pray my light will shine and the kids will get it—and go for it—no point doing "it" in the theatre or film—too expensive and too many compromises—I've found just the right way to propigate [sic] my vision in a pure form Thank you God!

I'm one of those kids. Arnold built new worlds, and struggled in all the ways building new worlds causes problems: no money, no recognition or widespread understanding. Eventually, he settled in Los Angeles and created Zanzibar, his studio/salon at 3316 Beverly Boulevard, where he spent the rest of his life world-building and expanded from film to music videos, plays, operas, ballets, and above all, his photography practice. When he died from complications related to AIDS in 1994, he left behind a vast body of work and behind that, an even bigger mass of sketchbooks, correspondence, and other materials from which his art was conceived, edited, plotted out, prior to its execution. These are the materials I was burning to encounter, nearly thirty years after his death.

Vishnu Dass, the director of *Heavenly Bodies* and current guardian angel of Steven Arnold's archive, came to occupy this fate in a series of psychedelically-fueled convergences. Shortly after we hugged hello for the first time, he initiated me into the collections, and we talked and swapped stories over the course of the next three hours as I looked through Steven Arnold's notebooks. Vishnu's apartment is set up as a sacred space: a place for meditation and deep contemplation, decked out with crystals, statues of deities, visionary paintings from different places and times, old family photographs. He describes Steven Arnold as his roommate; Steven has his own bedroom filled with paintings he made, self-portraits, portraits made by his friends, mannequins, costumes, and a large, old papier mâché head of a clown called Zanzibar he found at a flea market. Vishnu pulled out dozens of Steven's sketchbooks for me to look at, from his senior year of high school (1959) until his death in 1994. I hadn't asked for them, but he thought this is what I should see, and he was right. This was a special experience of bibliomancy, books picked *for* me to consult—singular, irreplaceable copies documenting acid trips, intrigues, a life dedicated totally to art.

In addition to being a major source of arcane, magical wisdom, these sketchbooks are a key to Arnold's work: every day, he would wake up and put his dreams and visions and ideas on paper, first thing. These sketches were then shaped into the works of art they would become: photographs, sets, the interior decoration of his studio. There was too much for me to look through everything on this first visit, especially as my consultation was paced by the ideal conditions of conversation. *Festina lente*: "make haste slowly," a popular antique-to-renaissance scholarly slogan visualized in old woodcuts and engravings as a butterfly on top of a crab, or a mast and sail on the back of a tortoise, or a dolphin wrapped around an anchor. I'm always looking for new ways to *make haste slowly* as a reader, as a writer, as a witch.

I thought of Thomas's words again when faced with a table full of Steven Arnold's sketchbooks, a room full of his knick-knacks, and not enough time to possibly look through them all. My life as a witch had been shaped by bibliomancy—the books I found from *Goosebumps* to Anne Rice to Leslie Feinberg to Marsilio Ficino on the early internet, the books that found me, the books I overlooked or forgot about or couldn't track down, the books I bought but didn't pick up to read until years later. Archives can be repositories for divination too. At the same time that they could reveal something to me about Steven Arnold's past, they could produce some vision about my future, about who I'd become from knowing him better. We could, for a moment in time, enjoy a shared fate. I had to trust that whatever would come, would come, and I just needed to be open to reading it. Here was bibliomancy in a wild and way-out collection of materials in the magical apartment of a stranger. I opened the first notebook to hand without thinking and received my first message from the beyond that Arnold had written in the Netherlands in 1964:

> Take a deep breath & be the pillar of strength your [sic] expected to be—The power is there—you need only call it out —

> WITH FORCEFUL conviction sustain THAT ENERGY & CREATE THE BEAUTIFUL FILMS THAT ARE TO BE YOUR LIFE—THEY ARE QUITE MAD AND unexplainable— THEY are VOICES OF YOUR SOUL—LET THEM OUT magnificently on FILM to baffel [sic] and delight a world OF young eyes and minds
> that intuitive magic is your key to productivity—

And immediately, a page from Arnold's 1967 journal told me: "IN THE SACRED QUIET SPOT / SIT AND LOOK IN / EVOLVE / GROW / READ WRITE / PAINT."

I took this generous and auspicious offering from Arnold home with me and work on a different book, a new book, the one that needed to be written most urgently: *Bargain Witch*, a record of the witches I have been and I have met, of the freaky spiritual underpinnings of my survival and enjoyment of life.

Reading is initiatory, writing is incantatory. I think that is, implicitly, always the case—readers are initiated into the knowledge hidden between the covers of the books they choose, and it alters their reality. Writers make marks that summon the attention of readers or invoke and converse with the supernaturally nonhuman in the form of dead people, deities, and dead people who have become deities. Channeled text and found text are inextricably linked to theories of creativity in all places and times. The major model for writing in the west—once again, the bible—is a centuries-long collaboration between the collective hallucination of a god and a litany of human scribes copying down that god's manifestations, acts, rules.

Or look earlier: the oldest known poems from the high priestess of Inanna, Enheduanna, are prayers attempting to establish communications with what we know as the planet

Venus. No text from Innana herself survives in response, but Enheduanna interprets all the good things that happened in her life as the other side of the dialogue. As a polytheist and an animist I want to set the bar high for myself and conceive of all reading as initiatory; any text can be ripe for self initiation. Sometimes it's a real challenge, a guided meditation from bureaucracy up to heaven: studying the California driver's handbook, struggling with taxes, stress-reading about healthcare enrollment. Following the text of my hormone prescription to a vast cosmic force that defies all reason or explanation.

I want reading to take me to some new limit; I don't want reading to blot or distract from my reality, but to enhance it, guiding me to new limits and articulations of living that I couldn't possibly have conceived of without books to lead me there. I can experience enhancement for cheap or free: pulp paperbacks, books lent by friends, library books. And I am in good company: I have drooled in many a witch's library, and agree with the great occultist A. E. Waite, self-identified "bibliomaniac," when he writes in an essay that "the Unknown World is ever at our doors, and that all things ultimately issue into the unknown. If this be true of every inquiry in general, it is true in particular of those which connect with literature and its substitutes." Later in the same essay he also says, "The best impressions concerning certain literatures are not derived actually by reading them," which I interpret in keeping with my own bibliomania: I can go wild for books, provided reading them gives me permission to go even wilder in life.[3]

Witchcraft itself is an exercise in book collecting as part of the work of extreme spiritual thrill-seeking, cosmic connection, spellcraft, and knowledge recovery. Witchcraft doesn't depend on books; it simply enlivens them and is embellished in turn. Books are portals and props for entrance into the unknown. The

---

3 A.E. Waite, "Dealings in Bibliomania," *Horlick's Magazine and Home Journal for Australia, India, and the Colonies* 1.4 (15 April 1904), 405-16.

cult of books leads to the occult at all levels of the practice and in many traditions: from the initiation of witches by signing the devil's book in blood, to the day to day use of books to record recipes, spells, and conversations with angels and demons, astronomical tables and botanical knowledge, to the more elitist practices of ceremonial magic, suffused with visions of the delivery of rare volumes bound in precious metals and crystal-encrusted covers. You can't understand witchcraft without its relationship to books, books that survive, books that have been destroyed, books that have been misread, and books that have never existed in the first place. Of course, this argument is just another way of justifying my life choices, which in turn reinforces my belief that books are magical vessels because I have almost exclusively chosen to work in places filled with them, among people who agree with me.

Reading has many modes and leaves behind many kinds of traces, but the mode of reading I'm always trying to enter comes from this lust for magic from books. I *want* reading to feel like finding my own name in the book of the devil, like inheriting a spellbook full of tried-and-true sex magick rituals, like looking into a crystal bearing a vision of the library of King Solomon which contains a lost, exquisite book that will change my relationship to the whole world. Ultimately these desires make me great at selling books. Applying these skills to a retail job lets me share my obsessions with others, and also have constant exposure to potential new obsessions: more books! Working at a bookshop was both a supreme expression of my spiritual vocation and a way to scrape together a salary with flexible hours. At the same time, doing this work at this particular bookshop, Treadwell's, opened me up as a reader, and cracked open my reading capacities to the group consciousness that forms from shared readings and sharing ideas as acts of love and spiritual connection.

I prefer the moments when reading is explicitly initiatory and writing is incantatory, so: books on witchcraft, books on magic. It's just more honest. I don't want to read writing that pretends it's not possible to be transformed, although I can work with that material, bend it to my purposes. *Magic*, a fourteenth-century English word for the art of creating marvels and miracles that can change the world. Squeezed in between my own early-twenty-first century context of dissociation as lost time and dissociation as endless imaginative potential, I want books to be marvels and miracles. I want this book to be an exercise in providing the raw material of bibliomancy, to be magic, to feel fated, to be a marvel and a miracle.

GO TO THE STONES

I needed to spend time among ancient standing stones, and I knew I couldn't go to Stonehenge. This was all thanks to the witches in my life. Stonehenge is too famous, they told me, so a visit could never be casual. And visitors couldn't touch the stones, whether it was among thousands of people there for the solstice or paying £60 to get the "VIP experience" with a group of thirty people that allowed to spend time within the actual circle. I'd done a cheaper version of that as a tourist years before and it was amazing but limited. The English Heritage website recommended: "If you wish to meditate during your visit, please be aware that there will be up to thirty people in your group, so may wish to consider booking the entire session." I didn't have £1,800 to drop, which I guess was a good thing, because I am bad enough with money to have spent it that way.

Luckily the UK and parts of Europe offer many cheap opportunities to commune with huge stones that bear an overwhelming feeling of significance in their placement, the embodiment of heavy presence. I longed for that presence, something older that tapped into the wisdom of a timescale beyond my human experience, but not beyond my appreciation. It had been less than a month since my mentor Lisa Jardine had died, and I needed to get away from London to grieve.

Stone offered me comfort everywhere I went; the cemetery in Nunhead, where I walked my dog every morning; Bunhill cemetery of radical thinkers where I went to take grave rubbings and speak to the ghosts of seventeenth century dissenters and their visionary heir, William Blake; in the Victorian extravagance of Brompton. All of London is a gravesite, but these are the places of deep earth magic I walked in as the reality Lisa's impending death sank in. Lisa was my mentor, my advisor, my friend, and something of the parental figure I didn't know I'd needed. She called me her apprentice, she called me her family.

I'd had months to see her and say my farewells as she grew weaker, we both knew this return of cancer would be the last. In the direct aftermath of her death I'd walk to St. Paul's Cathedral and sit in silence and pray and write sad poetry to copy out later in my journal with titles like, "My grief is my good fortune." Lisa was an atheist, but she loved the cathedral as a work of art and mathematical genius. She'd been a math prodigy as a child but had turned to the humanities, and among many books had written a biography about St. Paul's architect, Sir Christopher Wren. Something that fascinated her about Wren was his traumatized turn to work in stone. Wren's attraction to the medium was an attempt to create works of stable and lasting beauty, having survived a childhood during the English Civil Wars and years of violent upheaval in the 1640s, outbreaks of plague, and the Great Fire of London in 1666, which destroyed an earlier, wooden incarnation of the cathedral. In a world engulfed in flames, he set his sights on working with tougher stuff, and what better than the oldest tools the earth had to offer?

Wren's scientific experiments were grounded in his career in stone, his vocation as an architect, his interest in the (sacred) geometry of building space. He had been a founding member of the Royal Society, a social experiment in coordinating scientific experimentation and knowledge-sharing across the emerging disciplines of the time. Isaac Newton was a member, whose gravitational laws (and alchemical studies) changed how one might contemplate the universe. Robert Hooke was a member, whose experiments with the newly invented microscope made visible a trippy world of teeming life once completely invisible to the naked eye. John Aubrey was a member, whose interest in history, archeology, and antiquities of the British Isles led him to scientifically survey what he called the *Templa Druidum*, or the "Druid Temples" at Stonehenge and Avebury, written up in his *Monumenta Britannica.* Perception of space, light, time, and matter was changing dramatically for those who studied it in the closing decades of the seventeenth century, the period in history Lisa and I were both drawn to—we had met one another through our shared passion. During this period, everything had been miraculously changed in scale against a backdrop of unprecedented bloodshed and destruction: total crisis. It was a time of seeking out the miraculous and mysterious in order to try to make sense of it.

Sitting in St. Dunstan's Chapel, within the cathedral, I understood the awe Lisa had experienced among the stones there. My immediate impulse in grieving her had been to go to the places she loved or where we spent time together, and to seek out the writing of the seventeenth century virtuosos she had dedicated her life to understanding. She loved the voracious intellects of these men but never abandoned herself or her politics in pursuit of that love, and never conflated herself with her subject matter. In an interview from 1993 she said: "The bottom line is that I can never be universal man, so I don't actually want to be called a Renaissance figure because that's always universal man. What I am is an absolutely typical representative of intellectual curiosity in the late twentieth century and of a passionate commitment to change."[4] I had savored what there was to learn from her and her generation of feminist scholars; I had thought that my life's work would be among these people, but when she died, I realized that I would have to put that dream to rest too.

Sitting in the chapel, speaking to Lisa's ghost, reading one of her favorite universal men, Erasmus, gave me language to

4 Nicolas Tredell "In Conversation with Lisa Jardine" *Poetry Nation Review* 20.4 (April 1994).

describe my sense of loss. My favorite work by Erasmus was *De Copia Verborum ac Rerum*, which translates to, "On the Abundance of Words and Things," something of a textbook that gives lists of different ways to say the same thing, like a thesaurus, but for Latin phrases. I was and am all about copiousness, maximalism. But I noticed for the first time when revisiting it at St. Paul's that the longest, most passionate display of copiousness in the book is when Erasmus gives the reader over two hundred ways of missing a lost friend, or simply expressing the depth of friendship to a living friend: *Always, as long as I live, I shall remember you.*

I shall myself be delivered to Death before I consign you to oblivion.

I will forget my own name before I forget so rare a friend.

And my favorite: *I will change the world more easily than this mind that remembers you.*

This outpouring of loyalty written over five centuries ago guided me through the first days of bewildering loss. But I wanted more, a cathedral of my own to contain my grief. If Lisa had always been a little more scientific, like Robert Hooke and Christopher Wren, I'd always been a little more mystic, like John Aubrey and the side of Isaac Newton that was gay and into alchemy. Like a flash of lightning, I thought: I must go to the standing stones, to mourn in my own way.

The cheapest way for me to get to them was to make for Avebury, where I'd never been, and where the stone formations are thought to predate Stonehenge by a thousand years. I wanted to approach the stones by foot, so I took the bus from London to Devizes, a medieval market town where I'd booked a room for a few days in a bed-and-breakfast run by an older man who had spent his retirement training himself to walk on hot coals. He showed me to my tiny room but there was no banter, he dove right in: "I walk on hot coals for charity, but I began as a way to train myself to walk through the fire. I'd just survived cancer, but my whole life I'd been walking through fire. Doing it really changes you, it changes me every time."

Lisa had just died of cancer, and I sought the stones in part because I wanted to contemplate something vaster than my emotions. I hadn't considered the fact that everyone I encountered in the surrounding villages did too. There was no banter among strangers here, only deep sharing.

My welcome to the town was warm, a fire lit in every pub. I was recognized as a stranger, dressed in black, and caused intrigue as to why I'd chosen the middle of November to visit. The choice of the timing, clearly without hope for fair weather, and outside of any Pagan or Christian holiday, appealed to the people who'd rejected the city to be near ancient mystery day in and day out. It was the setting of a folk horror movie without the horror; people who might not identify as Pagan, or even as folk, but whose lives were deeply implicated and affected by the magic of place, in the long shadow cast by the standing stones.

I barely encountered anyone while walking the countryside. Every day it rained, every day the sun set earlier. I spent a lot of time tramping alone in the rain and waning light: to Avebury to the hulking stones and to sit in the stone circle; to the Neolithic tombs at the Long Barrow; to Savernake Forest to see the thousand-year-old Big Belly Oak; to Pewsey Village to see the White Horse cut into the hillside, since there would be no crop circles that time of year. Each night my clothes dried by the radiator. I'd brought with me a copy of Ursula LeGuin's *Earthsea* series and was reading it for the first time—astonished at how I had read her Sci-Fi but missed *this*? I wished I had read the books as a kid but felt equally thankful that the trajectory of my life had saved the experience of savoring it for such a place of pilgrimage. And I was thankful for her cosmology of magic as the remembering and mastery of ancient language, repeatedly described through Ged the wizard picking up a pebble and calling it by its true name: *Tok.*

I wondered what the true names of the stones at Avebury were, and then, what their names were when they were transported to this place thousands of years ago. The question of naming, and of a name invoking the magic of one's true nature, was a way to pursue a practically timeless spiritual question that has fascinated me my whole life: the idea of a soul in all things, which ultimately unites all things. I had skimmed the ancient Greek philosophers that argued about this idea of an underlying spirit animating the universe: what was it comprised of? Where did it come from? How did divine interconnectedness come to be? And to my understanding still, whether belief in this force could be described as pantheism, or animism, or pantheistic animism, it remained one of the most provocative and stunningly beautiful ideas born of humankind. There were times when it was a challenge—it's hard to see the World Soul on a rainy morning commute—and there were times it came easily, as here, marching through the rain down dirt roads that have held foot traffic for millennia.

The most dramatic entry or exit point to the stone circles of Avebury is through walking down what's known as West Kennet Avenue to the south of the circles, a path flanked by hulking pairs of stones that leads to another area known as the Sanctuary. The stones there were slick with rain but I could touch them, lean against them, sit beside them on my tarp when there was a break in the rain to sip tea from my Thermos and catch my breath.

This path led to the West Kennet Long Barrow, an ancient place of burial. Ducking and walking into the long barrow itself, inside the tunnel there is a profound silence that muffled all outside noise, a silence so dense that it spoke to me: *We have always mourned our dead, and made a monument of death, to better move through our grieving and pledge our remembrance.* I don't know how much time I lost there, only that I emerged to a darkening gray sunset. Nearby the entrance stood a cairn, a pile of stones with different meanings, but commonly made by wayfarers and ramblers to mark a useful point of their journey, another kind of remembrance. Among the eons of funeral rites that surrounded me, I was grateful to partake in this one with strangers—to make a mark meant for the living. I found a stone to add to the pile, then turned to return to Avebury. That was all there was to the ritual: to walk in the rain, to let myself cry, prostrate myself before the stones, descend into the grave, add a little pebble to a heap, and retrace my steps back. From the pub, I hitchhiked back to Devizes.

The whole of Avebury is situated inside a large stone circle. Within that circle, there are two others. Archeologists have noted that these areas are free from the "mess" of many early settlements: the animal bones, flint tools, and ancient debris of everyday Neolithic life, suggesting the area held some sanctity and was set apart by its creators, whoever they were. Like Stonehenge, there is much pleasure to be had in diving deep into the wide world of theories about what this place meant to its creators and the generations of descendants. Our contemporary moment is one of centuries-old embeddedness in total uncertainty.

I trust that we are not meant to know for a reason: the stones, calls sarsens, refuse all human narratives, but their presence is so full of vibrance that the experience of moving among them is enough. They freely offer the chance to grasp that there is meaning beyond human meaning, wealth beyond human value and necessity, time beyond human lifespans, and that feels miraculous enough. Walking among the stones, I've never gotten closer than feeling like the ant by the highway in the paradox about alien life: aware that something momentous is happening, but unable to perceive what, how, or why. I felt no more enlightened than the sheep grazing and shitting among the stones, my genetic makeup and my lifespan closer to them than all else. And this was the finest gift of my grieving, to feel finite and expansive at the same time, ignorant and aware in the right measure, open to accepting the earth's power that's beyond my imagination, open to taking up my own tiny place in its story. Every death is a rebirth, whether or not I can perceive it, but this time I knew, returning to London, that everything had changed, and my grief was giving way to a willingness to go deeper into the magic I found at the stones, magic that was all around me.

OUR LADY OF GLORIFIED RETAIL

The area Treadwell's Books was nestled in was a crossroads for magic dating back centuries. Such places of spiritual significance are ultimately non-denominational in their magnetism; years of layered associations and experiences give way to centuries of beliefs and traditions across a range of practices. It was a psychedelic experience to sit in any bench near the shop and consider all that had come before: Bronze Age bridges and mounds, Roman temples, walls and city gates, Anglo-Saxon cemeteries, Danish occupation, French occupation, rebellion and revolt, natural disaster. I imagined the map of London as a network of cobwebs made by different species of spiders connecting little villages grown thick and strong with use and movement, ever-expanding in their influence, hungry for more to get caught in the tangle of its streets and worship its gods through offerings of spirit, labor, or libations.

The past one hundred years alone had been rife with esoteric activity. We were located between a convergence of four areas synonymous with a magical, queer, and criminal underworld (called Bohemia when rich people were into it): Soho, Covent Garden, Bloomsbury, Fitzrovia. The occult was hidden in plain view at every street corner: the signs of old pubs like *The Rising Sun* and *The Wheatsheaf*, the ornate glass and mirrors of *The Fitzroy Tavern*; the architecture of the Freemasons' Hall and churches designed by Hawksmoor; the globally pillaged antiquities of the British Museum just around the corner, where I could visit likenesses of just about any deity I could dream of (and many that I couldn't) on my lunch break. I could draw a Tarot card and find its incarnation in the landscape: a cornice with three coins, a relief with blind Justice and her scales, the lion of Strength to subdue or unleash, the holy grail or ace of cups. Star, Sun and Moon; the graves of plague victims marked to represent Death and Final Judgment. The history of magical commerce ran deep here; there were other famed shops run by lifelong occult practitioners with famous customers: Watkins Books, with its association with Madame Blavatsky and Aleister Crowley; the Atlantis Bookshop, frequented by both Gerald Gardner, father of Wicca, and Ross Nichols, father of Druids. All around the core esoteric bookshops there was a glut of used bookstores that supported us in one way or another: places to find rare and out-of-print books on counterculture, folklore, and history.

We were tucked away on a quiet street around the corner from an old sunken garden where I'd eat lunch. At some point our building itself had housed a publisher of weird, esoteric texts: I found a 1964 edition of artist and occultist Katherine Maltwood's *A Guide to Glastonbury's Temple of the Stars*, with Treadwell's address on the imprint. The *Guide* was a book exploring the topography of Glastonbury and reading ancient myth into it, plotting the routes one could walk through the twelve zodiac signs she believed had been etched into the landscape by ancient peoples. It was a mix of artist's intuition and lifelong interest in Goddess spirituality, theosophy, freemasonry, Buddhism, and Arthurian legends. There was an analogy in the way I could read London, the magic of its landscape, the signs in the streets. Our street had exactly the kind of vibe to make such a synthesis feel possible: there was bistro lighting and outdoor dining at a place called *The Life Goddess*, and a few pubs where many a moot had happened over the years. A moot is a pagan meet-up where you can meet practitioners willing to talk shop and answer questions. Moots had become rare, but our bookshop grew to serve that need over the years, as a meeting place for young and old, initiated and interested.

Different magical groups would meet to use our basement: "Private Event" blotted out on our calendar was the sign for magical dealings. When I got the job at the bookstore, I was told that employees were expected to maintain "excellent astral hygiene," like those signs in restaurant bathrooms that read "employees must wash hands." It was important that the downstairs space, especially, was vacuumed every morning, whether or not anyone was using it, and purified with incense and banishing rituals regularly. Once a month a group of Druids would meet there, nodding and smiling as they padded past me in their hiking boots and cargo pants. Occasionally, one would walk with the aid of an intricately carved staff. Mostly they brought tea and cookies, and had a gentle discussion, leaving behind a little cardboard box with pound coins collected in donation. Sometimes a Thelemite we knew would work down there, but he'd been interrupted while invoking demons too frequently to use the space often; and besides, the Gnostic Mass was held in an event space over a vegetarian restaurant in Vauxhall. Then there were a few covens that met, as well as classes for young witches without a coven to learn more. There were workshops on goddess worship and scrying, Tarot and trance, and a few private rituals I took part in. In such a swirl of different prayers and invocations, I would come to see the importance of astral hygiene: banishing malefic spirits, working with cleansed and smudged objects, properly opening and closing the circle.

There were a few ways you might be drawn to the bookshop if you weren't already looking for it: a big, bright window display changed with the pagan wheel of the year—solstices, equinoxes, Beltane, Lammas, Samhain, Imbolc—or with juicy new publications by witches we knew. Each season had color patterns and magical items we'd incorporate into the display, taking silk altar cloths from a trunk where they were stored in the basement: reds, greens, blues, yellows, purples, black and silver and gold, depending on what we needed. Adding brooms, a sword, chalices, candles, lanterns, as needed. If that didn't grab your attention, there was a table out front with books for £1—bibliomancy for a bargain. We had devotees to that £1 table who'd buy its contents by the armful.

To the immediate right of the door was a community noticeboard, where people could leave fliers about magical events, businesses, and projects. The first bays of shelving contained regional histories and studies of England, Scotland, Wales, and Ireland—no magic at first, more history, moving into spiritualities of ancient cultures from there with an emphasis on Europe: Greece, Italy, and Mediterranean Europe, Northern and Germanic Europe, and Scandinavian Countries.

To the left were sections on folklore, mythology, anthropology, and theology. It was only once you reached the nearby checkout counter that you could really start to see the heart of the shop's holdings: a table of new publications and journals; a section for small, esoteric publishers (Scarlet Imprint, Fulgur Press, Three Hands Press, Ouroboros Press). Opposite the counter, books on witchcraft, Wicca, and rare books. The broad selection of esoteric, occult, and counter-cultural books at the shop offered something of a definition of contemporary witchcraft: it was a sum of many parts compiled by the intuition of the individual, a composite spiritual path drawn not only from engagement with documents naming and persecuting people as witches, but many other types of magical workings: from fortune tellers and magicians-for-hire, to cunningfolk and their remedies and recipes, freemasons and secret societies, and pagan civilizations and their myth cycles spanning the globe.

There was a reason that the shop required something of an outer-chamber initiation before getting to the goods—grimoires, books expressly about Wicca and the longer history of witchcraft—and that was the range of people who entered it, some of whom did not come in perfect love and trust. The surge in chic, media-friendly witches in pop culture and fashion did not alter reality for occult practitioners on the ground any more than trans visibility in Hollywood has made it any safer for us in the streets. Both realities cultivate dangers for the under-resourced—in my case, overlapping dangers. The truth about being a witch that anyone with Christian baggage will balk at the word. And many with Christian damage view their trouble from a Christian viewpoint, their joys and sorrows cast as a battle between good and evil, God and the Devil. Working in a shop with a window display of books about witchcraft and pagan gods is an open invitation to these people, many of whom are hurt or suffering in some way. A wounded person will reach for the nearest thing; trauma isn't eloquent, it drags you back to the scene of your horror and helplessness—it's time travel. And I get it. Of course traumatized people will think they are being pursued by demons, possessed or cursed by the devil. Looking for concrete proof of those explanations for struggle, grief and trauma, led people to our shop—a place they could take out their pain on, or blame as its cause.

People would enter the shop and threaten us with a burning at the stake; people would enter the shop and accuse us of harming children; people would become unhealthily fixated with the shop owner and look for her. They would call us, email us, relentlessly post on social media. People would look for their ex-girlfriend or ex-boyfriend at the shop—*She was a witch.* People would threaten to call the police on us, people would send letters to us promising eternal damnation. People would come to the shop in search of abusers who they'd claim as demons, devils, witches: *You're all devils, he must be here too.* Someone once manipulated a picture of the shop to look as if it had been set on fire and posted it repeatedly on social media, tagging us. Others would send newspaper clippings about recent witch hunts that had resulted in murder. People would enter the shop afraid, convinced they were under psychic attack, in need of help to lift a hex or curse. *I am sorry, we're a bookshop, that isn't a service we can provide.* People would want to steal or damage books as a passive-aggressive act of courage against the evil they thought we traded in. Or people would come in to forcefully sell us their self-published or homemade items—works written from a bad place, with ideas about witchcraft and religion that we did not want to trade in. One woman tried to sell us a bunch of ceremonial swords from the trunk of her car, whose provenance she would not attest to. *We are not dealing with used magical items at the moment, only books.* Men would come in a little too interested in Nazis and the occult, or Charles Manson and mind control. I would have to tactfully turn them away—*We do not carry books that espouse a magic as the subjugation of others. Try Amazon.*

These varying levels of distress were all visible—people were suffering, and I did not have the capacity or training to help them. I knew I could never resort to the police. Nor could I let things get out of hand to the extent that a bystander would intervene in a misguided attempt to help (that had happened at least once). All I could do was try to be compassionate, short-circuit the conversation, remain steadfast that the answers they were looking for would not be found here—the evil they sought was not part of the shop. All I could do was de-escalate: ask them if I could get them a glass of water, if there was a friend we could call for help. Give them the websites and phone numbers of crisis hotlines. The magic of the shop and my own belief in the transformative power of reading had to be subdued again and again: *We are only a bookstore. We only sell books, there is no harm in books.* Despite this visible suffering—ultimately a failure of the healthcare system—and despite occasionally working alone at the shop, I never felt afraid. I could remain steady. I could maintain an environment of calm for those in the shop.

⊛

Working magic by candlelight or moonlight creates a similar bodily reaction for me—of being in a dangerous situation. My heart races, sometimes the hair stands up on the back of my neck, I'll feel cold, and then hot. When this happens I feel like the magic is working—I'm getting down to a deeper, more ancient array of involuntary expressions, physical intuitions it sometimes takes my mind a little while to catch up with. I'm connecting with a vastness so gigantic that the only rational reaction *is*, at first, fear, as well as wonder. I remember in sixth grade, in preparation for holy confirmation, we had to pick one of the seven gifts of the Holy Spirit to study and write about. I picked *wonder and awe in fear of the Lord.* I was fascinated by the entanglement of emotions, that wonder could also provoke a holy terror. I felt that way at times, in the woods, or at night: how appreciation of beauty could turn to fear very quickly.

As for the other gifts of the spirit—wisdom, understanding, counsel, fortitude, knowledge, piety—whatever! I longed for extreme experiences in the dreary neighborhood I grew up in. The final gift of awe felt the most far out, the most un-fake-able, the most paradoxical, the coolest. I wanted to feel that way so badly. I was beside myself with excitement to be confirmed in the Catholic Church—the final sacrament of initiation, in which I begged the Holy Spirit to dowse me in tongues of flame. I prayed so fervently. I wanted to feel awe and fear as flames shot through my body and produced a gift of tongues. But the moment I was blessed with chrism, nothing happened. I wasn't sure who to blame; at that age, my parish and its congregants had already begun to appear to be a bunch of depressed hypocrites. Parents who bullied their children, children who bullied each other. Everyone hated dykes and faggots and I was a little of both in my way. It was a place of mean gossip, scarcity mentality, spiritual blockage. I knew that wonder and terror could be real, that the fire was out there somewhere in the world. I just had to find it.

There were times when I felt that way in ritual, and there were times I felt that way in retail. I could tell by the way people entered into the shop—my bodily alert system went off when something was wrong, when danger was afoot. Like ritual, in retail there was nothing to do but listen to myself. I could thank my body for giving me its excellent intuitive information—*Something is not right here, there is trouble*—and remain calm, collected. I used the architecture of the shop to anchor me: the checkout counter was about ten feet in front of the door, so I could clearly see, make eye contact, and greet anyone who came in. Some people were shy or distracted, that's fine; I didn't need to make eye contact to know if they were in some kind of psychic distress. The next step, if something seemed wrong, was to *stand up*. Standing changed the energy of the room, made me feel tall, strong, grounded. I would stand, and sometimes that was enough: they would startle, quickly browse the first shelf or two without really looking, then turn around and leave.

If they didn't, I would approach to say hello directly, ask if there was anything I could help with. That was to keep them from coming too deeply into the shop, which was basically a long room with an office in the back, and stairs going down to the basement where there were more secondhand books, our Tarot room, and that large event space carefully maintained for ritual. When people are troubled by sorrows that are old and abstract, they look to make their troubles feel more real, to find them in the world around them. My goal was to give these people nothing to find and nothing to remember us by. Keeping these souls close to the exit, shepherding them out, impressing upon them that there was nothing for them here, prevented their energy from lingering too long.

How to introduce the spirit of the shop that aided in this work: Lady Treadwell was definitely a *she*, and her presence was felt as a kind of ambient warmth and protection. Most of the cultural touchstones portraying "buildings as characters" either involve malevolent hauntings, or projections of mental illness, but she was neither. I started my job in midsummer, and she directly addressed me for the first time around Yule: I was given a Solstice bonus, £200, and Our Lady had signed the greeting card that came with it. Her warmth and generosity soothed my spirit, it felt good to feel cared for during a difficult time of the year. Then I stumbled upon an object consecrated to her presence, nesting in a room I didn't spend much time in, as old as the shop itself and dating back to its first location. I recognized her right away, because I had already seen this incarnation in a dream. *It is a pleasure to finally meet you—our personal Goddess*, I knelt to her incarnation in greeting, I kissed her but was sworn to secrecy: that I could not divulge its appearance or location to strangers. In this sense, to work with Our Lady of Treadwell's required me to fulfill what is known as the four corners of the Witches Pyramid, dating back to the nineteenth century writings of Éliphas Lévi: *To dare, to will, to know, and to keep silent.* I kept my silence, and she kept me safe.

Having our own personal shop goddess reminded me of an earlier time in college that had informed my patchwork spiritual practice. This was in a Latin class. I wasn't great at learning languages, I'd never immersed myself enough, only used their study to dissociate a little, to avoid things by diving into an excess of etymology, histories of words that grabbed me. I realized how bad my early education had been in grammar; I didn't really understand parts of speech, so I had trouble learning it in language class. There was a lot of shame around that, shame hiding an even greater shame. In this case, I'd signed up for *Summer Intensive Latin* to avoid my "boyfriend" and eventually use it as the reason to break things off—*I'm just so busy with class now, it's not you it's me.* I sucked at Latin, but it was easier to stumble over a brand new, very old language than to be faced with speaking the truth. It was an emotional summer, the summer my emotions were starting to bubble up and spill out everywhere, uncontrollably, all the time. I needed to come out and fuck all the women of my dreams! Instead, the old desperate self-destructiveness reared its head and I felt caught in the grip of despair. Everything made me want to cry. Even translating Latin got to me, the deep sadness of certain phrases as the teacher described them: the idea that the goddess Juno could harbor an unrelenting rage, *ob memorem iram saevae Iunonis*. "This is hard to translate into English," the teacher said, "It's like an anger so hot it lives forever, burns into a memory that can never be forgotten. It isn't really done justice words like unforgettable." I felt that way too, most of the time, frustrated in the knowledge that I would never let go of my anger.

And then, we had to translate the scene in *The Aeneid* when Aeneas recalls fleeing his homeland, carrying his old father Anchises on his back. Woken up in the middle of the night and forced to run, his father thought to take nothing save their *penates*, or "household gods," with him, mysterious deities worshipped privately in home shrines at the time, another difficult word to parse. I thought that was beautiful, the idea that home could be both sacred and moveable, providing you'd consecrated items to represent your household gods. It gave me comfort; in a world where I didn't feel much at home anywhere, I could make a home everywhere, and bring my gods with me. I might not be able to afford my own place, but I could afford little holy images and statues to infuse with holy protection. I wanted to know what these *penates* looked like, and found an example in a catalogue at the British Museum: a small bronze figure, about five inches tall, of a person crowned by leaves and bearing a cornucopia to represent abundance. Then, a 1595 engraving by Agostino Carracci depicting Aeneas and his family fleeing Troy: armored Aeneas heaves the elderly Anchises over his shoulders, the son's head bowed in toil and sorrow, the father's thrown back in shock. The old man clutches his son tightly with one arm, in the other, the heads and shoulders of two small statues peak out from the animal skin in which they are wrapped, held fast amidst a scene of carnage and destruction. *Penates*, always plural. I went home that night looking for what I could use for my own household gods: an old Teenage Mutant Ninja Turtles action figure? Some of the ceramic figurines from Rose Tea boxes my grandma had given me? I'd keep little trinkets around and think of them as my household gods, party gods, sex gods, gods of delirium, and gods of scholarship. The more unassuming, the better. Years later I knew right away that I had met a household god in her, Our Lady of the Shop.

Some of my ability to maintain the astral hygiene and serenity of the shop was in my nature: I know who I am and who I want to be, and neither of those people engage in violence. But I think some of this was also made possible by Our Lady herself. She had consecrated the shop as a sanctuary for all who would pass through its doors, beginning with the staff, who all had needed her protection. I would sweep and clean the shop each morning, and before unlocking the doors I would pray to her aloud: *Our Lady of Treadwell's, Help me to greet all who walk through its doors with love and compassion, and give me the strength to make of it a sanctuary of calm repose for all who need it, as you have done for me.* Most days, my prayers were answered. And when there was trouble, they were answered differently. I was able to maintain sanctuary by learning to listen carefully to my intuition.

Our Lady was visualized as Wisdom personified in the shop letterhead and merch, as depicted in the seventeenth century alchemical book of emblems, *Atalanta Fugiens*, or *The Flying*

Atalanta. *Atalanta Fugiens* is a trippy book of magical initiation that deploys image, music, and poetry to excite the reader into alchemical secrets of eternal life and wealth. There are images to decode, songs to sing, commentaries to unpack, deepening the sensual experience of reading. It's a particularly esoteric example of a genre of publishing we've lost: emblem books comprised of symbolic images unpacked through meditation, pithy slogans, poems, and comments meant to delight and inform on subjects of morality and medicine to love and religion. However out of favor emblem books have fallen, at Treadwell's we perpetuated the kind of reading practices that were part of it, and our Lady represented that too.

Our Lady of the Shop as we have adapted her, first appears in "Emblem 26," titled "The Tree of Life is the Fruit of Human Wisdom." She stands firmly, looking right into the eyes of the reader. Sunlight bursts from the clouds over her right shoulder, the tree of knowledge sprouts just beyond her left. In her outstretched arms she holds two unfurled scrolls: "Longitudo dierum et Sanitas" in her right, and "Gloria ac divitia infinitae" in her left ("length of days and health" and "honor and infinite riches"). The commentary paraphrases the Book of Wisdom, attributed to King Solomon, saying:

> They that are acquainted with wisdom have eternal perseverance, and they that are her friends sincere pleasure, and he that diligently enquires after her, shall receive much joy, for there is no unpleasantness in her conversation, but mirth and joy, and though wine and music do also cheer the heart of man, yet wisdom is more pleasant than them: for She is a tree of life to them that lay hold on her, and blessed at they that retain her.[5]

5 "Atalanta Fugiens: Emblem 26," *Furnace and Fugue*, https://furnaceandfugue.org/atalanta-fugiens/emblem26.html.

As a personification of Wisdom, Our Lady presided with great care over my education, and facilitated encounters with the most wonderfully knowledgeable and generous people, strangers and friends alike. Dangers aside, the shop was more often a crossroads for mystical and philosophical exchange and excitement—rotating casts of lecturers, the deluge of spiritual seekers who visited daily, and the shelves of books themselves, which offered a bird's eye view of esoteric spirituality as it had survived and mutated across disciplines for centuries. I would always be grateful for the unique way of learning in a bookshop, organizing the shelves according to the wisdom of retail. And because the books we peddled in promised revelation and enlightenment, we trucked in a kind of Glorified Retail. While the *Atalanta Fugiens* focused on the infinite riches of Wisdom in its purest form, we still had to keep in mind that there were bills to pay. Both aspects of alchemy—the quest for immortality, the quest for gold—kept us, I felt, a little more honest. Universities are completely shaped if not dominated by wealth, fundraising, and the advantages given to students whose accident of birth landed them with rich parents - all the while speaking and promoting a lofty language of purity and intellect. It's all propaganda. The hypocrisy of most places of learning did not apply to our bookshop; we were always clear about the honest need for the "infinite riches" to be more than metaphorical.

As for me, there were hustles within hustles. I worked at the shop three to four days per week, in addition to working for an educational non-profit, taking on freelance teaching and TAing, and then freelance editorial work. And I was still mostly hard up, always on the lookout for another way to make some cash. This often came about through the shop. For example: in one scam, I started selling hagstones wholesale.

A hagstone is a stone with a lucky hole running through it, like a donut, sculpted by the gradual erosion of water over years and years, tumbled in a riverbed or thrown by the tides along the shoreline. They're also known as adderstones—made from the petrified spit and cum of snakes. These descriptions are really horny animalistic sex magick we can't understand—it's never just a snake that makes an adder stone, they're formed within a massive entangled orgy of snakes sweating and spitting and stuck together (according to the *Natural History* of Pliny the Elder). From amidst a hissing, writhing hoard of these snakes is produced a magic stone Druids prized for its powers and wore around their necks.

Either way, hagstones are mind-blowing because they're either a thousand years old or four billion years old, way older and wiser than I'll ever be. Like most scams, I'm peddling access to awe and wonder, my own included. I got the idea to sell hagtones wholesale because I was wearing one, a string run through the hole, as a bracelet, to ward off evil. In British folklore, hagstones are worn for luck, to induce visions of faeries, to protect against thunder and bad weather, or hung over doorways to keep out malefic forces, or held beneath the cow's udder on the first pull to ensure its milk won't curdle, or tied around the necks of horses to prevent them being ridden to death to the witches' sabbat. If you were a farmer and found your horse sweaty first thing in the morning, it meant a witch had ridden that horse ("hag-ridden") the evening before. Eventually your animal would die from being ridden too hard, so putting a hagstone around its neck was a way to avoid such a fate (another name for them is Mare Stones). Personally, I felt like I was being Ridden to Death by Life and couldn't afford therapy, so centuries of folk wisdom would have to do.

I was also wearing the hagstone out of superstitious reverence: you never know who is going to walk through the door of an occult bookshop, and I could not let the customers and their incredibly draining magical needs get me down. In Ancient Greece, hagstones were known as Ephialtes stones—after the giant son of Poseidon, whose name means "nightmare"—and were hung over beds to protect from bad dreams and prevent visits by an incubus or succubus. Bad dreams and sex demons are also things to be wary of when working at an occult bookshop: the things you learn and the conversations you have can get into your subconscious and give you *truly unhinged* stress dreams that you absolutely cannot take literally or prophetically. And some of the people who come into the shop and flirt with you as part of their quest for *a transformative spiritual experience* are kind of demonic.

I was wearing the hagstone to keep grounded when a non-demonic customer pointed it out and said: "That's cool, do you sell them here?" That got me thinking: hagstones are made from streams of running water, running water is a powerful force that negates most malefic magic, and I needed a new income stream. There were so many humble ways to make money within the Witch Economy, and here was a new one presenting itself to me. Let's be honest about the alchemical aspect of witchcraft—a significant portion of magic is about making gold from shit, treasure from trash, rent money from thin air. Aside from worshipping the goddess (and, because of their holes, representing the divine feminine, hagstones are sometimes called goddess stones), making enough money to survive on the fringes of society is a key feature of being a witch. Even Eddie Buczynski and Herman Slater—proprietors of The Warlock Shop, a once infamous occult store in New York City in the 1970s—were known to sell their picked-clean chicken bones from lunch as oracle bones later in the day.

I needed the money, because I was discovering new ways of being broke daily: stretching pairs of two-week contact lenses to last six months, charging all of my electronics at work to save on energy consumption. In my flat, heat and electricity were run on a meter with a red key. When the meter ran out, I'd take the key to the shop downstairs and pay to put more energy on it. I had a piggy bank shaped like the Virgin Mary, covered in silver glitter, and I'd use literal pennies from it to top up the meter. I ate a lot of ramen. My patchy wifi came from the wine bar one door away. I'd leave my wallet at home because I couldn't use any of the cards in it. I could only go places by foot or by bicycle, rain or shine. Everyone I knew was getting priced father and father outside of London as rents rose, and I had taken on the struggle of staying closer to the center of town.

I could sell a mix of stones to my manager at the bookshop to make a quick £30 for groceries, the odd lunch out, and whatever else—gig tickets, beers—I'd need to keep up appearances, so no one would know how genuinely broke I was. I hadn't stopped drinking yet, but I couldn't afford to drink in excess, probably the silver lining, though it didn't feel that way at the time. All of my money went to rent on the only apartment I could find that would let me keep my dog; after that, money went toward buying him the expensive, organic, cold-pressed kibble the vet said would ensure him a long and happy life. My dog had saved my life in that way that non-human critters can, premium kibble felt like the least I could do.

One important thing about sourcing hagstones in London is cleansing what you find. I don't mean like in salt water under the right full moon. That comes later. I mean soaking them in bleach to clean off the literal human shit that's played a role in their erosion. The part of the foreshore where I was gathering these stones was battered by the River Thames, where there is a significant presence of human sewage and visibly decaying animal carcasses. I'd be picking through the stones and my dog would be trying to pick clean the bones of some dead fox or pigeon. In 1957, the presence of oxygen in the Thames was so low, and the smell of the water so fetid, it was declared to be biologically dead, although in recent years this diagnosis has been really turned around and there is a growing population of fish, eels, leeches, and—outside of London—seahorses, otters, and sharks. But suffice to say there is enough of gross shit and microplastics that you definitely need to clean these stones before wearing them, *let alone* working with them in a ritual.

Checking the tidal tables, I'd walk my dog to "our part" of the Thames foreshore, helpfully nestled behind a massive construction site near Borthwick Wharf. A quiet, fairly undisturbed part of the River where lots of stones and old shards of pottery dating back to the Middle Ages were daily churned up by the waters. A few minutes downriver the Cutty Sark was moored, an old clipper ship named after the revealing clothing worn by a dancing witch in a Robert Burns poem—a cutty-sark is like a crop top ("*In longitude tho' sorely scanty*"), and the witch in the poem danced so tantalizingly in it that it became her name. She's the figurehead on the ship's prow, lunging forth in all her fury, grasping a horsehair tail. We'd end our search for hagstones as close to Cutty Sark as possible, which felt like good luck. Wherever I'm doing magic I try to find the closest witch, to whom I offer my thanks.

The only people we'd see along the way were mudlarks—people with olive Wellington boots, metal detectors, shovels, and, most importantly, a license from the Port of London Authority to dig for buried treasure. As an unlicensed mudlarker, I could only graze the surface of the pebbled beach, no digging. But I didn't need to, making money from the pebbles themselves as I was. Walking my dog, storing my finds in poop bags, kept me inconspicuous. The profession of scavenging debris from the shore, sewers, and drains, is an old one in London and has many names: Mudlarks, grubbers, toshers, junkmen, rag-and-bone men, bone grubbers, bone pickers. This kind of work is done by night at low tide, an old branch of magic bringing together the poor, the outlawed, the desperate, the unemployable. Connecting with these scavengers across time felt like a ritual in itself; walking the routes of bone grubbers past, I felt a sense of homecoming, a sense of communion with a genealogy of archetypical outlaws. In those moments, history itself became the ultimate bargain, churning up old trash into a little spending money. At the end of the walk, I'd salute Cutty Sark in her slutty crop top, head home with heavy pockets, drop the stones in a bucket of bleach to soak all day, wash my dog's paws, and head to work.

One day a woman came into the bookshop with a homemade book titled *HAGSTONES*: ten pages of lore she had collected about the stones, a lot of it similar to what I'd found while trying to make sense of my latest scam (and to tell customers who were buying the hagstones, to drum up demand). I appreciated the coincidence, and the depth of appreciation for hagstones that her work had made possible, including one new invocation. In *Aradia, or the Gospel of the Witches* (1899), it is recorded that to find a stone with a hole in it is a special gift from the goddess Diana. According to this text, you must say a prayer of thanksgiving when you come upon *una pietra bucata*:

> I have found
> A holy-stone upon the ground
> O Fate! I thank thee for the happy find,
> Also the spirit who upon this road
> Hath given it to me;
> And may it prove to be for my true good
> And my good fortune!

The book concluds: *Remember, though, that legend has it that YOU don't find a hag-stone—IT finds you!!!* I wanted to check her source, so looked it up in a copy of *Aradia* we sold at the shop, a highly influential text in the witchcraft revival of the twentieth century. Like much of the source material for modern Wicca, it's difficult to verify. *Aradia* was recorded and translated by the Philadelphia-born folklorist Charles Godfrey Leland during his encounter in Italy with a mysterious "witch informant" named Maddalena, with whom Leland "became intimately acquainted in 1886, and have ever employed her specially to collect among her sisters of the hidden spell in many places." Who was Maddalena? Did she really copy down this "gospel" for Leland? And how many of these sources were pure fabrication from Leland himself, whose other books on German and Native American Folklore contain fictions from his own hand? Whether or not the source was Maddalena or Charles Godfrey Leland, human or divine, I found a stanza later on in the "Invocation to the Holy-Stone" that has stuck with me ever since:

> Great Diana! thou
> Who art the queen of heaven and of earth,
> And of the infernal lands—yea, thou who art
> Protectress of all men unfortunate,
> Of Thieves and murderers, and of women too
> Who lead an evil life, and yet hast known
> That their nature was not evil, thou Diana,
> Hast still conferred on them some joy in life.[6]

I'd read prayers about sinning and repentance and listened to a lot of Gospel, but I'd never quite heard a prayer to anyone, let alone the Moon Goddess, as a protector of outcasts without apology, ff people who led a life considered evil, yet understood by the Moon Goddess as not evil, and in fact deserving of happiness. The shop, the hagstones, the magic to protect me, had brought me a new way of speaking to the moon, a new understanding of the deep tradition of people like me—labelled evil day by day as the momentum of a transphobic British press escalated its moral panic—people who could worship the moon as nonjudgmental.

The synchronicity of stumbling upon a new prayer was not lost on me—Lady Wisdom, Our Lady of Treadwell's, had taught me to pay close attention, to be open to divine teachings from all who entered the shop. This was her education: *There*

6 Charles G. Leland, *Aradia, Gospel of the Witches* (London: David Nutt, 1899) 23-24.

are always gods among us! The mundane is sublime, the sublime is mundane! It was one of the greatest privileges of working in the occult bookshop. There, we could emphasize something that could be overlooked in other bookshops: the books we distributed promised enchantment, magic, and revelation. With that as a baseline for the information being peddled, there was a magical, fated quality to interactions. It was easier to enhance that feeling that when the shelves were lined with titles like *The Triumph of the Moon, 78 Degrees of Wisdom, Verdant Gnosis.* It was easier to notice by the light of a candle and a plume of Dragon's Blood incense. When there was a scrying mirror in a glass vitrine to your right (for sale), a wax replica of John Dee's sigil (for sale), and a large oil painting of two women divining tea leaves behind me (not for sale). When I played albums like William Burchette's *Guitar Grimoire* (1973) in the background, or Dorothy Ashby, or Hildegard von Bingen, or *Sabbatum, A Medieval Tribute to Black Sabbath* (2003), or Pentangle, Fairport Convention, and Trees. Keeping the shop lively, safe, and well-stocked was also about creating the right atmosphere for the right possibilities to unfold before the eyes of those who entered it. All of the reasons *anyone* would walk into an occult bookshop reduce to wanting to have *a transformative spiritual experience*, whether that meant asking for a book recommendation or arguing with me because, to them, I represented the devil. The balance between initiation and Satanic Panic, thinking magically and magical thinking, was a lot to maintain. It took focus and practice. But the reward was beyond material wealth, because I too got to have a transformative spiritual experience time and time again. During the years I spent working at Treadwell's, I received intense training in surrender to sacred encounters, a spiritual grounding that would anchor me in my life, my relationships, and my politics, and the ability to remain in grateful awe for the enchantment of day to day life.

WITCHES FOR HIRE

I remember the first time I was visited by Salem witches. When they opened the door, a gust of wind brought dead leaves in their wake. I felt sensitive to a slight drop in the temperature. It was the time of year when the veil between worlds is thickest, because that was the only time they were permitted to leave hearth and home. The power of these witches is so tied to place, the soil of the New England coast, and Halloween is such big business for tourism, it would be madness to leave town in autumn. The veil had to be pretty thick to bear such distance. They came through my door, cast an eye around the room, and made directly for me:

"We just got to London all the way from Salem, and this is the first place we've come!"

A certain kind of pilgrim came to our bookshop this way, rushing and breathless from a red eye, luggage in hand. As one of the most popular occult bookshops in the world, let alone London, we were a site of pilgrimage, and urgency was a sign of respect.

I had never met Salem witches, and I was a little starstruck. It's like a celebrity sighting among witches; Salem's reputation is larger than life. I was a Philly witch, and I'd lived in London for nearly a decade. The Philadelphia region never had its equivalent of the Salem witch trials: Pennsylvania was the colony people went to when they were kicked *out* of New England. In 1684 there had been one witch trial, presided over by William Penn himself, concerning a Swedish woman named

Margaret Mattson and her husband. Penn ruled that the pair *were* witches, but were not guilty of witchcraft, and further ruled that it was not a crime to be a witch by reputation. Just like that, witchcraft in Pennsylvania could be folk healing—cunning, broad, expansive, something other than heresy—a word that hung in the air and in recorded history as a death sentence. Pennsylvania witches could live and work in plain sight, their identities formed by some other trial or tribulation.

The trajectory of occult goings-on in Penn's colony was vastly different than what happened in New England and I was, on some level, heir to that freaky-folksy toleration in Philly. It wasn't a big deal to go to South Street and buy crystals and books at Garland of Letters, then get a slice of pizza at Lorenzo's. I'd stop by Harry's World across the street from the grocery store to pick up the Magic Flo I used to wash my countertops—it was anti-bacterial and drove away bad vibes. I could fit my magic into my everyday life without much fuss. Even the name of the store made it feel normal: *Harry's.* There was another crystal shop named *Rocky's*, and the idea that even Rocky Balboa, the Italian Stallion, could be a witch felt like the ultimate extended hand, part of the legacy of spiritual tolerance characteristic of the region. To be a Philly witch in London was even more relaxing: I basically had no reputation to uphold because, in a class system signified by voice, nobody could place my accent. I was starting from scratch, illegible. At the same time, working in an occult bookshop was the perfect chance to flex—to extend, to grow my sense of the supernatural or paranormal, fostering daily encounters with concepts of the divine, my own and everyone else's.

But to be a Salem witch *anywhere* is to work on a totally different level: everyone knows *something* about what went down in Salem, so the bar is set high when it comes to representing that history. And a concept of witchcraft defined by a seventeenth-century Puritanical worldview has a lot of Puritanical ideas about The Craft; it's historically very kinky when it's not totally upsetting. If you're a witch in Salem you're high profile, with all of the burdens of representation, competition, and skewed perspectives. Salem Witches are *not* like the other girls. To begin with these witches were a husband-wife duo. That's really old school, to be husband-wife magical partners; Wicca started as a fertility religion where seating and initiations happened in a boy-girl-boy-girl pattern. This duo channeled their magic into a company called *Bewitching Tours*, offering guided walks along the streets of old Salem, especially its cemetery.

This was around 2016, and the look of a witch at the time was heavily influenced by Stevie Nicks: a broad-brimmed hat, black skirts and a tasteful amount of tulle, a black leather jacket (but only late at night), and lots of cursed jewelry, all of it expensive-looking. But there were other subcultures of occult practitioners: satanic gays with painted nails and T-shirts that featured obscure bands, horror films, and drag queens from *Dragula* more often than *RuPaul's Drag Race*. There were solemn men and women who wore all black and worshipped gods that did not allow them a sense of humor. There were twenty-somethings who opted to dress for the Ren Faire, there were teens who pushed the look further into the realm of the fairies, wings and all. My colleagues and I all dressed like we were in the stage crew of our high school play: black jeans, black turtlenecks, black denim button downs, black boots. Except Johnny, who was making *Ocha* and wore white clothing from head to toe, his head covered in a white cloth, a time of spiritual purity and rebirth for him. The Salem witches stood out against us all with a kind of panache that is hard to pull off, dressed like regularly occurring characters in the supernatural series of the 1990s: *Buffy the Vampire Slayer*, *Angel*, *Charmed*, *The X-Files*. They both had on long black jackets; the woman's over a tight shirt of green velvet, the man more of a dandy in tweeds, a gold pocket watch tucked into his waistcoat. It was July.

There's a fin de siècle decadence for each century that trickles down into fashion, especially the fashion choices of heretics. The mass hysteria of the Salem witch trials in the 1690s (Bridget Bishop's torn "Red paragon Bodice"), the voodoo-revolutionary fervor of the 1790s (Romaine-la-Prophétesse's ribbons and women's clothing), the Satanic Catholicism of the 1890s (Huysmans's descriptions of bejeweled, expensive fabrics of Madame Chantelouve or Des Esseintes)—they all turned out their looks. So, too, did the mass media explosion in paranormal interest in the 1990s. Y2K cultivated an aesthetic of long black jackets, blood reds and deep burgundies, thrifting the leathers and velvets of the 1970s for those more apocalyptic times. Think: the scene in *The Matrix* when Neo finds Trinity in a nightclub. Think: Fairuza Balk in *The Craft* after she invokes all the power of Manon and can afford new clothes. The regular goth night in London—Slimelight, est. 1987—had a door policy: no jeans, no T-shirts, no sporty or athleisure wear. These witches would have been admitted into Slimelight, and still could move in broad daylight without attracting too much notice. In other words, they could move between worlds, as all true witches can. I loved their whole vibe.

"How's life in Salem?" I asked.

"Well, it's never been a better time to be a witch," they laughed.

"I bet. I can't think of many places where the tides have changed so drastically, from running witches into the grave, to practically being run by them!"

"It is truly a reversal of fate."

"Totally, I wish you could bottle that recipe!"

"Well, that's kind of what our tours are about: keeping this history alive, because people need it—they need a place like Salem, so they can connect with the past, believe in magic, believe in taking fate into their own hands, and turn the tides against their oppressors."

I'd always found the magnetism of Salem so confusing. As in, barely anything bad happened there, at least not comparable to the scale of bloodshed happening everywhere else at the time. By the 1690s, England was recovering from a period of revolutionary upheaval, beginning in the 1640s, that led to the largest loss of life in its recorded history—a fourth of the population. Then plague. Then war abroad. The northern colonies were populated by religious refugees who had barely survived persecution, only to recreate the exact structures of their oppression in a different place. It was a frightening, cautionary tale.

But it must be said: Salem matters because it happened mostly to white people, and so close to the time of the Founding Fathers of the United States of America, in a region that would give birth to Many Presidents of the United States of America. It is a relatively tidy tragedy within which to contemplate the worst of human behavior: paranoia, cruelty, bloodlust. The scale of death at the time—indigenous genocide, systematic torture and murder of enslaved people, starvation among colonizers themselves—all expendable pawns in the rollout of empire, an unimaginably vast force. Salem feels like a tree in that incomprehensible, unmappable forest. A landscape of the past that runs deep and feels powerful enough to threaten our sense of free will even now. Can we ever outrun the consequences of Salem in 1692? Or the construction of the *Foresight* in Deptford in 1570, a new style of ship that would contribute to the shift of global power to Britain? Or the marriage of Ferdinand and Isabella in 1469? The hardest thing about believing in ghosts is the scale: it just seems like there are too few of them compared to the horrible shit that has gone down, the spread of violence along lines of global trade and competition. My co-worker, Johnny, created his own Tarot deck based off of London lore and history that summarized the problem: Johnny's Blasted Tower card depicted the East India Company, a colonizing force founded in England whose creation had wreaked upheaval and destruction across the globe.

Salem is well-documented enough to contain glimpses into that trajectory, being one of Britain's early colonies attempting bloody conquest legitimated by courts of law—the testing grounds for projects like the East India Company. At Salem, the Puritans planted seeds of America's potential destruction by mass moral panic and infighting—strategies still in play that affected all of us who worked at or visited Treadwell's at the time, and beyond. Contemporary responses to what happened in Salem note the hypocrisy, how antiquated and even passé it was to execute women as witches. For the Quakers, who'd been prevented from an education beyond their own homemade grammar schools, who'd been roughly checked for witchmarks and run out of New England, some of them even executed by Puritans decades before, Salem was an example of how educated elites cannot be trusted and abuse their knowledge as power by sowing misinformation and paranoia.

The responsibility this burden of memory leaves on Salem witches is a tall order: there's so much to hold, an unwieldy legacy. The way in which the dead are remembered in Salem makes for many a restless spirit; the cemeteries are not quiet places of eternal repose but active sites for regurgitation and remembrance, a crossroads for witch commerce. This, too, was confusing and enticing to me: the idea that a place could be so bogged down by its own history that the remnants of its past only feel increasingly *present*, increasingly *prescient*, increasingly *pressing*. The more you think of it, the more you can't think about anything else.

"We know where the witches were actually executed, it isn't the place that's marked on maps and accepted by the mainstream," the witches told me. "We take our tours there, and hold vigils, it's a powerful emotional experience."

Many cultures have some form of professional mourners, but the idea of maintaining this intensity daily was overwhelming to consider. Talking to the Witches of Salem, I couldn't help but fear that the magic of the place was marked by a different kind of dark pact. Instead of bargaining with the Devil, it was the witches themselves with whom they were in an eternal relationship, a past they'd never live down, that would have their souls in the end.

At the time, I was finishing a dissertation in the history department of a university around the corner from the occult bookshop, and one of my big preoccupations was: *what do I do with my obsession with looking backward and into other people's business? When to look deeper, when do I avert my eyes, when do I shut them and stop looking? When to bury the dead, when to mourn the dead, when to let them rest?*

I asked the witches, "How long are you in town for?"

"Oh, just a few days."

They couldn't be away from their girls for too long, from sweeping their graves, from delivering their elegies. So, they would miss Slimelight.

The witch's archive is a fraught and fragile scattering of evidence. Must like the long history of queer, trans, and gender non-conforming people, the bulk of information about witchcraft has been generated under duress. Testimonies taken by panicked individuals suffering illness or the death of a loved one. Under interrogation after arrest. Under interrogation after time spent in squalid conditions with little food, warmth, or sleep. Under interrogation after torture. Christianity, the religion of bureaucracy, produces dogmas, laws, hierarchies, and governments based upon an interpretation of scriptures—that's a lot of paperwork! In its hunger to acquire wealth, property, and dominion over souls there is also the paperwork of heresy: tracts and treatises, testimonies and court records, in print and in manuscript. While journals of demonic and angelic communications detailing rituals, invocations, and visions survive, and recipe books of housewives and cunning folk, and folk knowledge handed down over centuries and recorded in story and song are also sources of information about *what witches do*, what we have of Salem witches are court records and angry diatribes written by angry men who cannot be trusted. What we can know and absorb about the Salem or Hartford witches—or, in England, the Pendle Witches, the Essex Witches, the Lincoln Witches, the Huntington Witches, and the Suffolk Witches—requires careful negotiation. The magic lies in the interpretation, not just among historians, but among spiritual seekers attracted to the craft.

I think a modern witch is someone who wants to find god, namely a god that hasn't been tarnished by association with all of the terrible things humans do to one another. As a teenager, witchcraft was the first form of rebellion I could grasp for, a trail of crumbs leading outside of Christianity. I followed the Devil to the edge of Christine doctrine, and when I stepped outside of it, he expanded into something much older. Once I was out there, being a witch became less about reading Edgar Allen Poe in the local graveyard and more about building correspondences between nurture and nature, hitching desires onto cosmic forces with the help of prayers and the elements. Being a witch became about having more information to sift through as time went on: from experience, from fantasy, from history. Finding a critical mass of characters whose fragmented remains contain a lust for the weird and a refusal to fully succumb to harmful systems of capitalism and white supremacy. Finding people who, in one way or another, offer the gentle suggestion: *There are other ways of being.*

Some driving contradictions in witchcraft: we know people were burned as witches in the past, but we can never know enough about what these people were actually like. We know Romans exterminated Druids in the past, but we don't know anything about Druids except from a Roman perspective. We know Pagan religions were replaced by imperial, forced conversion, and we want to practice that underdog religion because we've seen too much horror from a religion based on violent subjugation. So, the spiritual essence of modern witchcraft requires digging down into the past and finding what rings true for you. Assembling the right lore for the right occasion, building prayers into elaborate rituals from fragments and hearsay.

A bitchiness has crept into modern witchcraft that comes from thinking one interpretation is somehow truer than another, forgetting it was all an interpretation to begin with, a grasping in the dark. Browse an occult bookshop for more than a few minutes and you'll start to hear it, you can't help eavesdropping: witches dissing one another, claiming so-and-so doesn't know enough, or isn't initiated into the right line, or isn't doing *it* right. At this point in time, the squabbling is practically a tradition in and of itself: look to the conflicts between Aleister Crowley's followers after he died, or Gerald Gardner's, or Alex Saunders's, or really any group from the spectrum of ceremonial magicians to folksy covens of the past century-and-a-half, and there are power struggles over authority and inheritance.

The Salem witches had gossip from their own backyard: as a center of trauma reclaimed for the purposes of magical powers, witches have been drawn to Salem for decades, and there are various factions of Salem witches. The latest witch drama centered around a new magical shop that had opened in town, run by lesbians. "It's not that they're lesbians—of course!" They looked me up and down, a lanky butch dyke, never a girl, not yet a tranny. "It's just that they opened up a shop before they even knew any of us. They didn't even bother to introduce themselves. And now they're selling really expensive home goods, macramé, witchy welcome mats. And doing tours, like we do. They could have at least introduced themselves."

I asked how strange it was to be so steeped in history that happened centuries ago. Did people skip the living to jump back too quickly to the dead in Salem? "Yes, that's exactly it! They act like we're not even here."

What is a witch? What does it mean to claim being a witch? In the bookshop people would ask again and again: *Are you . . . you know, a witch yourself?* Everyone wanted to know who they were dealing with. The trick was saying YES in a way that was gentle to those who were asking the question more of themselves than of me, a way that gave permission. I would say to them: Yes, I am a witch. My life is structured like the tides according to the phases of the moon. I like working in the dark and occasionally feeling frightened of it; I anoint candles and burn herbs to give thanks to forces beyond my human understanding. I believe in mystery and change, and I long to embed myself in some divine pattern, something bigger. Sometimes it feels like a big, silly cosmic trust fall.

Or saying YES, I'm a witch, in a way that shamed the skeptics who wanted to laugh in my face, to make them feel like total losers for doing so—joke's on them. I don't believe in irony outside of the literary mode: most people who would take precious minutes from their finite life and walk into an occult bookshop in order to ask about witchcraft must, on some level, want to be part of it. But these people did enter the shop, did try to engage me in debate. I could laugh at these men. *You think you're smart enough to be the actual Devil's advocate?* I am the one getting paid to answer your questions. They were just wasting their own time, too uptight to surrender and so destined to miss out on all the fun. How sad that these skeptics would deny themselves pleasure for the safety of feigned aloofness, would choose the minor rush of brain chemicals released during conversation rather than the major one you get from drawing down the moon buck naked. There's a queer equivalent to this, too: when I worked in a gay bookshop, we'd get prank callers all the time, a voice on the other end of the phone laughing, asking rude questions, calling me a fag. The company line was: *Thanks for calling, I'm sure we'll be seeing you here soon.* Closet Cases!

Then there was a third YES: to the initiate witch who wanted some sense of my bona fides—*should they respect me, or not?* As someone raised in a hugely fucked up Catholic setting that nearly taught me to kill myself, I promised myself as a teenage witch that I would never look for god in organized religion again. My approach to these witches was to tread gently and not let myself get walked all over. There is an idea that belonging to a coven or being initiated into a particular tradition is somehow superior to self-initiation, but all I care about is spiritual ecstasy and cosmic connection, which I am certain I experience. As a self-initiate, I have nothing on my side but time, a handful of spooky encounters with the unknown, and shocking occurrences that make the hair stand up on the back of my neck with wonder and awe. I have basked in divine love, I have been shook by holy terror. I have run out of words to describe the majesty and beauty of beholding my life's unfolding within a golden, cosmic purpose that links me to the other living beings I've been lucky enough to travel with in my time on earth. I know what I know.

All of which is to say, a witch is nothing if not a relational being: relational to organized religion, relational to capitalism, relational to science, relational to a sprawling counterculture of freaks and weirdos and artists and seekers. I had a lot of sympathy for my interactions with visitors to the shop, who each had their own links to these big themes. We were all just trying to find a way to lick our respective wounds and make some meaning out of life. Life, which spares no one its ups and downs, its pleasure and pain.

Heresy was a major theme of my life, day and night. Alongside this job, I was a historian in training, finishing up a PhD on the revolutionary religious radicals of late seventeenth century England, a profusion of Christian heretics with very visceral, embodied names: Diggers, Levellers, Seekers,

Ranters, Quakers. Heretics who hated priests, heretics who hated monarchs, who were beaten and imprisoned for claiming that no mortal had any right to come between them and their experience of god. Sometimes they were described as witches, sometimes they were described as demons; overall, they were heretics and blasphemers. These groups were written about by establishment Church of England priests and scholars in lurid terms, described as swarms of pestilence, as "Hell Broke Loose." They were seen as serious threats to stability and power, as ill omens that had to be exterminated in order to bring about times of prosperity. One massive catalog of heretics was Thomas Edwards's *Gangraena* (1646), which grew by hundreds of pages in each new edition as Edwards added more descriptions of the blasphemy and religious heresy spreading around England like gangrene on an infected limb. The hallmark of spirituality among these condemned groups was their enthusiasm—a passion for discussion, debate, dissent, schism. They were always arguing, in person and in print; breaking up and starting new groups based on new visions, producing new spiritual outpourings from reading their translations of the bible.

The piece of scripture that Quakers returned to again and again to justify their spiritual outpourings came from 2 Corinthians 3:6: *The letter killeth, but the spirit giveth life.* It was part of their understanding of how the inner light, the presence of god in every person, expressed itself in the world. Reading in the spirit underwrote their belief that the bible ought not to be interpreted strictly and word for word, but actively and changing with the times. To follow the dead letter was death, but to read in the spirit of divine inspiration, to read from a place of enlightened wisdom, was the way to eternal life. This was the key to my own ideas about the divine, and the magic of divine communication: it was always changing, growing, becoming increasingly real in my life and in my soul if I cultivated it, it was expansive without ever being exhaustive. This view of the spirit—and of reading in the spirit—was unpopular in its time, unpopular in most forms of Christianity that have survived into the present, and it was very unpopular it my academic field

My boss, the Witch Queen of Treadwell's, who was also a dear friend, had once left academia and described her departure in this way: *I had to ask myself, would I rather study these themes, or live and experience them in my own life?* She knew her answer, and I knew my answer. Here in London, over three hundred and fifty years later, I had found the persistence of ecstatic heresy at my day job, surrounded in my waking life by people squabbling over their visions, their spells, their magic. The mystical underground was thriving in my place and time; I felt that the gossip and drama this created was just part of heightened spiritual experience, kicked up in the churn of wild enthusiasm. The challenge was not to take any of it too seriously or let spiritual difference harden into some kind of religious rivalry. Let everyone have their visions. Let everyone pray to their gods.

To keep myself grounded, I'd clock out from work and look at my schedule: was I spending more time in the circle of power drawing down the moon, or outside of it bitching? Swapping stories with the Salem witches and other shop visitors was enough: gossip *is* an energizing way to make fast friends and communicate shared values and tastes. And what they were really bitching about was commerce, which I could also relate to. I realized that we were both witches-for-hire in an expanding world, drifting away from the turn-of-the-century aesthetic we had all grown up with into something new. The witch economy emerging looked different: more expensive, with sleeker designs, crisp edges, minimal noise, line drawings. A sprouting branch on a family tree with roots that went deep. There was a new cohort of pretty, willowy witches emerging on social media expanding the boundaries and audiences of the witch economy, and we were trying to come to grips with it. Like punk, witchcraft had gone mainstream; the witches making the most money off it were not people we knew, and that was hard to stomach. I wasn't *unhappy* that they were eking out an existence in the world. But, I was skeptical. I was wary of all the ways in which I'd already seen revolutionary language, feminism, and queer politics taken up and very earnestly misapplied to the same old white (neo)liberal nonsense.

A few months later, the lesbians from that latest shop in Salem stopped by. Of course, they were totally lovely people. Of course, it was exciting to think that a lesbian-owned business would exist anywhere, let alone in Salem. And of course, there were two sides to every story: "We're slowly getting to know the place, it's very insular, there are a few very tight-knit cliques, it's hard to make friends, we're not sure how queer-friendly they are, but either way it's hard to go out on a limb like that." I knew that feeling all too well; I was the kind of person who wanted to know my neighbors as much as I was afraid of strangers knowing where I lived. But I told them I'd met a few nice witches the week before and recommended the tour: "Apparently, they let you take your dog, it sounded really good and well-researched, they were really friendly! You should check it out, maybe you guys can collaborate or something."

Most trial records and pamphlets about the persecution of witches document one-sided conversations about failed bargains between witches and their neighbors. The witch is conjured up as a figure to blame for failures with economic consequences: the death of livestock, the failure of crops, the illness and death of labor (children and adults). Nowadays, much of the infighting among witches has an economy of its own, boiling down to discomfort over *who* gets to make money through their witchcraft. From media attention in television, movies, and publishing, to running occult shops, to making money as a Tarot card reader. Before this was amplified on social media, it was true of places with tried-and-true histories of occult activity, like London, like Los Angeles, New York, and of course, Salem.

At our bookshop, we handed out a free map listing all the other nearby magical bookshops and occult supply stores and cites of interest. This reflected the true faith and power of the Witch Queen: it's an ultimate form of surrender to the Goddess to believe there is truly enough to go around for everyone. There's praying for abundance, and then there's acting as if abundance is the guaranteed norm. I wanted that, I would never choose to believe in a stingy god. But still, there was always drama in the witch economy: folks who acted in bad faith or who stole, or claimed to have a monopoly on something other people had been doing forever. I understood where the Salem witches were coming from on both sides: it's just *hard* to see someone doing the same thing as you, as if you don't exist. That felt like a human emotion dating back to the witch trials themselves. Still, at the end of every shift, however petty the squabbles, however juicy the gossip, I believed that even this dark side of witchcraft was about a longing for meaningful connection.

And that, to my mind, was the final mark of what makes a witch. After a longing to connect with the divine through nature, after a need to form a DIY spiritual alternative that resists the harm done by organized religion, after a tradition of disagreement and gossip in healthy doses as part of a balanced diet, witches do find weird ways to gently make enough money to get by in a hostile world. And they squabble over how that money is made amongst themselves. This comes up again and again in the trials: witches get caught performing services, or for seeking revenge when their services aren't contracted. Historically, the trials of witches detail obsession with the moment of the Devil's Bargain—the pact witches make with the Devil to gain their power. Endless testimonies speculate upon the moment the Man in Black appeared, the terms of his bargain, closing the deal through contracts signed in blood, sealing it with a kiss on the Devil's ass, concluding with fucking and the granting of little furry animals to do one's bidding. I was interested in the other kind of bargains typical to witches: offering their healing, their intuition, their insights into the future in exchange for subsistence. Or cursing when they were denied a basic means of subsistence. And witches *do* offer quite the bargain: it saves time and money if the Tarot reader is accurate, if the spell works, if the god listens.

SATURN'S BITCH

A little background about me: Saturn was in Sagittarius from December 23, 2014, to June 14, 2015, and then from September 17, 2015, until December 19, 2017. It was my Saturn return, the epic time in everyone's life when slow-moving Saturn returns to the place in the sky it occupied when they were born. In my case, the planet of discipline, decrease, the constraints and boundaries of space and time, was moving through my first house—my very self. It felt like a full hallowing out, a harrowing of my personal hell. The early months prepared me, in a sense, to work at Treadwell's.

Before this momentous astrological shift, I had a spiritual life. Dating back to my earliest visit to London, when I was there for a few months in 2007, I'd visited Treadwell's in an attempt to structure my freewheeling spirituality, by the twenty-teens I was hanging out there regularly. I worked at Treadwell's from July 2016 until July 2018, and from there the occasional guest shift. It was exactly the sanctuary where I was able to metabolize the lessons of my Saturn return, choose what to keep and what to leave behind. It was a place I could redraw my boundaries and renew my vows to myself: who and what mattered to me in life? How would I spend my brief time on this planet? And as Saturn is an agricultural god, the god that wields the scythe of harvest season: how would I cultivate the small patch of earth I had to live on, the place I occupied with my own two feet?

My Saturn return had its seasons. Saturn's first entrance into my first house mapped roughly onto the sickness and eventual death of my mentor and thesis advisor, Lisa Jardine. Visiting Lisa week after week to keep her company as she underwent chemotherapy amounted to more than just bearing witness to an intellectual luminary fighting like hell not to die. Lisa was family. She called her approach to her students an "apprenticeship," and she meant it: she had mothered me, fed me, looked out for me. Her warmth and kindness, her excitement and enthusiasm and even pride for my queerness, my weird interests, my politics, was not a love I had experienced before. It was such a simple kind of attention she gave me, one I hadn't realized I'd craved: she met me in my reality, rather than forcing me into some delusion or projection. She saw what I wanted to do, and she wanted to help me do it. She was an Aries, I'm a Leo, and we were fiery together, obsessing over each other and each other's obsessions. Losing her was like losing access to the sun, watching all its light and heat slowly drain away, but we spent whatever time we could together and I was happy to be there. And at seventy-one, however furious she was about dying and leaving behind everything she loved with such passion, there were also moments where Lisa reflected with gratitude on the life she'd led—the people in it, the places travelled, the work she'd done.

That, too, felt like a particular kind of Saturnian initiation: witnessing a scholar's death. A mind so active and sharp that she could both grasp that she was dying and equally grasp that it was in her essential nature to fight back against it until the very end. She'd had a life so full that she didn't want to give it up. I realized I wanted to be like that: I wanted to cultivate a life so rich and fulfilling that it would make accepting death much harder, the biggest challenge of my life. Death should be like that; we should all be so lucky. Until that time I'd had a lot of fun, chased my thrills and interests, but ultimately hadn't learned to value my life. I felt expendable. I'd seen killing myself as a viable option pretty consistently from childhood, had partied with a self-destructive edge. Watching Lisa die profoundly changed that. It made me want to love so many people so well that I'd suffer their loss until it was my turn to be missed. I needed to love and take care of myself to accomplish that. I wanted to experience all of the things that are most painful to lose: love, friends, adventure, fun, hilarity, the beauty of the natural world, the frenzy of good sex. I wanted to enjoy them all, voraciously, and then martial all of my courage and smarts and be spiritually adept enough to just surrender them and die one day.

I was very present watching Lisa die, and learn new things about herself through dying. I was learning new things about myself through the particularity of her death, the sweeping emotions and philosophy of it, how it felt to realize I'd found and lost a mothering figure in only three years. It took me another year of grieving to realize how it would also profoundly fuck up my prospects for any kind of job in academia. Lisa knew that; she'd warned me, and apologized in advance: *No matter how well-intentioned people are, they're not going to help.* She'd thought of everything! I'd brushed it off at the time; it seemed so meaningless and even vulgar to think I'd care about something as ridiculous as a job. Then things shifted into another season of my Saturn return: the death of a vivid dream. Writing up my final dissertation—submitted in September and defended in December 2017, just before Saturn left my first house—involved saying goodbye to Lisa in a different way, and letting go of a childhood vision of myself as a fulfilled and financially stable Professor of History. I had to loosen my grip and then let go of a plan I had been holding myself to since eighth grade, one that I'd basically made up out of thin air, with no firsthand knowledge or role models. I loved reading, I loved writing, I loved learning about the past. I was good at teaching and communicating that love—an academic job seemed like the perfect fit. I remember after two hours of being grilled by men in my thesis defense, one of them asked: *Where do you see yourself in five years? What's your dream job?* And I felt the initiation of a long leave-taking then and there: *Not this.*

A few months after Lisa died, the first and closest friend I'd made when I moved to England also died, out of the blue, of an accidental overdose. Rudolph. I woke up to a phone call filtered through a social media platform one morning, early in March, by a friend of his roommate who I'd never met. She'd found him dead in his room the day before. He was twenty-seven, he'd struggled with addiction, he'd gotten into chemsex drugs. It was horrific, everyone was in shock, there had to be an inquest and autopsy. He was a grad student at Oxford, so it made the local news there, and a reporter quoted the cruel judge of the inquest rather than anyone who knew and loved him. The judge said something like "What a waste of a life." We were all furious. I couldn't stop crying enraged tears, I kept dreaming of him. I journaled and wrote a lot of poetry in my notebooks, about how fags don't die by suicide or by accident, they die because straight people have created a fundamentally hostile world, populated by false categories of sick and well, crazy and sane, silly and smart, all traps to try to catch us and kill us. I vowed to Rudolph that I'd remember him and cherish the memories of him forever, and that in learning to carry the grief over all our dashed plans and schemes, I would learn to maintain an anger at the world that made his life unlivable. It was a miracle he had survived his childhood—a truly flamboyant and effeminate fag—only to suffer in this way as an adult. When Rudolph died, I had to completely redefine what it meant to love and be loved as a queer person in a dangerous world. I also had to reconsider how to be a friend, and how to ask for help from my friends.

The bookshop was a place where everyone took one another's spiritual and emotional development seriously. The Witch Queen regularly asked me, "How is your spiritual life?" My colleagues, the Tarot card readers, the friends and strangers who'd visit, all sought intense spiritual experiences, coincidences, revelations, to make meaning out of the world's enchantment, and that flavored even the most basic conversations we had. Part of the magic of the shop's owner was the magic of sanctuary: she'd always used the shop as a haven for people in fucked up or difficult situations. Over the years the employees had included the whole gamut of human suffering: people sobering up, escaping abusive relationships, out of prison and down on their luck, or discriminated against for being trans or queer, or just artsy and sensitive in a way that made "straight" jobs too hard. She'd let people crash on the couch if they had nowhere else to go. She had created a place where we all could take care of one another in our own way, each according to our capacities and talents.

It helped to be going through "A Hard Time" alongside people who legitimately cared about the state of my soul. People who acknowledged not only that *Yes, this is difficult,* but *Yes, pain can be a spiritual teacher, it can be transformed into something worthwhile, even if you don't know what that is yet.* There is hope and generosity in the kinds of gifts that witches will give to one another. It's a major compliment and vote of confidence to receive a thoughtful invitation to nourish your spiritual side: the emotional presence of a Tarot reading, the soothing comfort of an herbal tea blended especially for you. When I was having housing trouble, The Witch Queen found and consecrated a small wooden beam—a hearth—for me to light candles in to help find a home. These generosities became saving graces that grounded me and helped me stabilize—the spells worked. At the recommendation of one of the Tarot readers I got into reading the Orphic Hymn to Kronos (Saturn) whenever I felt overwhelmed. It called for "Fumigation from Storax." Storax was a black resin you could burn as incense. A portion of our salary each month came as shop credit; we could use it to buy books and incense, so I'd buy a bottle of Storax and fumigate my apartment on Saturdays at sunrise, the day and hour of Saturn:

> Consum'd by thee all forms that hourly die,
> By thee restor'd their former place supply'
> The world immense in everlasting chains,
> Strong and ineffable thy pow'r contains
> Father of vast eternity, divine,
> O mighty Saturn, various speech is thine.[7]

Being disciplined in the face of death never gets easier: in my case I was ultimately working a glorified retail job by day, finishing up my dissertation by night, and supplementing it with editorial work and teaching on the side. I worked three to four part time jobs at any given time. I was also restructuring my life from the information I'd received through grief, through loss. Initially I thought that for Lisa the overhaul was about how I could transform her love and mentorship into being a teacher and mentor to myself, and transform how I thought, wrote, edited, and channeled my vocation as a scholar into making a living. I thought for Rudolph it was about how I loved and spent time with friends, how I looked after my own body. But as time went on, these containers of self-improvement and clarification that I'd created to respond to death became overwhelmed, overfull, and I realized I had to go further in changing my day to day life. If the major response to loss was to strengthen and reinforce love as my life's priority, then my definition of love needed redefining. I realized I had to seriously overhaul my

---

7 Thomas Taylor, *The Mystical Initiations; or, Hymns of Orpheus, Translated from the Original Greek* (London: Printed for the Author and sold by T. Payne, 1787) 136.

marriage, even if it risked destroying it. And then I realized that, actually, I just had to leave it.

I'd met my wife when I was twenty-two. I'd wanted so badly for her to be the person I spent my life with, but my experiences of death and grief had laid bare how much we'd become estranged from one another. She had found her own life's purpose, and I'd encouraged it. I hadn't known enough of how to ask for what I needed, or advocate for myself. I hadn't realized how much I had compromised. The agreed-upon imbalance—*You want to become a lawyer, we'll get you through law school and into your dream job first, then I'll go back to school and do my thing, I'm flexible*—had solidified into habits, choices, consequences, responsibilities; how we spent our days added up to our whole life. I'd watch her at the end of each twelve-hour workday come home tired, remembering less and less of what I'd told her about myself, more and more concerned with the huge weight of responsibility she had taken on at work. The cares and worries and lives of her clients—the work she did was always more urgent than anything happening to me; it was *saving people's lives*. For a while I, too, believed that her work was more important than my needs. Whatever I asked for felt like asking for too much. I'd explain the same details about my life to her again and again. I'd notice how any conversation about changing our habits never went beyond words.

Initially I thought: *Not this, anything but this*. I couldn't lose her, we'd been through so much together: my coming out to my parents, her dad's death. We'd moved to London and started a life from scratch. I'd done everything in my power to help her get through law school; her family had accepted me like mine never had. How is it even possible to enter into a relationship with that much love and support, a desire to treat one another well, and then, gradually, unconsciously, lose it? I couldn't conceive of how I'd suddenly felt so small in a world of my own making. One evening she came home and found me crying—*again*—about Rudolph's death, and said to me, "How long do you think you're going to be sad about this? It's just too much for me to deal with right now." And, magically, that was my limit.

It changed my perspective on everything, even if we had come by our differences honestly and with no intention to harm. Of course it got way messier before ending, since like every doomed queer couple on the planet, instead of just breaking up we decided to "open things up" and date other people. The deep differences in our values, how we wanted to spend our time, what we needed from a partner, had gotten garbled and muffled in the language of consensual non-monogamy. But after seven years, we broke up. I was a wreck. My definition of love itself—what I thought had been my life's guiding principle, what I thought was the only true thing I had in the aftermath of major bereavements—had failed.

It helped to realize all of this in a bookshop filled with Pagan worldviews. One of my assets—a sense of flexibility, a sense that I could change my plans—was blown out of proportion. I'd made several grand gestures: *I'm not moving back to the USA, I'm changing my plans to stay here with you. And I'm not going right to grad school even though I've been accepted, I'm getting a job to help support the household.* These felt like momentary sacrifices that I would be richly rewarded for as time went on; they would appreciate in value. It seemed like a great idea, made through careful, loving discussion. I was too young to realize that our downfall was present in my behavior from the very beginning. Refashioning and redefining love was in part about rooting out Catholic damage. The love I had modeled for me at home and in Church was a love of self-abnegation and suffering: you showed your love, how *deep and hot* it was, by sacrificing yourself and your needs. It was the only way to really demonstrate love; love couldn't exist without these big dramatic gestures. It wasn't the real thing if you weren't crucifying yourself like Jesus Christ himself.

Love magic and love spells have a long and prominent tradition in Pagan religions. The Greek Magical Papyri, a large collection of spells and prayers found in Egypt in the early centuries before the Common Era, are filled with gnarly recipes to provoke feelings of love and lust, to bind and attract a lover. There's a spell to lead a lover to you that involves writing holy names with the blood of a donkey on a seashell. To petition the moon goddess Selene, you have to make a statue of her from clay, sulfur, and the blood of a goat, and she will in turn drag your desired lover by the hair and throw them at your feet. There are spells to make the subject of your desire sleepless, spells to make them sick. One from the Papyri that interested me was a love charm—to make me more lovable, harmless enough—but I couldn't find a copper nail from a wrecked ship with which to inscribe a piece of tin with the required incantation. In an even creepier ritual to draw a lover, you must make two figures out of clay, one of the god Aries in his armor and holding a sword, the other of your desired lover prostrate on their knees. Plunge the sword of Aries into their neck and write your desires on this prostrate figure: on their head, ears, face, eyes, shoulders, arms, hands, breast, heart, lower belly, genitals, buttocks, soles of the feet. Then stick thirteen needles in the body in each of these places saying: "I am piercing your brain, so that you remember no one but me, alone."[8] The spell ends with a long invocation to infernal gods asking them to attract and bind your intended victim, to compel them to love you. Not quite the redefinition of love I was looking for.

By the sixteenth century, love spells were an important part of the witch economy: spells survive for both men and women with a range of ambitions: attracting lovers, assessing virginity, assessing a lover's loyalty, improving fertility, promoting or preventing pregnancy, figuring out the gender of a child,

8 PGM IV 296-466, "Wondrous spell for binding a lover" *The Greek Magical Papyri in Translation*, edited by Hans Dieter Beetz (1986).

spicing up a long-term marriage. Sex workers were accused of using love magic—Queen Anne Boleyn was accused of casting love spells on Henry VIII—but there are also love spells not aimed toward sex or procreation as much as the admiration of others, including employers and social superiors. Although witch trials are highly sexualized, a lot of what survives of these is not linked so much to people called witches, but rather to magicians and cunning folk who made a mostly quiet living performing rituals on behalf of their clients. One manuscript that survives from this tradition combined love magic with spells to aid in gambling, hunting, and fishing. An example:

> Take a nutmeg and fill it full of holes then sweat it under. your left armhole three times. Then take some of your nature (semen) and some of your blood, being pricked out of the hill of Venus [in this instance, the base of the thumb] at eight o'clock on Friday morning, and put that in the hole of your nutmeg and then let it dry under your arm. Then take and give her the same, grated in drink or meat. Probatum ["Proven"].[9]

We sold a few books that included love spells, historic and contemporary, but not nearly extensively enough to meet the daily demand from customers. It was something that came up again and again in the shop: longing for love, or healing from heartache. The best I could do was to recommend the person treat his or herself to something nice, commit an act of self love, make a tea of pansies, also nicknamed heart's ease. Love magic was an elephant in the room: I did not feel comfortable encouraging people to engage in that kind of dark, desperate magic. "Look," I'd say, "What would happen if you did a spell and it worked? Could you ever trust the person?"

---

9 "Various Experiments for Love" *Everyday Magicians: Legal Records and Magic Manuscripts from Tudor England*, edited by Sharon Hubs Wright and Frank Klassen, 75.

This was the plot, essentially, of *Bell, Book, and Candle* (1958), my favorite movie about witchcraft and one which tackles the thorny question of what it means to fall in love. I'd recommend it to shop visitors: *Go on, draw yourself a bath and bring it up on your laptop.* But ultimately, I couldn't tell them much about love magic because I myself was stumped as to what love could possibly be in the aftermath of so much grief. It would take years of discipline initiated by Saturn's return to my first house to rebuild and redefine. And many years after that to accept that cultivating a loving relationship is both a lifelong struggle that must center on the self, and one of the most worthy spiritual pursuits through which I have learned to relate to others.

RITES OF SPRING

The Witch Queen shared lore about the Spring Equinox I could find no record for in books. She said she'd been told of a ritual she had never tried, though she'd lived in the same neighborhood for years. It went something like this: at sunrise at the onset of spring when light and dark have equal measure, go to the highest point in your parish, and greet the sunrise. This is to announce your presence to the land, and pray that it may keep and protect you, and bring bounty into your life.

"Want to try it this year?" she asked.

"Yes! Yes! Yes! I can't wait!"

At that time the highest point near us was, we determined, Crystal Palace, a big old park in South London. It was named Crystal Palace because the Crystal Palace, a massive glass and iron behemoth built to hold the first Great Exhibition of 1851, had been moved there from Hyde Park in 1854. Although the building burned down in 1936, Crystal Palace maintains to this day highlights of outdoor Victorian entertainment: manicured gardens, fountains and obelisks, a maze to wander around, a lake to paddle boat in, and a series of thirty-three huge model dinosaurs made in 1854. In addition to the dinosaurs my favorite part of Crystal Palace's history was the British premiere of cast-iron public urinals in 1951, a big moment in the history of public cruising and gay sex.

We arranged to meet at 4:30 AM by the bus stop nearest the park, while it was still dark, to give us time to find the best spot for sunrise at 6:03 AM.

Typically, my Spring Equinox celebration was a riff on that of Scott Cunningham, gay solitary herbalist witch whose *Encyclopedia of Magical Herbs* was invaluable to me, and a bestseller at Treadwell's. Cunningham's ritual is beautiful: simply bring as many flowers into your house as you can. Fill your cauldron, fill your pots and pans, pack your altar, strew petals on the floor and place flowers in your hair. I loved how he wrote: *"Invoke the Goddess and God in whatever words please you."* Cunningham advises to touch the plants and flowers, to spend time in silence with them, to thank them for their companionship: *"I walk the earth in friendship, not in dominance."* I'd eat pomegranates and honey on toast among my daffodils and roses, and to cap off what is a celebration of the return of a green and fruitful world, I'd jerk off as many times as I could until exhaustion, my special prayer for a season of sunshine and blossoming, creativity and abundance.

That year my Spring Equinox, also called Ostara, was already shaping out to be spectacular: I splurged on tickets to see the English National Ballet dance Pina Bausch's *Rite of Spring* (*Le Sacre du Printemps*, composed by Igor Stravinsky and first performed in 1913). This was one of my favorite pieces of art, but I had only devoured it on YouTube: a 1975 recording of the deeply visceral, astonishing performance in which a woman is chosen to dance until she dies, in sacrifice to unknown gods. Bausch's genius choreography—bodies contorting in the pleasure and pain of worship, circling and pushing in a herd and surging occasionally in individual ecstatic expression—is intensified by the ground on which it is staged, which is covered in soil that ensures the dancers become increasingly filthy as they sweat and dance for their lives.

To prepare myself for this and for my 4:30 AM meeting I decided to take a long hot bath to warm myself and wake myself up. Cleansing is important before ritual, whether it's a bath or shower. But bathing just feels magical no matter it's done: hot water is enough to get the heart racing and the blood flowing. I like to embellish a bath with anything I have to hand: candles all around, branches of rosemary and jasmine buds thrown in, salts to exfoliate, oils depending on the situation, in this case some citruses to help wake myself up. Hydrating carefully while bathing, drinking green tea with lemon and honey.

A few days after my ritual with The Witch Queen, I would watch this music unfold in person: how the choreography seemed to begin before the music, as workers wheeled four large dumpsters of soil onto the stage, dumped them in unison, then used long rakes to spread it evenly. I was close enough to breathe in the damp smell of earth, like chopped beets, as it was tilled and kicked up by the dancers in their furious movements. But I was too excited about seeing Pina Bausch's choreography in person the evening of the ritual, so instead of watching that on YouTube, I opted for the video that first taught me about Stravinsky's ballet as a child: Disney's 1940 psychosexual fever dream which Susan Sontag once described as exemplifying "certain formal structures and themes of fascist art," *Fantasia*. My apartment filled with daffodils, my bath filled with herbs and blowers, I settled down to focus on the animated portrayal of the birth of single celled and then multicellular organisms on earth, their breeding and growing and emergence from the sea to land, evolution into dinosaurs, then extinction and destruction, all backed by Stravinsky's bizarre rhythms and prominent bassoon.

At 3:45 AM I bundled up and got on my bicycle. The distance to Crystal Palace wasn't technically that far, but as it was the highest elevation, the journey included huge hills, and I wanted to leave time for the drama that would involve cycling up them in thirty-eight degree weather.

We met at the bus stop. The Witch Queen knew the exact place to go where there was a gap in the wrought iron fence for, I imagine, teenagers, witches, and horny queers to enter after hours. We allowed our eyes to adjust to the darkness, navigated our way to entrance and ascent to a place where we could watch the sunrise. We walked mostly in silence, enjoying the crunch of our feet and the special feeling of having a shared purpose in a place that was meant to be off limits. She had long been a loving friend to me, and a fair and caring employer, and we could enjoy the quiet by night as much as we enjoyed inexhaustible conversation by day. Finally, we came into a clearing where there was a large stone staircase leading to a kind of promenade and plateau in the park. It was perfect. At the top of the stairs on either side, there were two huge sphinxes. Monuments from the Victorian craze for Egyptian culture, that looked a little like Pamela Colman Smith's illustration of The Chariot card. "*We are going to watch the sunrise sitting on some friggen stone sphinxes!*" I shouted. We laughed and hustled up the final stairs. We each chose a mythical beast. We sat and breathed deeply, the sky turned lighter and lighter, and we raised our hands in greeting to the rising sun.

CALIBAN AND THE WITCH (2004)

When I worked at the bookshop, witch after witch after witch would ask for Silvia Federici's *Caliban and the Witch: Women, the Body and Primitive Accumulation* (2004). Caliban and the Witch is a Marxist-feminist interpretation of the witch trials in Europe that follows from Federici's work in the 1980s with Leopoldina Fortunati on *Il Grande Calibano* (1984). It was a slightly difficult book to order, and comparatively expensive, so we didn't stock it in great quantities. It's also primarily an academic work by an academic writer. The presence of witches within the book is confined to one chapter, mostly overwhelmed by wider contexts: historic, cultural, philosophical. After talking to customers or watching them leaf through a copy, it seemed like people *wanted* to want to read the book, or wanted the book to be something it wasn't, and above all felt embarrassed about not having read it. I tried to turn them on to other witches' writings: Starhawk, Rachel Pollack, and when it came out, Kristen Sollee's *Witches, Sluts, Feminists*.

Customers desired the book to be (this I crowd-sourced) vivid and richly researched descriptions of witches themselves—what they did, why they were persecuted—from which to draw a spiritual lineage, and the tools to incorporate these witchcrafts into broader, anti-capitalist arguments *for the present*. But the title is explicit, in a way: Caliban, a monstrous character from Shakespeare's *The Tempest,* is tormented and held against his will in the play—punishment for being the son of a witch. The witch is his mother, Sycorax, a long dead character we never meet but only hear of in relation to Caliban's present suffering. Sycorax is condemned by characters the audience is supposed to sympathize with, like Prospero. From a magical perspective the play offers an interesting double-standard: the elite conjurations of a rich nobleman, Prospero, are applauded, even though Prospero uses his magic to colonize and rule the island of his exile, and later he's restored to his dukedom in Milan. Caliban, a native of the island, is punished for the foul witchcraft of his Algerian mother, Sycorax. This double-standard of *who* was condemned and persecuted as a witch in the early modern period has been unpacked, beautifully and persuasively, by post-colonial writers and other feminists.

But much like Sycorax the witch in *The Tempest*, witches are fairly absent from Federici's sweeping analysis of the transition from feudalism to capitalism. Federici's witch is a composite figure, an archetype of feminized power, its exploitation and suppression, rather than a named historic subject with any specificity. Mostly her presence is in the form of faceless dead women and a mounting death toll. This relative absence doesn't necessarily weaken Federici's insight and analysis, her grand synthesis of heresy and class—it simply keeps the work of digging through the history of witchcraft unfinished, in need of active revisitation.

> Why, after 500 years of capital's rule, at the beginning of the third millennium, are workers on a mass scale still defined as paupers, witches, and outlaws? How are land expropriation and mass pauperization related to the continuous attack on women? And what do we learn about capitalist development, past and present, once we examine it through the vantage-point of a feminist perspective? It is with these questions in mind that in this work I have revisited the "transition" from

> feudalism to capitalism from the viewpoint of women, the body, and primitive accumulation.[10]

Crucial to Federici in *Caliban and the Witch* is the revolutionary tradition of circling back to the "transition to capitalism" in order to search for clues to its undoing, seeds of its destruction. This is an act of divination—looking in the guts of the past for ill omens—that I wholeheartedly agree with and partake in myself. For her, the witch trials are a flashpoint for better understanding the creation of capital by waged work, and the unwaged, feminized labor of reproduction, child-rearing, and housework that was a precondition for capitalist accumulation. Or as I think of it: the figure of the witch is relational, the body of the witch is an intersection of forces. The work of witchcraft lies in understanding these intersections and harnessing their meaning for our own purposes.

As an initiate of Hekate, I'm always working at the crossroads, the traditional place of her worship—usually I'd find a crossroads as close to cypress trees as I could, her favorite. At my last place in London I found a particularly powerful crossroads in a park, marked at its fork by three cypress trees, a perfect offering to the triple moon goddess on earth. Spellwork is all about combining as many of the most powerful symbols in one place as you can, the more the better. There's the crossroads we make magic at, and then there's the crossroads that map onto our own bodies: classed, gendered, racialized, sick or disabled, aged, it all flavors the magic we make, the intuition we have to work with. By candlelight I have dipped my fingers in the ash leftovers of burnt offerings to Hekate and drawn these crossroads over my chest, my belly, my thighs, my arms, imagining myself to be a crossroads for her worship, my spells to be vectors of intersection with my stars, my life choices, my

---

10 Silvia Federici, *Caliban and the Witch: Women, the Body and Primitive Accumulation* (New York: Autonomedia, 2004) 11-12.

victories and defeats, my experiences that lie beyond victory or defeat, my basic needs and loftiest ambitions.

> The most important historical question addressed by the book is how to account for the execution of hundreds of thousands of "Witches" at the beginning of the modern era, and how to explain why the rise of capitalism was coeval with a war against women . . . My work here is only a sketch of the research that would be necessary to clarify the connections I have mentioned, and especially the relation between the witch-hunt and the contemporary development of a new sexual division of labor, confining women to reproductive work. It is sufficient, however, to demonstrate that the persecution of witches (like the slave trade and the enclosures) was a central aspect of the accumulation and formation of the modern proletariat, in Europe as well as in the "New World."[11]

Between *Caliban and the Witch* and Federici's follow-up book, *Witches, Witch-Hunting, and Women* (2018), there's a fairly major but uncommented upon adjustment: from "hundreds of thousands" to "thousands" of witches burned, and in most regions, "dozens." That's good: times have changed, scholars have worked with the records related to witch trials and adjusted the death toll over a period of three hundred years, from millions to tens of thousands. But I think this silent adjustment poses a significant problem for a book that argues the witch trials to be akin to the slave trade and the enclosure of land as a central event in the history of capitalism. The witch trials *in no way* meet the scale of enslavement or the colonization of land, by a very, very long shot.

That the tools of the persecution of witches (legal and technological) were rolled out on an exponential scale

11 Federici, *Caliban and the Witch*, 14.

in colonized places is of great significance not only to understanding how capitalism works—extraction, brutality, power in the hands of a very limited number of people—but also to understanding the need for coalition building at every crossroads. We have been carefully torn apart, on an individual and collective level. This might have been reflected in Federici's initial text, as the research existed then to describe the trials in proportion to the broader evils of Christian imperialism, but because *Caliban and the Witch* is primarily a work of Marxist-feminist philosophy, engagement with witches is sparse, lacking in detail and specificity, and engagement with archives is entirely absent. The endnotes of each chapter are enlightening, all of them from secondary sources, and one would have to read the actual documentation of trials to be precise about the nature of the crossroads where witches lie.

Federici's source material is all secondary, and even when revisiting *Caliban* in 2018's *Witches, Witch-Hunting, and Women*, the secondary material on witches themselves remains largely confined to work written in the 1970s and '80s. Federici hits her stride when she is talking about contemporary violence against women, especially the postcolonial rollout of vigilante witch hunts. Federici is at her strongest when forcing the past to yield a prototype for the present: a feminist who resists capitalism. This work is all up to date in its citations and analysis of twentieth and twenty-first century witch hunts. This is important political work, and "the witch" is only significant to Federici when she aids in this political work, when she screams a rallying cry.

It is also painful work, upsetting, overwhelming, which is why I feel ambivalent about its tone and method. It tends to fit an aspect of the queer- and trans-feminist spaces I've run in for a while now: outraged by the brutality of the world we live in, we rally against it by taking it out on each another. *Do you know how many trans people were murdered last year?* Yeah, I do, because I'm trans and also because that's kindof the first thing anyone knows about trans people, our death count. *Do you know how they tortured and burned witches?* Yeah, I do, because I'm a witch and also that's kindof the first thing *anyone* knows about witches, the guts and the gore. Rather than assuming the witches who came into my shop needed to hear more about violence, I took for granted they'd been exposed to the horror firsthand and deserved a break. A space to wander and wonder, in relative safety and serenity. Time to read against the grain of violence that is so hard to make meaning out of, time to read beyond retraumatizing themselves, time to read the things that will nourish them to show up to the protest when the time comes. Time to read about the ingredients of the spells they will cast. These desires were not satisfied by *Caliban and the Witch* or *Witches, Witch-Hunting, and Women*; in focusing on the political stakes of witch trials there was no room for spirituality, and no room for the body—the body of the witch, the body of the reader. The proverbial sexuality of witches was only invoked in the book after women had died on account of it. The brilliance of the book—a revolutionary synthesis of sources—is its downfall for witches. *You don't have to read this book to be a witch,* I'd tell these customers, mostly young women and queers. *Read this book if you want to stay angry, read this book to know more about history. But it's okay to spare yourself.*

AN ABC OF WITCHCRAFT PAST AND PRESENT (1973)

A good book to start with to inform a witchcraft that is wild, feminist, and free is Doreen Valiente's *An ABC of Witchcraft Past and Present*. It's a real who's who and what's what of twentieth century Wicca, and it offers a rooted and playful adaptation of historical and archaeological sources from someone who was there nearly from the beginning. Combine it with Valiente's autobiography *The Rebirth of Witchcraft* (1989), and Philip Heselton's *Doreen Valiente: Witch* (2016) and you have an unholy trinity of information to really understand the cultural context for Wicca and one of its founding mothers, as well as her sassy sense of humor and love of football and horse racing.

The A to Z format of *An ABC of Witchcraft Past and Present* and its index of further themes is incredibly useful to read cover to cover, to dip into for synchronicities, to keep on hand in the magic circle or by your desk. The Four Airts, Magical Alphabets, Amulets, the Antiquity of Witchcraft, Apuleius, Aradia, Artemis, Astral Plane, Astrology . . . the book consolidates a lifetime of study, interest in folklore, and experience working with various magical groups. And Valiente is also a bargain witch: her magical collection of objects, which still survives intact to this day, is a largely thrifted affair. She knew how to spot a magical deal in the wild, and she knew how to consecrate and pour power into these knick-knacks. There are many tips in this book about how to do that: how to make a scrying mirror from an old picture frame, how to consecrate a knife to be your athame, how to make charms from everyday bric-a-brac.

One entry, "The Black Fast," was lifted and turned into a group ritual by my colleagues and me at Treadwell's. The Black Fast was a name given to a kind of fast that involved forgoing all animal products, meat, and dairy, a kind of veganism with intention. It came from the trial of Mabel Brigge, executed for witchcraft in 1538 for supposedly fasting with the intent to kill King Henry VIII. Valiente calls it, "Fasting to aid concentration for some particular purpose" and extolls it as an old example of the tried and tested "occult potentialities of the human mind." We at Treadwell's met after work one day to agree upon our own Black Fast, veganism undertaken with intent to curse the Tory government, and slow the effects of their withdrawal of Britain from Europe.

> Mabel Brigge protested at her trial that she had only used this method to compel a thief to restore stolen goods, and hence its purpose was a righteous one. However, a witness against her claimed that she had admitted using the Black Fast to bring about a man's death, and that the man had broken his neck before the period of the fast was completed.[12]

I consulted the *Letters and Papers, Foreign and Domestic, Henry VIII, Volume 13 Part 1, January-July 1538*, the printed government records from the time period that chronicled Mabel's trial and execution, and sure enough, Valiente's description was precise to the extent that she must have consulted the same documents herself. There was nothing more that was needed than her instruction, and so we agreed to abstain from all meat and dairy, and met month by month, chanting "*Whither, whither*" in hopes of slowing the conservative

12 Doreen Valiente, *An ABC of Witchcraft Past and Present* (London: Robert Hale, 1986), 41.

consolidation of power in the local elections. That spring, the Conservatives lost thirty-five seats in Parliament and the neo-fascist UKIP lost just about every seat that had been up for re-election. But this turn of the tides was not enough to change things, we would have had to coordinate the Black Fast on a much larger scale.

The people, places, events, artifacts, and symbolism the book draws together will thrill any reader with new obsessions to pursue and new rituals to try out. But the long entry on "Witchcraft" is really all that is needed to self-initiate; and her introduction defines why anyone might want to do this in the first place:

> It has been argued by skeptics that witchcraft cannot possibly be a genuine religion, because it has no sacred book, no sacred liturgy, nor anything which identifies it with the other religions of mankind. The reason, however, why witchcraft has none of these things, is that it is older than these things. Witchcraft is as old as mankind itself; and it does not begin from books. It begins in the heart. Anyone who has a sense of wonder, an imagination that can respond to the moods of nature, who is not satisfied with the glib answers of the intellectual and materialist, who has curiosity and awareness—that person has the beginnings of witchcraft.
>
> I became a witch many years ago. That is, I was initiated into one of the various branches of the witch cult in Britain today; and since that time I have made contact with other sections of the cult and been initiated into some of those also.
>
> I have danced at the witches' Sabbath on many occasions, and found carefree enjoyment in it. I have stood under the stars at midnight, and invoked the Old Gods; and I have found in such invocations of the most

> primeval powers, those of Life, Love and Death, an uplifting of consciousness that no orthodox religious service has ever given me.[13]

In her updated introduction to the 1986 edition of the book, Valiente folds this knowledge and experience into excitement about the emergence of feminist and lesbian-feminist covens, for example, naming and applauding Starhawk's beautiful and influential book *The Spiral Dance: A Rebirth of the Ancient Religion of the Great Goddess* (1979). This gets to my favorite thing about Doreen Valiente's writing: she believes one hundred percent in the spiritual power of naming yourself a witch and all of the dedication that entails, and one hundred percent calls people out on their bullshit when they try to turn witchcraft into a dogmatic religion that relies on a fixed fundamentalist approach to "authoritative" texts. This is even reflected in her humble title, An ABC, not The ABC. The power of her "wisecraft" or witchcraft is its ability to change, shifting over time to address and incorporate political need and to remain a comfort to the oppressed. Her deep knowledge effects change in two directions, showing the ways in which a politics of feminist liberation survives at the heart of what we know about witches of the past, and the ways in which our present language allows us to better apprehend the resonance in order to move forward. To her, the defining feature of witchcraft is that it remain a living tradition, and therefore, change shape as it travels and is adapted to the needs of the witches who feel called to it.

---

13 Valiente, *An ABC*, Introduction.

ORIGINAL CRONE

"You don't look like a witch."

A significant proportion of men who walked into the occult bookshop reacted to me that way: You don't look like a witch.

This was 2016 and the 1968 Women's International Terrorist Conspiracy from Hell (W.I.T.C.H.) had been revived, was making the news. They were anonymous, so the news media had obviously filled in the blanks with the sexy, stereotypical pop cultural witches leading up to that moment: the white girls from *The Craft*, *Charmed*, *Bewitched*; Samantha Robinson in *The Love Witch*, a movie that had just come out. A few got singled out for Media Coverage: thin, young, pretty, with long hair and generational wealth who earnestly identified as "crones" and "spinsters." As if their earnestness were enough to strip these archetypes of their meaning, as if fragments of history survived exclusively to be garbled for commercial purposes. I guess the bigger problem was, it seemed to work for them. The latest craze was monetizing the meaning of "crone" and "spinster," and I was depressed about it. And angry; it was suspiciously in sync with the white feminism in the air, those T-shirts that said things like, *Strong Is The New Pretty*, or dieting teas called names like "Cleanse" rather than "Starve." Every generation has its own distinct kind of false consciousness.

History with a capital "H" is mostly a matter of garbling source material to valorize the consolidation of wealth and property, making us accept it as normal. The trickle-down of history as a discipline conceived of within capitalism creates conditions in which no subculture is safe, no outlaw is outlandish enough to avoid being "reclaimed" and put to work to make money. Wealthy white twenty-somethings were calling themselves crones. The President of the United States of America was calling litigation against him a Witch Hunt. Lana Del Rey and many others on Twitter posted instructions to hex him. All of a sudden everybody was a witch?

The figure of the witch has always been relational to a culture in crisis—some of the women and men killed in the "Burning Times" of the fourteenth through seventeenth centuries testified at having become witches twenty, thirty, forty years before they'd gotten arrested. Times had changed, some sickness or famine or crisis emerged, and suddenly they faced trial, torture, and execution.

> She saith, that about one and twenty years since she began saying her Prayers in the evening about bedtime, there did appeare unto her three Spirits, one in the likeness of a young man or boy, and the other of two Puppies . . .[14]
>
> One old woman confessed that she had beene a Witch the space of above fifty years, in which time she also confest that she had done many very wicked things.[15]
>
> . . . of the age of eight and fiftie yeeres, [he] confessed that he had used the practice of Witch-craft from his childhood, and that he had bin trained up in the same by his olde Graundmother, a woman dead many yeares agoe . . .[16]

14 John Davenport, *The Witches of Huntington* . . . (London, Printed by W. Wilson for Richard Clutterbuck, 1648) sig. A3.

15 *A True Relation of the Araignment of eighteene Witches* (London: I.H., 1645) 3.

16 *A Strange Report of Sixe most notorious VVitches* . . . (London, Printed by W.W. for T. Pauier) 1601, sig. A3v.

Maybe you're not a witch unless you're caught, or you're hexing during a crisis. I love love *love* Lana Del Rey. And the hot new crones I'm generalizing about weren't evil, just imprecise. It was my problem, not theirs. I needed to develop a spiritual capaciousness that could withstand the ravages of capitalism and release me from my growing resentment that only certain types of people were making money by calling themselves witches (the rest of us just got treated badly regardless of what we called ourselves). The same was happening in queer and trans circles: a generation of influencers changing the world through modeling underwear was emerging, but in my friend group, we were still unable to afford hormones, were cursed and spat at in broad daylight, and a drunk man had recently tried to set his Rottweiler on us while we were hanging out in front of the local library. The argument for visibility was only making more visible an extreme imbalance in resources.

It was a spiritually murky and confusing time, and we were all part of the same weird ecosystem: unemployable enough to want to make money from witchcraft. Or, disillusioned enough with how money worked to call it what it was: a value system based on magical thinking and bloody hysteria. Aka, witchcraft. But who gets to be a witch? It's a deeply contested status throughout all of history, one that didn't touch most magicians for hire who lived during the centuries of witch panic. This was all good for business, however exasperated I felt.

There was something witchy about it all: the deep anxiety caused by political instability in the UK and USA, the yearning for spiritual paths that could calm and ground despite all of the uncertainty. An essential truth of witchcraft as a spiritual path is that it's always a revival, a reconstruction from fragmentary evidence and faulty memories stitched together to imagine *who* witches used to be, *what* they used to do, and *how* their lives and beliefs and rituals might be recreated. To be a witch in the twenty-first century you must yield to the frustrating lack of evidence, and Surrender Responsibly. The leap of faith isn't in divinity—*duh, of course the divine exists, have you SEEN what flowers and fish and stars look like?*—but in humanity, it's in how humans have contacted the divine. It's harder for me to believe in humanity than to believe in divinity. It's a challenge to believe that humans have been doing a version of what you've been doing for millennia, that doing it connects you to some big family, and that's why it *works*. I have no problem attributing my good or bad luck to a gorgeous, unknowable force. But it's really hard to believe in family after the experience of being born into one.

On the bright side: this was 2016 and I guess I didn't look like a witch! Which was way better than it being 1966 and me not being welcome among witches (queer), or 1866 and me not being allowed to be a witch (died in a coal mine), or 1766 and me not being allowed to be a witch (died disguised as a sailor at sea), or 1666 and me being burned as a witch (heretic), or 1566 and me being burned as a witch (heretic again), all the way back until time immemorial. It was a helpful spiritual exercise to imagine the constraints of my life transposed into different time periods. I don't have any illusions about how bad it's been, and I'm using my witchcraft to make the best of it. And the best thing about being told the same thing over and over is you can come up with a response you really like. "*You don't look like a witch!*" a "Documentary Film Director Looking To Interview Teenage Witches" said to me one day as he walked into the shop. "I know, "I'd say, "that's so you won't see me coming." I'd work my magic on him, keep the conversation going, slowly writing down fake website recommendations on Post-it notes to hold his attention while actual teenage witches came in and out of the shop behind his back, speaking out a spell of protection in real time.

Working in an occult bookshop was about being mysterious and a little sinister in the right moments, to create a Unique Customer Experience for the wide array of self-identified witches who came. Creating the energy of the scene from *The*

Craft when they first enter the occult shop to steal supplies for their magic: Lirio (played by Assumpta Serna), the witchy shop owner, grabs the hand of Sarah (Robin Tunney) who is about to pull back a black curtain, and says: "*That's not for you.*" Like that, I was there to apply all of my reading and spiritual practice and dramatic timing to the right pressure points, telling people what they needed to be initiated into a magical and transformative reading experience based on where they were in that moment, but not beyond.

Later in the movie, Lirio takes Sarah behind the curtain, and what she encounters there scares her away. Which translates, in the actual occult shop I worked in, to lost sales. For a while, our basement was under construction, so we cordoned it off to the public with a velvet rope. When people tried to peer down the steps I could say: "*That's not for you, not yet.*" When I could elevate the intrigue that way, I was guaranteed a sale.

"You don't look like a witch!"

It was 7:00 AM, four hours before the technical start of my 11:00 to 7:00 shift, and they were filming my reaction to the prompt: *You don't look like a witch!*

"Um, well, witches are everywhere among us—the point is, we can look all kinds of ways, but mostly we don't want just *anyone* to notice us . . ."

I tried to sound mysterious, but I probably just sounded awkward. I had agreed to open up early because the film crew for a Japanese television show about magic was in town and asked if they could film in the shop. I would be paid cash-in-hand (£300) for doing this, and as usual I sure needed the money.

Filmmakers of all levels and abilities were always asking to film in the shop: in exchange, these students or auteurs promised us *publicity*. It was exhausting explaining again and again that, as a busy bookshop, we didn't need publicity, but we did need the space free to serve its purpose: book browsing! People love to ask for something hugely vain and inconvenient by explaining how it will be good for you. I have no idea where folks have learned to talk or act like this, but it feels very patriarchal, and it happened all the time. If they'd been honest and gracious about needing a huge favor, I might have at least tried to help. But for filming, we used a pre-formatted email to respond to these inquiries, complete with a cost for renting the shop hourly, in addition to paying the staff member who would oversee the shoot. Once we asked to be paid for our time, the querent usually disappeared. This time was different: the TV show was legit, and the crew also wanted to pay extra *to interview a real witch*, and for me to do a spell for them. Something about making money this way energized me, made me feel like the modern-day equivalent of a witch who had to live on the margins of superstitious villages plagued by bad weather, tough luck, and dynastic family feuds, scamming my way to my next meal. Yes, I will work a spell for your cash, and the spell will work because it was my money spell all along.

Butchdyke, buzzcut, exhausted from never sleeping enough, underweight from not eating to avoid getting periods, dressed like a frumpy librarian with a purple and magenta argyle sweater I'd bought on clearance at the Gap in high school over a decade ago, I noticed the entire camera crew's faces fall, one by one. I wasn't a sexy witch. I didn't even have the decency to wear all-black. "*Are you a boy or girl?*" One crew member asked. I struck a match to light a stick of dragon's blood incense again and again for the camera, my wrist limply flailing. They didn't know how to direct me to change my style, so I camped it up more each time. They asked if I could wear a classic, pointed hat to enhance my look, so I put one on that we kept as a Halloween decoration for the shop. Mortification of the flesh is a pathway to sanctity; moving through and beyond humiliation, I could enter into the perfect mode to create ritual for them in the next segment.

I had my own directorial vision for the spell I would be filmed working. I was imagining the opening of Kenneth Anger's *Inauguration of the Pleasure Dome*, where Samson De Brier slowly adorns himself with rings and a string of diamonds. I wanted that energy and tight close ups on magical still life as it is drawn into active assembly. I thought it could be more subtle, a close on my hands with a mortar and pestle grinding up borage "for courage," making a tea; carving WISDOM and the sigil of Jupiter into a purple candle and anointing it with oil, then using the oil to anoint my third eye; lining and copying out the magic square of Venus onto a piece of paper with a quill and green ink, lighting it on fire and dropping it into a cauldron. I'd had this idea that I would hold shards of different crystals in my mouth—amethyst, citrine, malachite—suck and spit them into the cauldron.

Instead they'd brought their own prop wand—"Like H★★★★ P★★★★★©!"—and filmed me waving it in big circles and in various poses.

"We'll edit in the sparks! Can you say something in Latin?"

That got us to where they had wanted me to go the whole time: *H★★★★ P★★★★★©*.

"Is this the kind of shop H★★★★ P★★★★★© would come to before going to school at H★★★★★★★© School of Witchcraft and Wizardry?"

So, it had come to this. Of course, I was the perfect age to have a deep, indelible knowledge of the Boy Who Lived, H★★★★ P★★★★★©, even if current spirituality didn't really have anything to do with the books and personally I had felt totally betrayed by their author.

"Yes, this is exactly the kind of place Harry would have to come to get books for school: in this section we have books for the History of Magic, or for Potions class, for example."

"And did you learn all of this at H*******©, School of Witchcraft and Wizardry?"

"Oh, no I'm afraid I never got my letter. I'm self-taught, what's called a hedge witch; a solitary practitioner."

"So, you can be a witch or wizard even if you don't get your H*******© letter?"

This I could work with, I could adapt what I'd prepared: "Yes, exactly! We welcome all spiritual seekers here—there is nowhere you have to have gone to school, and no book you should or should not have read. I believe that all magical knowledge and occult wisdom should be available to all people—it's up to the individual to desire the pleasure of its pursuit. As A.E. Waite says of the Hermit Card in the Major Arcana of the Tarot"—and here I pulled the card itself off the top of a deck I'd left on the desk where I'd planted it—"*the beacon in the wizard's hand intimates that 'Where I am, You also may be' . . . the Divine Mysteries secure their own protection from those who are unprepared.* If you're ready, you'll find what you're looking for on these shelves. And even if not, you're still welcome to browse, sit on the couch, read, attend a lecture or workshop."

"CUT! Let's try again and let's stay on the topic: Has H**** P*****© ever come into this very shop?"

And: "Can you show me a magic spell—maybe one to banish a banshee?"

And "Do you have a section of books to defend against the Dark Arts?"

At my lunch break, I rode my bike to the bank to deposit the £300 so I'd be able to use my debit card again—not a bad exchange rate of cash to spells. I never saw the footage and don't know if it ever aired on TV.

A lot of scholarship and pop culture focuses on the persecution of witches, but I don't like to limit my household gods to hassling the spirits of the extremely ill-served. I like scrappy historical witches who did more than get murdered. I like to celebrate the miracle of dying by natural causes, I read of witches who died of natural causes in order to pray that I and my friends will die that way too. I had wanted to make a pilgrimage to Mother Shipton's cave for years. Mother Shipton, an iconic witch whose face launched a thousand facsimiles. What does a witch look like? For centuries, the visual history of witchcraft was by and large a history of Mother Shipton.

Mother Shipton, aka Ursula Southill was born around 1488 and died in 1561. The cave she was born in, and moved back to later in life, is located in Knaresborough, Yorkshire. Mother Shipton is a wonderful witch to venerate on your altar: from the late seventeenth century onward, the legend of her life and her prophesies made for a popular printing and merchandising tradition. There's plenty of source materials to recoup for your altars, for hundreds of years you could buy little pamphlets about her, poems about what she predicted, prints depicting her with the devil, or an imp, or in her cave. Later that expanded to board games, homewares and crockery, door knockers, and even more chapbooks and broadsides. A lot of the rhyming prophesies are clearly counterfeit, or FanFiction, depending how you look at it; things she is not documented as saying but and attributed to her long after her death. She was a witch who leant her voice to many other anonymous witches, who gave us the earliest Witch Merch, not unlike some of the novelty items we occasionally sold at our shop around Halloween: "My Other Car is a Broomstick" bumper stickers, "Hex Appeal" mugs, wooden "Danger! Witch Crossing!" signs.

But it's way bigger than that: any depiction of a cartoon witch with a big, crooked, warty nose and a hunched back is in its essence a depiction of Mother Shipton. She's the Original Crone, the legendary hag whose grotesque features still look back at us in Halloween costumes and decorations. Some say Queen Elizabeth II's face was the most famous face in the world, printed on money, stamps, and official portraits. I secretly hope it's Mother Shipton's, but we just haven't counted her that way; printed in cartoons for centuries, so much of the cheap paper doesn't survive to be counted and wasn't respected enough to preserve.

My first encounters with witches were all versions of Mother Shipton: as a child I was afraid of a life-sized doll of a witch my aunt put in her living room around Halloween, convinced she would come alive and hate me; my fear turned to intrigue when I first saw the Wicked Witch of the West zap Dorothy's red slippers. My intrigue turned to attraction around the same time, when I saw an old crone's face by an entry in my grandma's almanac describing how, during the blue moon that summer, witches would dance naked in the woods to celebrate. Naked old women dancing! I wanted to see that. I loved Witch Hazel in Looney Tunes, I loved Witch Hazel in Disney's Trick or Treat. I enjoyed the twinge of arousal I got from being afraid; my fear turned to love, there wasn't anything to be afraid of after that. I loved these women who owed their big noses and hearty laughter to Mother Shipton. Honoring the reality of her life and power requires a deep dive into centuries of exaggerated perceptions captured in various pop cultural media and memorabilia. It's a rich store of historical information that, by virtue of its sheer bulk, you can neither dismiss nor take too seriously, the perfect conditions for serious spiritual self-evaluation. On my altar I keep a cast figure of Mother Shipton in the form of a little brass door knocker I found at the Bermondsey Antiques Market.

The details of Mother Shipton's life are unreliable and literally murky and hard to read—if the pamphlets about her that were published nearly a century after she died are to be believed.

In *The Life and Death of Mother Shipton*, printed in London in 1677, "R. Head" writes in the introduction that, while on a trip to a monastery in Yorkshire, he found Shipton's life story:

> I was informed by a Gentleman (whose Ancestors by the Gift of King Henry the Eighth, enjoyed a Monastary in those parts) that he had in his keeping some ancient Writings which would in that point satisfie my desire, were they not so injured by Time, as now not legible to Read; however, I not despairing to find out their meaning, with much Importunity desired to have a sign of them; which having obtained, I took the best Galls I could get, beat them grosly, and lad them to steep one day in good white-Wine, that done, I distilled them with the Wine; and with the distilled Water that came off them, I wetted handsomely the old Letters, whereby they seemed as fresh and fair, as if they had been but newly written; here did I find her Life and Prophesies copied out by an impartial hand, which I have in this Book presented to thy view.[17]

Head literally makes a potion of oak galls, white wine, and water, and wets an old collection of letters to make their writings more legible in order to recover the story of Mother Shipton. The story that follows locates the source of Shipton's power to foresee the future in her father, the Devil. Orphaned at age fifteen, Shipton's mother Agatha meets and agrees to marry a "comely" man, the Devil in disguise. The Devil then reveals himself to Agatha, and initiates her into his power, in a description that could have been lifted from the records of the witch trials themselves:

---

17 *The Life and Death of Mother Shipton* (London: Printed for B. Harries at the Sationers Arms in Sweithings-Ally, near the Royal Exchange in Cornhill, 1677) sig. A2.

Now could my lecherous Devil stay no longer, but he must needs walk a corant with his Mistris into another private room, and there courted her to lust; the simple Girle consented, and so they both went to bed together, with the Ceremonies of Marriage. His touches (as she confessed wot the Midwife that delivered her of her Devilish Off-spring) were as cold as ice, or snow. After they had lain a little while together, he told her what he was, and what she must do hereafter, if she intended to live happy and delightful days. First, he told her that he was no Mortal, but a Spirit immaterial, and not burdened by a body, nor houndred by any material thing; So that I can when I please pierce through the Earth and ransack its creatures, and bring what precious things I please from thence to bestow on those that serve me. I know all rare Arts and Sciences, and can teach them to whom I please. I can disturb the Element, stir up Thunders and Lightnings, destroy the best of things which were created for the use of man; and can appear in what shape or form I please. It will be too long to discribe my power, or tell thee what I can do; but will only tell thee what thou shalt do. That being done, I will give the power to raise Haile, Tempests, with lightning and Thunder; the Winds shall be at thy command, and shall hear thee whither thou art willing to go, though never so far off, and shall bring thee back again when thou hast a mind to return. The hidden treasures of the Earth shall be at thy dispose and pleasure, and nothing shall be wanting to compleat thy happiness here. Thou shalt moreover, heal or kill whom thou pleasest; destroy or preserve either man or beast; know what is past, and assuredly tell what is to come.[18]

18 *The Life and Death of Mother Shipton*, 3.

After taking the Devil's bargain, Agatha slowly begins to waste away, finally dying in childbirth. When young Ursula is born, she inherits all the power promised by her father who visits her daily in the form of a cat, a dog, a bat, or a hog, and is cared for through childhood by a nurse. In school, she becomes famous for her grotesque appearance, and her quick learning: "she exactly pronounced every Letter in the alphabet without teaching. Hereupon her Mistriss shewed her a Primmer, which she read as well at first sight, as any in the School, and so proceeded in any Book was shown her." Eventually she is kicked out of school for taking revenge upon students who make fun of her: "some were pinch't and yet no hand seen that did it; others struck speechless when they were about to say their Lessons, not being able to utter a word." The book concludes with a long description of her prophecies, interpreting them to the year of its own publication in 1677, and ending with still more prophecies that had yet to be fulfilled, including "the overthrow of the French, or some great disaster to that Nation, with several other Revolution." Despite its focus on the monstrous appearance of Mother Shipton, overall these continuously printed stories and the details of sex, death, and Devil-given magical powers are often positive and even reverential to Mother Shipton, at a time when witches and heretics were still persecuted.

The weirdest thing about driving into Knaresborough on pilgrimage to Mother Shipton's cave was the intense feeling of déjà vu that came over me as the buttery, gray northern sunlight was blotted out by trees. A feeling so strong I was convinced I'd never experienced déjà vu before that moment and haven't since. Any other time had paled in comparison.

In scientific terms, driving into Knaresborough inspired a kind of brain failure in me. My temporal lobe and hippocampus made a faulty connection. And apparently I am more prone to déjà vu because I

- Have a high level of education
- Travel a lot
- Remember my dreams
- Hold liberal beliefs.

Even if scientists know how déjà vu happens, they don't know why. So I was left to my own devices, awed that my body had allowed me to experience—illusion or not—the momentous sensation that I had *made this journey before*, a sensation I couldn't force or fake. Belief in magic had always given me this—involuntary bodily states of awkwardness that I was thankful for. At that thought, another sensation I couldn't force or fake hit me: the hair on the back of my neck stood up. Everything felt heightened, prime conditions for a good time.

I'm not even suggesting that I knew Mother Shipton, or was Mother Shipton (even if Father_Shipton has been a screenname I've used over the years). One of the most exciting things about Mother Shipton's Cave is that it's the oldest tourist attraction in the United Kingdom: it's been marked as a "heritage" site since 1630. Since then, pilgrims like me are charged a small admission fee to enter the forest, the cave, and gawk at the petrifying well that's just next to it. It was cool to imagine the possibility that I have been visiting the same tourist attractions again and again across many lifetimes, amassing the same campy merchandise and taking my photo in front of the same rock formations, engaging in the same earnest worship of crones.

To get tickets into the forest where Mother Shipton lived you must go into the gift shop where they sell them. It's the perfect fusion of the holy through the profane: in the shop there are waxen dioramas of Mother Shipton at a cauldron, panels that tell her story, multiple old fortunetelling machines—Zoltar, Lucky Lady. Most prolific of all throughout the large room are petrified objects, positioned everywhere. The real source of mystery and intrigue and the reason the area has been a tourist attraction since the 1630s is the dropping well near the cave, a well so rich in sulfate and carbonate that leaving items there causes them to be encrusted in a ghostly white shell of minerals.

Objects petrified in the well hang from the ceiling of the gift shop: baseball mitts, top hats, officer's hats, slippers, shoes, tea kettles, dolls. On display under a glass case is a petrified cowboy hat worn by John Wayne, and there are petrified teddy bears everywhere. If you order in advance, you can buy one from the shop upon your visit. Outside and hanging from the rock formation dripping with water are long, ominous ropes of little teddy bears strung up to petrify. A nearby placard reads: *"As early as 1538 Henry VIII's Antiquary travelled here to research and write about it. He wrote:- 'A well of a wonderful nature called the Dripping Well, for out of great rocks it emits water continually, the water is of such a nature that what ever is cast in and is touched by this water turneth into stone.'"* This was John Leland, who in the same decade had toured much of the great libraries in England before their dissolution and destruction, and would spend much of his life searching to recover what he'd seen disappear before his very eyes. Another pilgrimage I have yet to make is the so-called Leland Trail, following his footsteps in Somerset in search of books, antiquities, old churches, and megaliths.

Mother Shipton's cave itself is not very deep—inside, a spotlight backlights a bronze statue of the old crone herself, and you can press a button that plays some audio: the sound of a storm, the sound of witches' laughter. Behind the statue, in the deepest part of the cave, I groped in the dark until I found a high shelf of rock to place my offerings to her: a hagstone I'd painted in goldleaf, a shiny penny, a mixture of herbs. I prayed to her like some people pray to the Virgin Mary: *Protect me, light my path with your wisdom and understanding.*

PUPPIES ENOUGH

Cotton Mather's Wonders of the Invisible World, compiled in 1692, circulated by manuscript and word of mouth, then published in 1693, stoked the flames of the mass panic over witches in Salem, encouraging their capture and punishment. In the book he argued for the legitimacy of spectral evidence. Spectral evidence was a feature of testimonies by accusers: they claimed they had seen ghostly visions, or apparitions of those they were condemning as witches. Controversially for the time, at Salem such visions were accepted as proof that the witch had entered into a relationship with the Devil. Susanna Martin—the Salem witch nearest and dearest to my heart, if I were forced to choose—was a victim of this argument; spectral evidence was used to convict her. But Susanna Martin had a hot take of her own against this madness, which Mather recorded in his chapter on her trial:

> Magistrate. Pray, what ails these People?
> Martin. I don't know.
> Magistrate. But what do you think ails them?
> Martin. I don't desire to spend my Judgment upon it.
> Magistrate. Don't you think they are bewitch'd?
> Martin. No, I do not think they are.
> Magistrate. Tell us your Thoughts about them then.
> Martin. No, my thoughts are my own, when they are in, but when they are out they are anothers. Their Master—

> Magistrate. Their Master? who do you think is their Master?
> Martin. If they be dealing in the Black Art, you may know as well as I.
> Magistrate. Well, what have you done towards this?
> Martin. Nothing at all.
> Magistrate. Why, 'tis you or your Appearance.
> Martin. I cannot help it.
> Magistrate. Is it not your Master? How comes your Appearance to hurt these [people]?
> Martin. How do I know? He that appeared in the Shape of Samuel, a glorified Saint, may appear in any ones Shape.[19]

Susanna Martin knew her bible: the appearance of "the Shape of Samuel" comes from the Book of Samuel, in which King Saul seeks out the "witch of Endor" in order that she might conjure up the spirit of the prophet Samuel. One of the few mentions of necromancy in the bible, it was a flashpoint for debate over the existence of witches, the power of spirits to take the form of holy men, and whether it was okay for Christians to consult fortune tellers. Susanna Martin was taking part in a centuries old intellectual debate with serious earthly consequences for her in particular, when she agreed with theologians like John Calvin, who believed the ghost to be a demon appearing in Samuel's form without any involvement of the spirit of Samuel. A deepfake Samuel. The bible, Calvin argued, sets a precedent that shows the Devil is able to appear in the form of people without their consent. Susanna Martin argued that the same had happened to her.

I love Susanna Martin as a smart, sharp reader. I love Susanna Martin as a woman who values her interiority—"My thoughts are my own, when they are in"—and who stands

---

19 Cotton Mather, *On Witchcraft Being the Wonders of the Invisible World, First Published At Boston in October 1692 and now reprinted with additional matter . . .* (New York: The Peter Pauper Press) 113-114.

up for herself. But the longest and most detailed accusation against Susanna Martin, and the reason I have come to love her most, centers on spectral puppies. Cotton Mather calls it a "truly admirable" story, told by John Kembal, Martin's neighbor. Kembal testified twice against Martin: first accusing her of killing his cattle, and next of setting these ghostly black puppies to attack him. The story: Kembal had considered buying a puppy from Martin, whose bitch had given birth. But she would not give him his pick of the litter, so he decided to buy from another neighbor. Taking his business elsewhere without even bothering to follow up with her was infuriating. When this news was relayed to Susanna through her husband George, she was overheard by another neighbor named Edmond Elliot to exclaim in anger: *If I live, I'll give him Puppies enough!*

So, *Puppies Enough* is the title of this horror movie. A few days later, as Kembal left the woods on the way home, he saw a black cloud arising in the northwest and "immediately felt a force upon him" which made him unable to avoid tripping over the stumps of trees in his path. Suddenly

> there appeared unto him, a little thing like a Puppy, of a Darkish Colour; and it shot backwards and forwards between his Legs. He had the Courage to use all possible Endeavours of Cutting it with his Ax; but he could not Hit it: the Puppy gave a jump from him, and went, as to him it seem'd, into the Ground. Going a little further, there appeared unto him a Black Puppy, somewhat bigger than the first, but as Black as a Cole. Its Motions were quicker than those of his Ax; it flew at his Belly, and away; then at his Throat; so, over his Shoulder one way, and then over his Shoulder another way. His Heart now began to fail him, and he thought the Dog would have tore his Throat out. But he recovered himself and called upon God in his

> Distress; and naming the name of JESUS CHRIST, it vanished away at once.[20]

The hallucination moves from being puppy-like, to being a puppy, to being a killer dog, and according to Kembal he told no one of the encounter. The next day Susanna Martin allegedly asked that same eavesdropping neighbor Edmond Elliot about Kembal, because, "*They say, he was frighted last Night.*" Eliot responded: "*With what?*" She answered: "*With Puppies.*" She said she'd heard tell of it about the town, although Kembal claimed he had mentioned the matter to *"no Creature living."* These and eleven other testimonies against Martin resulted in her execution on July 19, 1693; Cotton Mather records that her plea throughout was: *"That she had lead a most virtuous and holy life."*

Susanna Martin's alleged outburst—*I'll give him Puppies enough!*—and the canine apparitions that follow exemplifies the tragedy of the Salem trials, which elevated everyday experiences of neighborly tension and cooperation, eavesdropping and finger wagging, into a whole new stratosphere of fear and delusion. Close your eyes and picture the scene Kembal describes: an adult man walking along a trail with cart and axe, veering off the trail and stumbling, blinking and rubbing his eyes upon the sight of a small creature that increasingly looks like a puppy, a playful puppy, a puppy with the zoomies moving too quickly to be *cut down* by the man's axe. A puppy beginning to look more like a dog—you know those ungainly puppies who are like six months old but already huge and clumsy as they try to catch up to their growth spurt. Like most grown men I have observed, he has a filthy temper that turns violent quickly. The entire world is oriented toward coddling and soothing this man's anger, but in the backwoods of this British colony there is a shortage of that kind of female labor. The clumsy excited puppy disappears as the man trips and falls and cries out, enraged. Imagine

20 Mather, *On Witchcraft*, 117.

dredging that story up in court in hopes that your neighbor be punished with death. I could cry when I think about how the story survives, not as a weird tale of puppies hallucinated in the wilderness, but as a nail in the coffin of a murdered old woman who claimed her innocence to the very end.

There is no straightforward spiritual or historical path to women like Susanna Martin, linked to witchcraft and the Devil against her will, against her soundest arguments—arguments otherwise respected and published when voiced by men. Susanna Martin's not a witch—if I'm to respect her dying wishes—and yet when I assemble together the parts of her called witch by her murderers, it's meant to be a gentle shorthand— a gathering of all the things she was punished for in order to sing their praises. To call her witch is a citation of impossibility: the impossibility of ever knowing anything about her beyond spectral evidence. To call her witch is a warning: barely anything survives from that long ago that *isn't* spectral evidence at this point. Who is to be trusted? It's unfair that she died to prove the finality of so many failures: of her neighbors to appreciate one another's humanity, of the courts to protect anyone, of me myself, a self-appointed and earnest heir, longing to understand once and for all where I've chosen to come from.

But I can connect with Susanna Martin over puppies. *I'll give him Puppies enough!* is the kind of thing I would say if I was angry. I am a fairly gentle person, and I am superstitious about cursing; I like to insult people proportional to the problem at hand. I'd be upset if I lost money I had counted on from a neighbor. And I love dogs, I love my dog and would be insulted if I had puppies that someone overlooked for the puppies of another. My first heresy, as I remember it, was puppy-related: *I don't want to have children. I will have puppies instead.* I remember telling my teacher in third grade, feeling the room get uncomfortable. Some kids laughed. The teacher took me aside and said kindly but firmly: *You can't say that, Brooke.* I asked why not. *You just can't, it's not right, it's not how things work, when you're older you'll understand that it's a sin.* I remember thinking: *You are not going to stop me from having puppies.*

I knew it would have been a miracle to give birth to puppies, but I believed wholeheartedly that such a miracle was possible for me. I could imagine the holy card: instead of the little children of Lourdes being visited by the Virgin Mary and a dancing sun, I would be visited by the gift of Puppies. An interest in all things dogs and wolves dominated my childhood; I was desperate to prove I deserved a pet, and to do so I researched all I could about their care, the different breeds, their evolutionary histories. This deep love brought me to the crossroads of another heresy: one day in school, Sister Vincent—an angry, ancient nun who should never have been forced to follow her vows of obedience into the work of teaching children-ranted in class about the nature of our souls, heaven and hell. We fifth graders were dirty and would probably go to hell, she said. Our souls were already stained with mortal sin. But more frightening than that, Sister Vincent (who we called Sid Vicious), said that only humans had souls and therefore could be saved—there were no animals in heaven. I remember sobbing at home with my dog Champ in my arms. I couldn't imagine a God who would create animals and not love them; I couldn't imagine the spirit of Champ's personality to be without a spark of immortality, just like mine. To comfort me my mother gave me the best advice she ever would: *Don't listen to her, heaven is what you make it, God is as loving as you could imagine, and more.* It was my first lesson in conceiving of a divinity outside of the punishing God of organized religion. I am sure she didn't mean for me to begin to split God into a pantheon of deities and intelligences that I would eventually make offerings of blood, sweat, and cum to, but the pathway was miraculously opened that day.

A weird, intimate relationship to the animal world is one of the patterns among the witch trials that I am most attracted to, and I use these accounts to recover otherwise unknowable people to myself. I can at least understand and connect with the desire to commune with animals. Reading through the transcontinental sprawl of pamphlets about witch trials, the feature of testimonies against witches that takes up the most space describes their relationship to animals. Today we'd call them familiars or pets; at the time they were called imps—a vegetable word in its origins, meaning "young shoot," that becomes animal and occasionally human in its meaning around the time of the witch hunts. It's always been strange to me that the presence of animal intelligence and relationships is not better represented in the pop cultural representations of witchcraft, which tend to sideline the immense power of these critters to focus on the human.

The documented obsession with describing witches' relations to animals, feeding them with their own blood, is an integral part of making a pact with Satan. It reminds me of how Donna Haraway describes her relationship to her dog in the opening to *The Companion Species Manifesto*: "Ms. Cayenne Pepper continues to colonize my cells—a sure case of what the biologist Lynn Margulis calls symbiogenesis. I bet if you check our DNA, you'd find some potent transfections between us."[21] My history of witchcraft is also a history of transfections and mutually beneficial exchange.

Here's a testimony from *The Wonderful Discoverie of the Witchcrafts of Margaret and Phillip Flower, daughters of Joan Flower,* (and yes, Phillip is a girl's name in this pamphlet!). In it, the Devil appears to Joan Flower:

---

21 Donna J. Haraway, "The Companion Species Manifesto," in *Manifestly Haraway* (Minneapolis: University of Minnesota Press, 2016) 93.

> He came more neerer unto them, and in plaine tearmes to come quickly to the purpose, offered them his service, and that in such a manner, as they might easily command what they pleased: for he would attend you in such prety formes of dog, cat, or Rat, that they should neither be terrified, nor any body else suspicious of the matter. Upon this they agreed, and (as it should seeme) give away their soules for the service of such spirits, as he had promised them; which filthy conditions were ratified with abhominabled kisses, and an odious sacrifice of blood, not leaving out certain charmes and conjurations with which the Devill deceived them, as though nothing could bee done without ceremony, and a solemnity of orderly ratification.[22]

In another case from 1646, alleged witch Elizabeth Weed was forced to testify, and described over two decades of witchcraft, with the Devil appearing regularly to fuck her, and give her puppies that she named Lilly and Priscill who would suck her blood in exchange for harming humans and cattle respectively:

> She saith, that about one and twenty yeares since she being saying her Prayers in the evening about bedtime, there did appeare unto her three Spirits, one in the likeness of a young man or boy, and the other two of two Puppies, the one white and the other black: and that which was in the shape of a young man did speak unto her, asking her, if shee would renounce God and Christ; shee answered, shee would. And the Devill then offere'd her, that he would doe what mischiefe she should require him; and she must covenant with him that he must have her soule at the end of one and

22 *The Wonderful Discoverie of the Witchcrafts of Margaret and Phillip Flower* . . . (London: G. Eld for I. Barnes, 1619) sig. D.

> twenty years, which she granted. And saith, that he came to her about a week after, about ten of the clock in the night, with a Paper, and asked her whether she were willing to seale the Covenant, shee said she was, then he told her it must be done with her bloud, and so pricked her under her left arme and made her bleed in the place, a great lumpe of flesh did rise, and hath encreased ever since, and he scribled therewith. And being demanded what light was there, she answered, none by the light of the Spirit, and presently he came to bed to her, and had the carnall knowledge of her, and so did divers times after, and saith, the other two Spirits did then, and at other times come into her bed also, and suckt upon other parts over her body where shee had Teats. Being demanded the names of the lesser Spirits, she saith the name of the white one was Lilly, and the blacke one Priscill, and that the office of Lilly was to hurt man, woman, or childe; and the office of Priscill was to hurt Cattell when she desired. And the office of the man-like Spirit was to lye with her carnally, when as often as she desired, and that he did lye with her in that manner very often . . . [23]

Part of the Devil's bargain is, after you agree to give him your soul, you get imps that do your bidding, usually one to kill humans, and one to kill cattle. Here are some statistics I culled about these killer critters: they have taken the forms of a white dog, a kitten, a mole, a cat, a white rat, puppies, field mice of different colors, dogs with hoglike features, snails, snakes, hornets, wasps, sparrows, frogs, polecats, a gray kite, and black rabbits.

A litany of their names: Pretty, Pussy, Hiss Hiss, Rutterkin, Lilly, Priscill, Tib, Jane, Grissel, Greedigut, Jarmara, Vinegar Tom, Hoult, Elimanzer, Wynnow, Jeso, Panu, Tomboy, Jesus,

23 Davenport, *The Witches of Huntington*, sig. A3.

Jockey, Sandy, Mrs. Elizabeth, Collyn, Littleman, Prettyman, Dainty, Susan, Besse, Margaret, Amie, Jack, Prickeare, Frog, James, Sparrow, Robyn, Rug.

The places they are reported to suck witchblood include: under the right ear, under the left ear, "the inward parts of her secrets" (vagina), under the arms, the breast, under the tongue, on the roof of the mouth, on the crown of the head, "in their fundament" (anus), "above the private parts." Typically the devil would give you your own personal imps, but sometimes another witch would. Susan Cock inherited her mouse, also named Susan, and her yellow cat Besse, from her mother Margery Stoakes after she died, according to *A true and exact relation of the severall Informations, Examinations, and Confessions of the late Witches Arrainged and Executed in the County of Essex* (1645).

I dreamt of my dog Frankie the night before I found him, two days before I met him and adopted him. It was the first dream I'd had of a dog that wasn't Champ, the rescue terrier I'd grown up with, my only consistent childhood friend. Frankie came to me helpfully in the dream I had closest to waking, and I woke up in a great mood: "I just dreamed of a dog that wasn't Champ!" I told my atheist wife. "In the dream I was the big spoon to this kindof scruffy reddish terrier who came and turned around and around and then nuzzled up to my chest. I think this means I will find my dog now!"

I'd been looking for nearly a year. It had been my dream to adopt a dog while working on my PhD, but somehow the animal shelters of London didn't have dogs that fit my little flat; or when I found one, he or she had already been adopted. I wanted to adopt a terrier in honor of Champ, for love of their particular personality traits: sassy, mischievous, wise and self-knowing, with a tendency to become tyrannical if allowed. I pulled up my computer and started the search again. Terrier-rescue.co.uk came up. There was the dog in my dream! *Fonze, Red Fell Terrier Mix, 2-3 years old.* I called the number immediately and got a woman named Diane, who grilled me for 2 hours to determine whether I was *up to the task of adopting a terrier.*

"They're strong willed," she said.

I could hear an eruption of barking in the background.

"I have six at the moment, and two more I'm fostering. People think they can handle them just 'cause they're small, but they can't, and then we have to take them back. I'll need to see your whole flat and any outdoor areas."

I took her on a virtual tour using my camera phone.

"You'll have to patch up that small opening on your balcony—he'll escape through it."

Sure enough, within a year he chewed and escaped through that precise spot to try to get at a neighbor's cat sunbathing in its yard. Diane moved on to the portion of the interview where she put me into different scenarios.

"Say you're busy writing or working and the dog wants to play with you. What Do You Do?"

I told her the truth—that I looked forward to adapting the pace of my life to the needs of an animal. That if I was asked to play, I trusted it was a sign that what I needed at that moment was to play. That if I was asked to go for a walk, I would delight in it. That if I was asked for a treat, it was a reminder that I too needed a snack. She seemed satisfied.

"I just have to ask—are you planning on having children?"

I smiled to myself as I assured her, thinking back to my early heresy, that I had no interest in having children, and never had.

"I just have to ask because I know people. . . people like you can do that now. And I had a friend once, we're not friends now, who swore up and down she wouldn',t and after she adopted one of ours it turned out that she did want children. I took little

Charlie in after she gave birth, he's with me now. I'll tell you the same thing I told her: The Dog Was There First!"

This fanaticism felt like a clear path into witchdom, or at least, an extremity of belief in animal companionship that would have been tried as witchery for centuries. She'd lost a friendship by suggesting that her friend either not have a child or send the child away, put it up for adoption rather than the dog, that they were equal beings but that the dog had been there first. I loved that. It reminded me of a man I'd met who knew Doreen Valiente: "I've never met someone who treated everything with such dignity," he said, "who apprehended the soul of every person, animal, plant, object. "

That kind of animism felt like old, old magic. I began to reappraise terrier-rescue.co.uk. The website looked about the same age and level of technical ability as the early internet angelfire websites that had informed my teenage self-initiation into witchcraft. Terrier-rescue.co.uk was basically a simple online message board with threads for each dog up for adoption. Each thread served as a profile of the dog, with pictures and attributes, and stories and pictures posted from volunteers who had walked the dog that week. Staffordshire Bull Terriers, the Pitbulls of the UK, featured plentifully, as they did at most animal shelters. Many of the terriers were described as "In Rehab," that is, dangerous or violent, and being gently rehabilitated for adoption by the loose network of old crones who ran the organization on a volunteer basis.

Over the next twenty-four hours I spoke to Diane, and then Delia. Diane, the hardliner, also called my wife to give her a sound talking-to after she got home from her job. Even though the dog would be my boon companion, and I was its primary mother-father, Diane was concerned that my wife had never grown up with or cared for animals: "It's a big commitment and you need to know what you're getting into!" My wife was enthusiastic but a little checked out; the workaholism was already beginning its full takeover. At last, I was given a time in which to meet the final volunteer, named Doris, at the shelter just outside of London on June 1, 2014.

A few years later, in a consultation with an astrologer, she asked: "WHAT happened to you in the first week of June 2014?" I knew right away: "That's when I adopted Frankie." It was written in the stars. Bringing him home that day changed both of our lives, and in the years that would come, spending my days with Frankie taught me all about how to love again in a new way, both for myself and the people in my life.

I didn't like the name Fonze and changed it (Diane left me an angry voicemail: "You shouldn't change his name right away! He's already been through so much change and confusion you'll just confuse him more!"). But that's not how we experienced it: Frankie was alert and responsive to his name right away. He was curious, energetic, and affectionate. But he was very quiet and didn't wag his tail. He was also very nervous outside of the house, watching his back at every turn, straining to chase animals, skateboarders, John Deere landscaping vehicles. It would take an extra hour on his walk to help him find the right place to do his business, he was too nervous to let his guard down. After a few months I heard him bark for the first time; then he started wagging his tail, initiating play, eating more, and keeping on the weight. It was a time of deep contemplation and transfection: we'd walk and walk and walk, ten, twenty miles in a day, observing one another, taking turns following one another's whims. It brought me into my body and into my daily life in a totally different way.

Connecting with his animal nature and needs, learning how to read his multitude of doggy ways, communicating in every language but speech, allowed me to see the shape my life was taking. Example: I thought Frankie would be a pub dog, lying at my feet while I sipped a pint and read or scribbled in my notebook. But he was too highly strung for that, growling at any man, child or dog who entered the room. So, I went to pubs less—I ultimately needed to quit drinking. Example: We didn't have a yard, so Frankie needed to be walked three or four times per day. I stopped staying away from home for long stretches, traveling widely, partying through the night. Considering the needs of his tough little body led to a new appreciation for the needs of mine. As our bond grew, as Saturn moved into Sagittarius that December, I had unwittingly prepared and furnished myself with the ideal companion through my coming Saturn return.

Frankie was there for me as I lived by the cycles of the moon: he was my watchdog at the crossroads at each new moon, he was there to run with wild abandon in the fields near our home under the light of the full moon. Usually his curiosity kept him busy at home and on walks; he could be very independent and pursue his own interests and smells. If he was awake, he was always up to something. But in ritual, he changed remarkably. He would neither participate nor vacate, just watch carefully. *Preside.* Outdoors he would resist if I tugged to bring his lead into the circle of magic I'd drawn in the dirt or sand. An uncharacteristic, otherworldly patience would descend on him—he would sit and watch. He, who always wanted to escape, slip his lead, find some smell and follow it into a fight, or track down trash on the street to feed himself, could sit without my holding his lead, and watch. He'd appointed himself my guardian and took it seriously. Consecrated to Hekate, to whom all dogs are beloved (and in ancient times, sacrificed), his sense of purpose was just to be present with quiet, watchful eyes. But his change of personality was jarring—so unlike him—that it added a spooky quality to whatever I was up to: *It's working. We are not alone.*

Whenever I'd leave Frankie for more than an evening, he'd begrudgingly let me pray over him to Hekate. I'd light candles and use them to set alight a few dried twigs of lavender to trace a circle around him, praying: *Hekate, Triple Moon Goddess, Mother Maiden Crone of the Crossroads, Dread Queen and Bearer of the Key to All Doors, I am your loving servant, hear my prayer: Protect and care for this creature Frankie, who is beloved to you, and beloved to me.* Frankie would glower at me if the smoke got too close and I would kiss his forehead three times.

Only once did I call upon Hekate when Frankie was in immediate danger. It was March, we were in the countryside at my girlfriend's family home. I'd only been there once before. The fields and woods surrounding it were deep and dark, and beyond them, small country roads with no light, then highways. It was around midnight, and the moon was nearly full. We'd all gotten back from dinner late, and I needed to take Frankie out before bed. I slipped his harness on and took him to the driveway where there was an old wooden gate leading into the fields beyond. I saw him disappear into the darkness at the end of his lead, and felt the tension that comes when he darts to chase something. I jerked forward and back and felt the empty lead return to me—Frankie had gone under the wooden gate and somehow slipped his lead! I heard the slight ring of his collar as he ran off into the night, but could see nothing.

I ran to follow the sound, sloshing in the wet, marsh-like conditions of the field, screaming his name. It was like a nightmare-dark, cold, wet, slow-moving, no one to hear you scream. I had no idea where I was running, only the fear that Frankie had no idea what he was doing, and that I couldn't lose the sound of him—if I lost him he'd surely be gone forever, roadkill. I realized I needed to be quiet to hear where he was going. I heard birds scatter from a nearby tree so ran toward that. I looked up at the waxing moon and prayed out loud: "*HEKATE, MOTHER I BEG YOU TO REUNITE ME TO THIS DOG WHO IS BELOVED TO US BOTH. I PRAY THAT OUR TIME TOGETHER DOES NOT END HERE.*"

I was crying. I could hear his collar faintly tinkling in the distance and followed that, my feet and legs soaked with cold water, then got to the edge of the field where it became too thick to move on easily. I stood on a tree stump and flashed my phone light ahead into the woods; it barely registered beyond a few feet. "*HEKATE! I BEG YOU, RETURN MY DOG TO ME, THIS CREATURE WHO IS BELOVED TO US BOTH!*" I stayed very quiet and listened carefully, then caught in the distance the green glow of an animal's eyes in the night. I started to wade my way through the scrub and bracken; the eyes came slowly toward me. I got closer and realized it was Frankie walking back toward me. At that point in the five years I'd had him, he'd never bothered to come when called, regardless of what food I had on hand. Shivering and wet, Frankie walked right up to me and let me scoop him up, with a docility out of his character. I had never known him to give up on following his nose.

When I got back inside, soaked and truly freaked out, it turned out we'd only been gone fifteen minutes. No one had heard me screaming or registered anything was wrong. It became apparent what had happened to Frankie in the woods. He'd run headlong into a patch of young nettles, and the sting of them had sent him back to me. The nettles were sacred—as any plant that both harms and helps, poisons and cures is—to Hekate, the Goddess of the Witches.

Frankie has a magic of his own that it took him about a year to feel comfortable revealing to me. At first I only heard it: after his walk, I'd give him a treat, and he'd bound into the living room to eat it on the area rug. I'd be in the kitchen and I'd hear a strange, unsyncopated drumming coming from down the hall, like a complicated tapping on the floor. By the time I made it to the living room he'd be sitting unassumingly chewing on his treat. Nothing to see here. After a few times I followed the sound quickly and quietly enough to see what it was: the drumming was Frankie jumping around the treat. He'd pretend to creep and pounce and jump away from it, then roll over and leap up and land, then circle and bow. He'd work his body like a little wolf hunting, stalking, pouncing on the treat and then jump back and begin again from a different angle. I felt like a scientist out on the savannah witnessing a rare mating ritual among a species thought long extinct. The moment he noticed me watching he'd stop and gobble up the treat. Nothing to see here.

"Frankie is a dancer! He makes up his own dances to play with his treats! You have to see it, it's always different, the little moves and feints, he puts himself through his paces! It feels so magical!" I told anyone who'd listen.

Over time I didn't merely witness the dances by stealth—he would let me watch openly, but never photograph or film. If he noticed me bringing out my phone he would end the show by eating the treat. A whole mythos emerged from The Dance: he was actually an incredibly underground, transgressive performance artist who refused the accolades of the surveilled and straight world. You could only learn about his work through overhearing it, choosing to follow the sound, and even then, you had to have built a considerable amount of trust through shared meals and walks. First, you were initiated into Frankie's pack; then you could be introduced into His Mysteries. Frankie danced to celebrate abundance and nourishment, he danced to honor the hunt that his ancestors had forsaken for human companionship.

Other transgressive performances I'd seen from him beginning in those years: leaping into the air to catch an old crow that had just taken flight, thus bringing upon us both the ire of an entire murder of crows—they followed us everywhere with their bitter cursing for weeks, recognized us for years. Slipping his leash in old Nunhead Cemetery to find and face a massive, legendary feral cat that lived deep in the wildlife protection area. Prancing in procession with the Jack-In-the-

Green of Deptford every May Day, barking at the bells of the Morris Dancers who followed. Refusing all food to save room for the discarded chicken bones he found himself on the street; and the most extreme: sniffing, eating, and shitting out used condoms he found in the park.

Meanwhile, the dances became more elaborate the safer and better cared for Frankie felt. Now I could watch from start to finish, and they became longer, with acts and encores. He would gently take the treat from my hand and I would watch as he took it to the bed or to the office or to the living room and throw it. Wherever it landed, he would work his way toward it while drumming his erratic, complicated rhythm, adding little growls and sneezes. He would announce the end of the performance with one loud cough—HACK—then remove the catalyst by eating it. I would clap wildly and say "BRAVO! BRAVISSIMO!" He would wag his tail and run over to take his bow. Sometimes he would do it when there were guests over for dinner—but only if they were trusted and had properly appreciated him. But, like Prince when I saw him perform back-to-back shows amounting to five hours for £10 at the Electric Ballroom in Camden in 2014, he continued to refuse to be filmed or photographed. Something both performances had in common was the wild abandon to an art form, total surrender. That surrender was predicated on confidence, or ultimately, feeling safe—another lesson in the bare necessities I would have to work to bring into my life, the grounding and trust and self-confidence, if I was to be able to abandon myself to art, and all of the things I loved about life.

I remember a time in the summer of my childhood, walking my dog Champ. I ran into some boys from school and they said: "*Oh, so this is what you do on your day off? Walk . . . your dog.*" A few laughed. It was meant as an insult. I remember feeling angry and saying something like: "*Yeah, that's right. This dog is more fun than any of you.*" I'd get bullied in all kinds of ways, tripped and kicked in gym class, avoided in all team sports. I overheard my parents arguing about it: "*I don't like that they call her by boys' names.*" They called me Slim Jim, Jimmy Cricket, Daddy Long Legs. I didn't mind them, actually liked they were boys' names, but something about the way my parents said that about me made me feel sick: in the end, I was the problem. In school, kids tried to start a rumor that I liked dogs "too much" and was "too obsessed." "*Brooke, like-likes dogs. It's gross. She doesn't like people.*"

I remember deciding I didn't have time to bother caring so I don't know if it caught on or not, and I didn't have friends at that point to lose over it. These people had nothing to offer me; I knew for certain I wasn't missing out on anything with anyone. I was telling the truth—no one had anything to offer me that I didn't find boring. But of course, like witches and queers of times past, I faced strange accusations of bestiality. Because humans who are inhumane—or children treated inhumanely and mimic it—can't understand, can only defile and cheapen the love and companionship they haven't opened themselves to experience. They also can't understand the lifelines people build when the love they long to experience is illegal or brutally punished: it's no accident that as the total horror of puberty began to set in, and all of the humans around me betrayed me, all that remained were Champ and the neighborhood dogs. In a sad neighborhood with people suffering too much to consider surrendering their bigotry, I intuitively fell in with creatures who offered me socialization and positive self-reflection without judgment. They kept me from total depersonalization; it kept me alive. I was taking part in a tradition dating back across hundreds of years of maidens, mothers, crones; the dispossessed, the pathologized, the criminalized.

Years later, the firm belief in a witchcraft that relied upon finding companions that were not strictly human set me on my path to working at Treadwell's. Months after I adopted Frankie, I found out that The Witch Queen who ran the bookshop had adopted a terrier, too. Our shared experience opened up into a deeper friendship and intimacy; we'd walk our dogs together, share stories about the wonders and struggles of their care. It put us into deeper contact. It's just true that one of the mysteries of life is that you sync up with people whose daily schedules and tasks resemble yours. Some of those strangers become benevolent figures in the background of your day-to-day activities; some of those strangers become dear friends. That autumn, I began to spend more and more time with this Witch Queen and her darling dog—whom I would grow to love, cuddle, and walk through the gardens of Bloomsbury—in the basement of the bookshop, eventually the door that had been opened would become a job, one that would require me to tap deep into my sense of vocation and spirituality. Hekate, mother of dogs and opener of doors, had availed herself in my life in so many ways, for so many years.

I imagine myself in all ages and times among the cunningfolk who named animals of their daily life. I too have let the seasons of my life be shaped by their whims and needs, let my days be filled with revelations big and small on account of the attention we pay to one another. In turn, I feel named and identified by these animals, humanized by them, in keeping with one evolutionary theory that supposes wolves to have chosen humans for domestic symbiosis thousands of years ago. This theory is known as the "garbage dump theory," given the role human garbage played in luring wolves to make the choice to domesticate themselves. I'll take it. But certain humans are better fit than others to cultivate for this kind of domesticated interdependence. It's their loss.

I believe that there is a love and care and kinship to be experienced with non-human creatures that cannot be had among humans. I would not want to love or be loved by, care for or be cared by, or feel kinship among humans the way in which I have from animals. The more species I can encounter the more expansive my heart becomes as it seeks out different tones and colors of appreciation, understanding and difference. Love expands across so many horizons of being, of the meeting of souls in so many different incarnations. The first few months after adopting Frankie did reflect back to me how poorly I loved myself; in that way I do believe he saved me from floating away into a life of excessive partying, a life of starving myself to avoid my period instead of seeking healthcare. It was a quick revelation with slow and far-reaching implications—I saw the work I had to do—and then we moved on to the next ten years, in which there has been so much for us to experience together. There is a special quality to a love that can grow outside of the judgment or paranoia or resentment or fear that human minds and language kindle when in contact. Frankie was just like: *No Fucking Way. Dogs don't do regrets. Dogs don't do shame.* If I felt that way around him, it was my problem alone. Our relationship is immense in its simplicity: he wants to sleep cuddled up to me so we can hear each other's hearts beat. He wants me to take him for walks, and play, and watch him dance. He wants to enjoy whatever I'm eating, and have meals to himself. I want no metaphors or conflations between the different kinds of love I've experienced, including my love for Frankie. Just because I learned how to trust and be trusted by Frankie does not mean I know how to do it with humans; I'm just better practiced at being aware that trust is important to cultivate in all its different forms. The distinct experiences I've had with Frankie are not transferable to anyone else, nor is the love. But that love and trust has helped me in ways no other living thing has, to better identify and name what I want, what I need—or don't want and don't need—from other people. This too is a kind of love magic, which is probably why so much of the encounters between witches and their imps are sexualized in the sensational and bizarre documents that survive the witch trials. Love remains a mystery and a perversion to those whose lives are fueled by hatred and violence.

I pray daily to the creatures of the world and my local environment that I could not be human without. That my ancestors could not have become human without: bees and insects too numerous to fully grasp, dogs and cats, the foxes of my old neighborhood, the possum of my latest neighborhood, the little brown hummingbird I see each day sipping from honeysuckle and sage. I do not believe my humanity possible without our interconnectedness, animal live as I both see them and as they remain hidden to me—occulted. The Wild Occult, the Pet Occult, the Plant Occult, the Mycelial Occult, the Arboreal Occult. And so on, a litany of living things no better and no worse than me. Animism—one of the oldest spiritual philosophies, belief in a soul of all things—remains both the most seductive lens through which to appreciate the world, and the greatest challenge.

I, TITUBA, BLACK WITCH OF SALEM (1992)

I love the fictions that make inroads into deeper truths, like Maryse Condé's *I, Tituba, Black Witch of Salem*. It's a work of historical fiction that recovers the life of Tituba, a scantily documented woman who was the first to be accused of witchcraft in Salem, and who survived the trials only to disappear from the historical record. *I, Tituba* teaches us how to reconsider the past with sharper eyes, and is one of the best books about witchcraft, full stop.

Other favorites that get the mood of ritual just right: Sylvia Townsend Warner's *Lolly Willowes*, Shirley Jackson's *We Have Always Lived in the Castle*, the mix of psychology and occult philosophy in *The Sea Priestess* and *Moon Magic* by Dion Fortune, and the philosophy of magic in the *Earthsea* cycle by Ursula K. LeGuin, and. But unlike these books, *I, Tituba* is unflinching in its portrayal of violence and brutality, set against the backdrop of the Middle Passage, where the stakes of being denounced as a witch are compounded by the experience of being Black. We couldn't stock *I, Tituba* in the bookshop since it wasn't easily or cheaply available from our distributors, translated from French, and published by an academic press. I'd come across *I, Tituba* in the library at college, but never a copy in the wild. All I could do was send hungry readers on a quest: *You must find this book. There are first editions, even signed first editions, to be found online cheap. Try to get the hardback edition from 1992, the design is better, it feels better in your hands.*

Do whatever you can to get it for your library, you won't be sorry; every magical library must have a copy of this book. But you must steel yourself to read it.

Condé admits, in an interview included with English edition, "I'm not a witch myself, I'm just writing about a witch, but I don't have any knowledge of witchcraft." But in the epigraph to the novel she writes that *"Tituba and I lived for a year on the closest of terms. During our endless conversations she told me things she had confided to nobody else."* Part of the stunning authenticity of the book owes to the fact that it is the best kind of channeled text: Tituba divulged her secrets to a great writer who, not content with raw channeling, undertook both the craft of a great novel and the due diligence of researching seventeenth century magical texts and recipes to better understand the world she had been given the task of rebuilding.

Tituba's early life is debated by scholars: she was an enslaved person brought to New England from Barbados, although it is uncertain if she was Black, or Indigenous, or both. *I, Tituba* offers a spiritual solution to this uncertainty through depicting the syncretic religious practices in the Caribbean where Tituba came from and where Condé was also born and raised, a few islands to the north, in Guadaloupe. Regardless of Tituba's origins, her life would have been steeped in a blended spirituality of resistance against brutality and white supremacy and the transatlantic trade, a mix of Indigenous spirituality and Traditional African Religions. Condé conjures a lost world of knowledge handed down in secrecy to trusted individuals, rooted in the land, with lush descriptions of local flora and fauna, wisdom coming from wise women, and spirits tied to their place of death, bringing together religious traditions from Indigenous and enslaved people. At first this knowledge, which Tituba receives from an older woman named Mama Yaya, survives under many names that are not witchcraft: healing, cunning, conjuring:

> Mama Yaya taught me about herbs. Those for inducing sleep. Those for healing wounds and ulcers. Those for loosening the tongues of thieves. Those that calm epileptics and plunge them into blissful rest. Those that put words of hope on the lips of the angry, the desperate, and the suicidal. Mama Yaya taught me to listen to the wind rising and to measure its force as it swirled above the cabins it had the power to crush.
>
> Mama Yaya taught me the sea, the mountains, and the hills. She taught me that everything lives, has a soul, and breathes.[24]

It is only after she has learned all she can from Mama Yaya, when she first feels attraction for the man who will become her husband, John Indian, that she is exposed to the notion of a witch:

> "Ow! What are you doing, little witch?"
>
> He was joking, but it made me think. What is a witch? I noticed that when he said the word, it was marked with disapproval. Why should that be? Why? Isn't the ability to communicate with the invisible world, to keep constant links with the dead, to care for others and heal, a superior gift of nature that inspires respect, admiration, and gratitude? Consequently, should the witch (if that's what the person who has this gift is to be called) be cherished and revered rather than feared?[25]

As a child Tituba had been driven from the plantation where her parents were enslaved—freed but essentially left for dead—and as a young woman she lived in a cabin on the outskirts of town, cultivating magical knowledge. The price of her love for

---

24 Maryse Condé, *I, Tituba, Black Witch of Salem* (Charlottesville: University Press of Virginia, 1992) 9.

25 Condé, *I, Tituba,* 17.

John Indian is incalculably high, as it brings her back within the brutal plantation system she had been able to avoid. Trained by Mama Yaya in the meantime, her reputation as a healing woman further endangers her in the context of a society where her healing gifts and knowledge are recast as witchcraft and devil worship, and fear of rebellion against enslavers is high.

I love how Tituba's experience and Maryse Condé's sensitivity to language blend as one. As Condé explains in the interview: "Tituba was only doing good to her community. Could she be called a witch? I don't think so, and the book is there to prove it." Through Tituba's perspective, the novel holds the complexity of reclaiming witchcraft, as Tituba both rejects the title at first, and then embraces and redefines it in her own terms. Her passionate ambivalence, moving between *I am not a witch, you have no idea who I am, to: I am a witch of my own definition, I am much more powerful than you could ever imagine,* expresses a truth of what it means now, hundreds of years later, to seek guidance from a spirituality that celebrates refusal. Contemporary witchcraft requires blending together practices from many religious traditions—only look at the New Age Movement to see some clumsy examples—in a world that is still struggling for freedom from the legacy of the Middle Passage. The oppression of Black and Indigenous women like Tituba, alongside the less numerous executions of poor white women and men for witches and other forms of persecution shown in the novel (for instance, against Jewish people), makes the many facets of "witchcraft" into one common cry for a spiritual foundation in solidarity across oppression.

Reflected in the local nature of healing and spellcraft that Condé depicts is idea that every region of the world has its folk remedies, its superstitions, its ways of speaking to the dead, its magic and miracles. This is a practical truth of witchcraft as a spiritual practice—when local knowledge reigns, authority will always remain decentralized, there will always be more to learn, many types of witchcraft, infinite witches. Microcosm of the macrocosm, this plays out over the course of Tituba's own life. While on her voyage to New England, Tituba's healing is required of her to care for the children of the Puritan preacher Samuel Parris. For the first time she must adapt her magic to her new environment:

> I was lacking certain items required for practicing my art: the trees in which the invisible spirits repose, the condiments for their favorite dishes, and the plants and roots for healing. What was I going to do in this unknown and inhospitable land across the sea? I decided to make substitutions . . .
>
> My prayers did the rest.[26]

This syncretic practice only increases after Tituba lands in the freezing New England wilderness. The pain of separation from her homeland Barbados worsens in its spiritual dimensions for Tituba, cutting her off from easy access to the company of beloved spirits, including Mama Yaya and her parents, and requiring her to seek out new spirits in the new land to teach her about all the different, new herbs within her reach. Her study is arduous, and time consuming.

I, Tituba contributed to what I felt was the core of my job at the bookshop: be kind to those who sought to set themselves up as witches, and equally, be precise about the immense work it takes to emotionally, intellectually, and spiritually disentangle and recover from the religious institutions that have failed us—or, at worst, tried to kill us. Recommending books that honestly lay bare the long history of this failure, while offering generous openings, alternatives, and imaginative paths for readers, would be the simple, practical way I could contribute to a much bigger picture. It also wasn't lost on me that, throughout much of the records of witchcraft that survives in western culture, books take center stage—and yet, their contents remain secret: the

26 Condé, *I, Tituba*, 45.

Devil's own book, the magician's grimoire, the recipe books of cunningfolk, the book of secrets of the alchemist, books of shadows kept by contemporary Pagans. All these remain closed, privileged sources of information for initiates. Demystifying a spiritual path through distributing books in broad daylight—once a heresy, in modern times a scandal—felt like a form of advocacy I was particularly suited to undertake, not only because I loved books, but also because I had enjoyed firsthand their sustaining powers.

The final aspect of *I, Tituba* that I love and why I recommended it to readers, is with the hope that every witch would consider historical recovery part of their magic:

> It seemed that I was gradually being forgotten. I felt that I would only be mentioned in passing in these Salem witchcraft trials about which so much would be written after, trials that would arouse curiosity and pity of generations to come as the greatest testimony of a superstitious and barbaric age. There would be mention here and there of "a slave originating from the West Indies and probably practicing 'hoodoo.'" There would be no mention of my age or my personality. I would be ignored. As early as the end of the seventeenth century, petitions would be circulated, judgments made, rehabilitating the victims, restoring their honor, and returning their property to their descendants. I would never be included! Tituba would be condemned forever! There would never, ever be a careful, sensitive biography recreating my life and its suffering. And I was outraged by this future injustice that seemed more cruel than even death itself.[27]

Art and history have always had a reciprocal relationship: we need art to help us imagine the stories we have lost,

27 Condé, *I, Tituba,* 110.

forgotten how to recognize, have yet to rediscover. And so too can witchcraft underwrite a spiritual means of engagement with historical loss, steeped in its own beloved, time-honored recipes, traditions, and lineages. Working a ritual is always, in part, an act of history making: repeating words and deeds known to have worked before, building our own flourishes and offerings into the silences left in all records. As much as witches are asked to divine futures, those who do so with the most finesse are often those best informed about our pasts.

IT NARRATIVES

Items travel and accrue meaning; the older they are, the more hands they have passed through, the more accidents and adventures they have survived. One example: The robes I wore in ritual were always hand-me-downs from other witches, in particular, a golden robe made out of a mixture of silk and polyester. The robe had served me in a ritual invocation of Sophia, I had worn it in a Mithraic rite in which I played the Sun, I had worn it in a ritual reconstructed from the writings of the actress, suffragette, and occultist Florence Farr, I had worn it in the woods while performing a version of the Rites of Eleusis for a friend's bachelorette party. It got *around.* I'd catch glimpses or anecdotes about other times and other people who had worn the gold robe and fantasize about the other experiences imbued in the fabric beyond my own sweat and dead skin cells.

When I worked in a special collections library in collage I remember a particular collection of eighteenth century novels there: little octavo or pocket-sized books in shiny brown leather with spines stamped in guilt lettering, called novels of circulation, also known as "It Narratives." I was fascinated but never got around to reading any until much later. "It Narratives" are a mode of eighteenth-century storytelling that show the world through the subjectivity of an object moving through it: an old shoe, a stagecoach, different forms of currency, a doll, a book, a quire of paper, a teacup. Another approach to this form of storytelling was to speak from the vantage point of an animal, usually a dog. I imagine the objects on my walls and shelves and on my altar existing in this narrative tradition: having stories of their own to tell of magic, mystery, the silly things humans get up to in the dark.

These novels use the vantage point of objects to tell larger histories that cover many lives and in some instances, lifetimes. One of these novels that I started to read and couldn't put down was *The Adventures of a Black Coat.* Full subtitle: *Containing a Series of Remarkable Occurences and Entertaining incidents, That it was a Witness to in its Peregrinations through the Cities of London and Westminster, in Company with Variety of Characters. As related by ITSELF.* The novel opens with a weighty exchange between an old coat and a new coat that's been recently stored in the closet alongside it. The Sable Coat begins to tell his life story, one filled with downward mobility, rejection, crime and debauchery—against its wishes it is a jacket of the underworld. Initially cut as goth mourning attire for a government official to wear following the death of a princess, after the period of mourning ends the coat is gifted to a favorite servant, who then consigns him to a merchant in Monmouth Street who rents out clothing: "Here properly I may say I began to exist; my heart dilated with joy at the prospect of seeing life."[28] Overall, the adventures of the often-judgmental coat are about British social mobility and scam culture. He's rented by servants and soldiers aspiring for better jobs—a civil servant who wants an ambassadorship, he's rented by actors, by a con-artist who steals luxury items from the rich as part of an elaborate bling ring that works across coffee houses, auction houses, fine restaurants, jewelers, and the opera. The coat ends up in prison on the back of a poet in debt, is traded to a quack doctor. The world of artistic and cultural exchange and social mixing is a spectrum of dashed ambitions and scamming, people down and out on their luck trying to turn things around.

28 *The Adventures of a Black Coat* (Dublin: for Robert Bell, 1762) 17.

It Narratives predate the spiritualist practice of psychometry, or token-object reading, by a century, but in essence the leap of imagination is similar: objects have spirits that can tell stories if only we know how to listen and interpret them. The word "psychometry," just means "measuring the soul," and was coined by Joseph Rodes Buchanan in 1842: "The Past is entombed in the Present!" he wrote, "The world is its own enduring monument; and that which is true of its physical, is likewise true of its mental career. The discoveries of Psychometry will enable us to explore the history of man, as those of geology enable us to explore the history of the earth."[29] While this practice is couched in the world of spiritualism and psychic mediumship, and derided as a pseudoscience rather than a far-out fringe of animistic thought, it never felt far from a description of my work as a historian, spending time handling old objects and documents in deep contemplation, asking and occasionally begging them to tell of their stories and experiences. And there was also overlap between my intellectual pursuits and my spiritual life: as a witch, I was always erecting altars for this or that spell, to petition this or that god or spirit, to call in certain themes and energies into my life. And to do that to the best of my ability, I sought to incorporate charged objects with exciting and lurid histories.

Anyone can build an altar. The main thing that distinguishes an altar from an assemblage, shrine, or diorama, is change. And the law of change is expressed first and foremost through cleaning it: sweep away the dust, refresh the candles, dump the water into the earth and wash the glass and refill it. Add flowers or food, then compost them. Burn the incense, disperse the ashes. Altars undergo their own cycles of decay, death, rebirth, infused with intentions and prayers, the changing seasons and shifting stars. You live alongside them, come face to face with your intentions and prayers every day until it's time to

29 Joseph Rodes Buchanan, *Manual of Psychometry: The Dawn of a New Civilization* (Boston: F. H. Hodges, 1893) 73.

change again. Some things will change daily, some weekly, some seasonally, some year by year—different scales of time to reflect on. At Treadwell's we sold a few items for altars: candles, herbs and incense, cauldrons and thuribles to burn them in, the occasional statue of a god or goddess in metal or stone. A magical antiques dealer would come in from time to time with rare items he'd sourced: a bronze statue of Inanna, a clay oil lamp featuring Artemis, a wax disc bearing the Seal of Truth used by John Dee. One artist made painted wooden facsimiles of the Stèle of Revealing, a seventh-century BC Egyptian slab central to followers of Aleister Crowley.

Building an altar is like planning a dinner party for the unseen forces of our lives, and, like planning a dinner party, it's one of my favorite art forms. Whether I've been on a strict budget—only sourcing what's free—or whether I've been able to really splash out, the shifting constraints are fun. To work with Saturn, you might cut corners or spend nothing to show that you are disciplined and frugal before petitioning the god. To work with Jupiter or Venus, you might actually throw a dinner party for your friends first, extend the altar into the whole room for a time, charge it with love and laughter, spend a little beyond your means. Other charged objects find their way to my altar from walks and hikes and travel: certain crystals, bones, pieces of sea glass I've painted with gold, ceramics made by friends or artists I love, talismans like the old brass door-knocker with the figure of a Mother Shipton on it. An amulet with the Virgin Mary that belonged to my grandmother. There are items I've had on my altars that I bought for a dollar, and items I've had that are worth several hundred; cheap souvenirs from seaside tourist towns, prints from the eighteenth century. Sometimes what I want for my altar—an owl of Minerva excavated in a Roman settlement on Folly Lane in St. Albans; a second century Etruscan coin stamped with the goddess Hekate—is impossible to acquire, so I've drawn it on the finest paper I had ready, and that had to do.

Everything accrues meaning over time: I know a witch whose paintings of various goddesses were rendered for her by a dear friend. When she unveils one of the paintings for use in ritual, appreciation deepens into remembrance of all the prior times they'd been used and of the painter, who'd died long ago. An old bottle I bought at an antique shop in Rye to fill with rock and driftwood and old pieces of fisherman's rope near Derek Jarman's house in Dungeness—capturing the power of a place of opposites, where desert meets ocean meets Nuclear Power Plant meets Queer Garden sanctuary—deepens in meaning and power whenever I place it on my altar. I am able to vividly recall each time I've done so over the years, and why. To place an object on my altar is part of the magic of correspondences—building relations between myself and my desires up, up, up into the cosmos. But to place an object on my altar is also an animistic challenge: I must consider the soul of the object in its own right, its survival and passage over time, the environments that made possible its creation and movement. Its possible uses after my death. Its own possible loss, or destruction.

TRANSSEXUAL HEX

I am not nostalgic for the past, I just think history is the ultimate bargain: saving time from having to reinvent the wheel, saving time spent feeling isolated when there's nothing new under the sun, saving time from making the same mistakes. A treasure trove to mine for ideas, obsessions, lovable characters, under-appreciated oddities. Here is a prayer I recite more or less before entering into a research process:

Archives are for divination, History is a speculative fiction.

The future is foretold by what records are kept. Each version of the past determines a future by its telling, its teaching, its circulation and safeguarding, the way it is metabolized.

From the fragments of information that survive in clay tablets, papyrus, parchment, paper, photographs, film, it is always possible for alternative futures to be imagined.

Archival research is a fortune teller's business: shuffle through the catalogues and search engines, the aisles and the files, and from the vastness of contents, choose.

Given how much survives and how much is lost, even my most educated choices are subject to chance.

Like oracle bones, like Tarot cards, like tea leaves, like runes, those choices will be influenced by other forces beyond my experience.

The patterns I notice from these records, the stories I am able to piece together, the meanings I am able to assign to each, will be a mix of desire and serendipity.

The accident of survival, the constraints of time and space and the limits of my imagination on any given day.

I multiply this by the millions of subjectivities possible among the living and the dead.

I choose the future you'd like and write the history of how it came into being.

I trust I will find what I'm looking for; or, it will find me.

I can only claim a history of witchcraft dating back to my own childhood, to the stories and spells I have encountered and felt a strong attraction to. I honor my predecessors—by blood and by choice—through the affinities I have with their ideas and deeds. I look for those acts—acts of magic, spellcraft, acts of relating to the world or refusing it—that resonate with me, and find my history that way, its elusive and sometimes illegible documentation. Sometimes I simply inherit the responsibility of telling the stories I find. Sometimes I inherit the responsibility of continuing the work or the spell contained in the story. For example, I have inherited the spell hinted at in a newspaper article entitled: *TRANSSEXUALS HEX ROBIN MORGAN*.

Little information about how *TRANSSEXUALS HEX ROBIN MORGAN* exists beyond the single newspaper clipping from the July 18, 1973 issue of *The Advocate*. It describes how, after Robin Morgan verbally attacked and incited violence agains the transsexual musician Beth Elliott at the West Coast Lesbian Conference, a group of dolls put "a voodoo curse" on her in self-defense. They were the Miami Beach chapter of the Transsexual Action Organization (TAO), an activist group founded in 1970 that spread from Los Angeles across the country to Miami, across the ocean even to England.

I trawl the archives, beg to know more details from this hex, beg and pray. I decide to make a facsimile of the newspaper clipping and meditate with it for more insight. I print out a copy of the article, put on Beth Elliott's album *Buried Treasure*, and spent hours one evening, painstakingly drawing a photorealistic image of article, typefaces and all:

> Although Robin Morgan did not attack any of us personally, her attack on Beth Elliott is viewed as one against all of us. The curse is a mild one and has been placed by Cuban transsexuals associated with the Santería-Lucumi religion. We love women and have no wish to harm them unless we are harmed, thus the curse was not made with evil or destructive intent. Apparently that would only echo back upon the curser. It will, however, act as a restraint. She will suffer because of her attacks upon transsexuals, without a doubt.

This portion of the article is a quote from TAO Vice President Colette Goudie. Getting lost in the fine details of the article, taking not a single word for granted, transcribing with my pencil slowly and carefully, puts me into a scribal trance state, which is the goal. I want to sink into trance and see what comes to me, if anything, of that ritual, and this is what I see:

> *A woman dressed in red approaches a freshly painted white door. She holds a watermelon under the crook of one arm. Her well-manicured hand with red stiletto fingernails presses the doorbell of an apartment in a deliberate sequence: one long, a short and a long, then three long buzzes. After a pause, she is admitted into the apartment: the door opens into a room bathed in candlelight.*
>
> *The woman offers the watermelon to her host, who is wearing a long blue dress. They embrace, and then she is embraced by five others. Each have covered heads and bodies adorned with beaded bracelets and necklaces. They are building an altar: on a table covered in a blue silk tablecloth they have placed an image of Our Lady of Regla, adorned with fruit, shells, seven blue candles, seven bottles of sea water. The watermelon is added to the altar.*
>
> *Thick yellow corojo butter melts in a pot on the stove. It is transferred into a large bowl and drops of indigo are*

mixed in, creating a psychedelic swirl that turns a deeper and deeper color, until the warm butter is uniformly blue. Corn meal is sprinkled it, then seven little Tetí fish, then a pinch of salt, and then finally, a cotton wick. The mixture is left to harden.

Another bowl contains a paperback copy of SISTERHOOD IS POWERFUL *(1970), edited by Robin Morgan. For a long time, cooking oil is poured over the book, submerging it completely. Five eggs are placed to float on the oil and then sprinkled with cinnamon. A cotton wick is inserted.*

Two women carefully bring the two bowls to the altar and place them beside the watermelon, into which letters are being carved: R-O-B-I-N-M-O-R-G-A-N.

The seven women congregate, one of them puffing on a cigar, and begin to pray together.

At the end of the vision, I burn the facsimile and give thanks. In the absence of more information I must pour my own self into the gaps in the story. I must imagine all of the spells and hexes transsexuals have performed across time—it costs nothing to hex, and is therefore within our agency and power to pull off. I grab a copy of *SISTERHOOD IS POWERFUL*, bind it in black thread, and drown it.

I was a transsexual who hexed in preschool. Transsexuality is a spiritual as well as a physical path that requires incredible self-discipline and self-initiation. It does not surprise me that when I scrutinize my life consistently and with discipline, the earliest memory of a witchcraft before the words entered my vocabulary was a transsexual hex. My preschool was called CHURCH OF THE ATONEMENT. The memory is as clear as the Disney movies and Universal Horror films I watched a hundred times at that age: Miss Snyder, one of the teachers, crouches down and is watching me playing with the other boys. We're playing with our Ninja Turtles action figures and, as ever, I am Leonardo, the leader. I can feel her watching us, overshadowing us. I feel what I would now describe as self-conscious.

"Where did you get that toy?"

"It's mine, Leo's my favorite."

"You can't have that. It's for boys. Put it away."

When she walked away I remember starting a new game, calling the corners with the Ninja Turtles: Leonardo Donatello Michelangelo Raphael! Getting my friends to play this new game: *Teacher Overthrow.* Our goal was to draw the mutant powers into ourselves and use them to overthrow the classroom so we could play how we wanted. We were separated as usual during naptime, because I was always made to go to the other end of the room, an experience of forced feminization I didn't care to understand. My first Book of Shadows was the blueprints for the overthrow: drawing the positions all of my action figures would need to occupy to seal off entrances and protect the classroom once I'd banished the teachers and taken charge. At this point everyone called me Leo, because like Leonardo the turtle, I was the leader of the operation. During naptime I would not sleep but meditate, like I saw Leonardo do in the cartoon. During drawing time I would finger paint (more power, to use the body) symbolic representations of my Miss Snyder being fired and exiled from the school. I instinctively knew it wouldn't work to represent it literally, but that I could concentrate my will and intention on the symbolic representation (lots of XXXXXXXXXXXXs), and it would happen. Like magic.

The result of the ritual: I was separated from my friend every naptime but still allowed to play with them and with the toys I wanted. Another teacher, whose last name was my first name, and who was so sweet and calming, suddenly entered the picture and presided over my playgroup, getting in Miss Snyder's way and keeping her away from me. I was able to keep people off my back for a few more years.

⊛

Having come across the newspaper clipping, I felt I'd inherited the responsibility to keep feeding what was started when a group of Transsexuals Hexed Robin Morgan from Miami in 1973. Unlike inheriting wealth or property, inheriting spells is infinitely scalable: the inheritance is split by as many people feel the call. Maybe you.

My spell is also a spell of precision: at the same conference where Robin Morgan spewed her vitriol against Beth Elliot, she identified herself again and again as a witch and founding member of W.I.T.C.H., ending her speech with a reading of Doreen Valiente's *Charge of the Goddess*. In reviving *TRANSSEXUALS HEX ROBIN MORGAN*, I am also working to disentangle the confusion and misidentification of witchcraft and feminism with this particular form of hatred and transphobia, to return to a witchcraft that dismantles patriarchal systems of power and the unnecessarily cruel bio-essentialism that fuels them.

Magic is ninety percent intuition, ten percent research. The more you gather knowledge and materials, the more you enhance and magnify the reach and capacity of your intuition, the more tools you give it to play with. Stuff yourself with books and ideas, then leave them all behind as you step naked and alone into a candle lit circle of salt. What you remember as you speak to the gods will be the exact, perfect, intuitive combination of what's needed for the situation. In this case I remember I have inherited *TRANSSEXUALS HEX ROBIN MORGAN* and, as per the article I don't want to hurt her, just end the immense pain and danger her bad ideas have caused others.

KIDDIE GRIMOIRE

A key desire within witchcraft as a spiritual practice is to find an unbroken spiritual alternative to the Abrahamic religions. It's such a deep human desire that people have made up lineages to support it. For me it was more personal—belief in magic is simply the lineage I have with myself, every version of myself, from my earliest memories. I would sit, and contemplate, and try to pray. The older I got, the harder it got, sometimes—eventually, as an adult, it took me hours of meditation to arrive at a prayer I felt comfortable chanting. That prayer was: *Let every sign be a sigil, every object a talisman, every surface an altar. Let everything be sacred and infused with holy meaning!* A sigil is a magic symbol. A talisman is a magic thing, like a good luck charm. Altars are for making offerings to the gods. The point of the prayer was to come up with something I felt like I could wholeheartedly say every day for the rest of my life. The point of the prayer was to be grateful for the sigils, talismans, and altars that I had found or made for myself since childhood, the things that had sustained me. The point of the prayer was also to challenge my perception: to remember that anyone could see the world this way, and that seeing the world this way would ensure that I was living according to my own principles. The prayer could be a warning too: if I wasn't experiencing a world suffused with meaning, magic, sanctity, and divine presence, I needed to rethink my priorities.

In the 1690s the book that mattered to witches, at least according to their captors, was the Devil's book, a supernatural book that seems to exist more in fantasy than reality. By the 1960s the book that mattered most was the *Book of Shadows*, a concept formalized by Gerald Gardner and adopted by covens following his approach—a witch's personal manuscript kept in secret and restricted in access depending on the degrees of initiation within the craft. The *Book of Shadows* is, Doreen Valiente has shown us, a phrase coined by Gerald Gardner to describe the book of rituals and spells he created for his coven, sometime after he finished writing *High Magic's Aid* in 1946 and its publication in 1949. By the 1990s, with movies like *The Craft*, books had taken on a different level of significance for witches: many guides to magic-making and compendiums of spells had been published, including books of shadows.

These books of shadows are imbued by their makers with a desire for a greater antiquity than the mid-twentieth century. They often appear to look like ancient tomes, with leather binding and distressed covers. In Gardner's case, he claimed the texts within to be centuries old, until Valiente pointed out that they had come from the writings of Aleister Crowley and early twentieth-century freemasonry. The desire for deep antiquity doesn't stop there: the word grimoire itself—another word for a book of rituals and invocations—has similar pretensions. The *Grimorium Verum*, or *True Grimoire*, published in the eighteenth century, claimed to be a translation from a text written in 1517, a total fabrication, although its contents do have similarities with sixteenth century books. The sheer will and longing that drives these forgeries is moving to me spiritually: people yearn to be part of an old tradition, to rediscover long lost information that will make them feel at home in an alienating and harsh world, and I think that's beautiful.

Visitors to Treadwell's would ask me, "*Do you have a Book of Shadows?*" And I would say: "My spells and rituals are documented across decades of notebooks, maybe someday I'll consolidate things."

Paper was and is the dominant, constant, most excellent substrate of my life. Having fingers sticky for paper, a will to make my own little books and pamphlets, goes as far back as my memories; so long as memory is chief informant of my identity, paper is too. The scaffolding of these earliest childhood memories is the knowledge that my dad worked for a paper company. It was the coolest: there was a cupboard in our house filled with paper samples. Like any poorly paid job, it made sense to take as much free stuff as was given you to compensate. Different paper stocks were named after different animals, and this produced wild ecology in my imagination. Was it false advertising to name the papers after animals whose habitats were surely seared by the chemicals used to make paper on a mass industrial scale? Or were the animals kept safe from harm, while human communities suffered the effects of ecological racism downriver? These questions would come much later. Back then, there was only rummaging around the paper cupboard that towered over me, learning the different names given to different qualities of paper that delighted me: Lynx, Timberwolf. Images of muscular bucks and elk wrapped around five hundred sheets of bleached white paper that I could fold into little booklets, staple, and draw in.

My dad would describe the paper mills owned by the company like a bedtime story: *The paper mill is a building so big he'd say, that it has its own weather system. It's own climate. It could be sunny outside and seventy degrees, but inside the paper mill it could be fifty degrees and raining.* I pictured the paper mill as a whole world, its vastness overwhelming. The timber, I imagined, were grown inside the paper mill to speed up production. Lynx and timberwolves lived there, darting through the trees in pursuit of smaller woodland creatures; creeks ran through it, but they didn't have dirty needles in them, like the creek near my house I wasn't supposed to play in. Rather than stuffed in cupboards, the paper products were suggestively, thoughtfully scattered around the mill, for people to pick up and use. Like milk and honey, which we'd been taught about at school. My milk and honey was paper and ink. Paper Planet. I wanted to live there.

In the cupboard, matching the stationery, there were baseball caps, branded pens, pencils, small magnifying glasses to look at the paper's grains up close. Swiss army knives with handles the green color of the company's logo. I used the magnifying glass to look at bugs, the penknife to whittle, the pens and notepads to draw on the notebooks I'd made from the paper stock the critters I'd spotted on the outskirts of Philly: a groundhog, a robin, grey squirrels, young rabbits under our deck. I wore the baseball caps. This must have been the first merch I loved: the paper company's sigil and motto, A " symbol of quality in the world of paper."

This gave me an idea for my first business: I could make good money on the paper goods, folding and stapling these sheets into notebooks for people to write and sketch in. Because the paper was free, I could sell everything at a bargain and undercut competitors—like the place my mom liked to shop, *House of Bargains*. My products would have another added value: bespoke decoration. I would decorate the margins of lined pads of paper by hand, to embellish what future customers would write there. The notebooks had themes: for collecting autographs, for recipes, for poetry, for magic spells and incantations, for identifying rocks and minerals, for identifying plants, for identifying animals, for writing a novel or script. I'd learned the phrase magnum opus from my uncle, and my sales pitch was: *Write your magnum opus TODAY!*

Like any good salesman I had a passionate but healthy relationship to my product: I found it hard to commit my own writing to the paper, so that meant I'd never use up all of my stock. I found the paper so beautiful, its woven texture so lovely in its blank, pristine state, there were times I couldn't bear to write on it. On some of my earliest feelings of frustration and hesitation—I wouldn't want to waste the paper by writing on it too hastily, but the wait to think of something really good to write down would pile up, and so blank it would remain. Being a stationery salesman would let me deal with the beautiful paper stress-free; I could enjoy the pleasure of holding it, and then sell it, its temporary custodian. On the side, I would occasionally offer my own writing, but only the best of it: handmade wilderness survival guides and birdwatching logs for local enthusiasts. A book of recipes I made up for cooking over a campfire. A script for a TV pilot about the dogs that lived in my neighborhood. A book about things I liked to think about while fishing. And of course, a book of spells and magic lore.

Another question visitors to Treadwell's would ask of me: *What's the first book of magic you used?*

We didn't sell that book, because my earliest initiation into came through schlock—black-and-white *Universal* monster movies my uncle taped off of the TV for me—my favorite was *Abbot and Costello Meet Frankenstein*—and *Goosebumps* books. The first books I really remember loving and reading voraciously and repeatedly were those *Goosebumps* books by R. L. Stine. He was also the first and only person I have ever written a fan letter to. I loved the bright color combinations and the drippy font used to spell goosebumps and I loved the cover illustrations by Tim Jacobus, which toed a line between pulpy and ethereal. *Goosebumps* were the first books I read and identified with the characters: Grady, who gets to become a werewolf in *The Werewolf of Fever Swamp*, Ricky, getting to one-up his bullies in *Calling All Creeps!*; Freddy, discovering a secret passage to a vampire's coffin in his very own house in *Vampire Breath*.

Goosebumps also introduced me to the idea that books could be magic in both senses of the term. It's 1994 so I'm nearly eight. My best friend lives up the street and doesn't go to my school: Eddie. Eddie is the youngest of four brothers and his family has a big yard with a huge oak tree. We pool our collection of *Goosebumps* books together in a lidded box and tie a rope around the handle. Then, one of us climbs the tree to the top (we take turns who gets to go first) carrying the rope, then dropping it to the other. We use a branch of the oak tree to create a simple pulley system, the person on the bottom pulling the rope to hoist up our books, then tying the rope around an exposed root. Tucked into the box was a precious response I'd received to my fan letter with a digital reproduction of R. L. Stine's autograph—the holy grail! On the other side of his letter thanking me is a complete list of all available Goosebumps books, which I use as a checklist for my reading. *The Scarecrow Walks at Midnight* is one of the books I've read most, and it depends on books as magical tools.

The Scarecrow Walks At Midnight puts the reader within the POV of the propertied classes: *"Jodie loves visiting her grandparents' farm. Grandma's chocolate chip pancakes are the best."* The propertied classes have access to luxury commodities not shared among the farm workers. But this summer, things are different: Jodie notices her Grandma Miriam and Grandpa Kurt are acting strange; they seem tired and anxious, and they have stopped making pancakes. Also changed is the strange, malevolent charisma of their farmhand, Stanley, and Stanley's son, a disenfranchised kid named Sticks. The source of this change in the balance of relationships is that Stanley has a book:

> "My book," Stanley replied mysteriously. "My superstition book."
>
> Uh-oh, I thought. Stanley shouldn't have a book about superstitions. He was already the most superstitious person in the world—even without a book.
>
> "You've been reading a book about superstitions?" Mark asked him, watching the brown worms crawl over the soft dirt.

> "Yes." Stanley nodded his head enthusiastically. "It's a good book, tells me everything. And it's all true. All of it!"[30]

That, and the fact that the scarecrows that guard the farm's cornfields have begun to come alive. Jodie experiences the terror of the scarecrows firsthand in a series of run-ins with moving, walking, stalking Scarecrows. They have gained life from a magic spell cast by Stanley from his "superstition book"—clearly a grimoire of some kind. I did not wish to identify with Jodie so much as Stanley with his book of folk wisdom and remedies. Reading and re-reading this book transformed my relationship to both reading and making books in general, including spell books of my own.

My early spellbooks don't survive, but I can recreate some of their secret knowledge from memory:

Altars

I have built strange altars since childhood. Maybe all childhood is an exercise in building strange altars, bringing little trinkets charged with significance together into whatever assemblage your imagination dictates. Playing make-believe is pure witchcraft. All of the most sinister witch trials try to deny witches their power by accusing them of worshipping fake gods and living under too many delusions, executing them anyway. Reading through records of trials and testimonies feels, first and foremost, like reading through a brutal assault on the human imagination.

I have many memories of building altars. The first happened pretty much every day at bathtime. My terms for taking a bath were this: in order for me to get into the tub, my parents had to let me streak first. I'd run around the house naked and then dive into the bathtub. Once in the bathtub I would tear off little

30 R. L. Stine, *The Scarecrow Walks At Midnight* (New York: Scholastic, 1994) 14.

pieces of a bar of soap and sculpt them into things—animals, little bowls—and assemble them on the ledge of the tub. Then I would make a potion in the sculpted bowl, from little dabs of shampoo and conditioner. I loved the green bottle of Prell shampoo, but felt really lucky if there was Head & Shoulders because the milky blue color felt properly creepy, like a potion should be. I would mumble made up words while mixing the potion in the bowl, use water to knead it altogether, and anoint myself.

> He himselfe impresses or inures the marke of the Beast, the Devills Fleshbrand upon one or other part of the Body, and teaches them to make an Oyle or Oyntment, of live Infants stoln out of the Cradle (Before they be signed with the sign of the Crosse) or dead ones stolne out of their Graves, the which they are to boyle to a Jelly, and then drinking one part, and besmearing themselves with another, they forthwith feel themselves imprest and endowed with the faculties of this mysticall Art.[31]

I can plug the gaps in my childhood memory with descriptions from the witch trials themselves, their eerie resonances stretching over hundreds of years to harmonize with my kindergartner imagination.

> Imps let witches know to be ready on all Solem appointments, and meetings, which are ordinarily on Tuesday or Wednesday night, and then they strive to separate themselves from the company of all other Creatures, not to be seen by any: any night become come, they strip themselves naked, and anoint themselves with their Oyntments. Then are carryed out

31 John Gaule, *SELECT Cases of Conscience TOUCHING VVitches andVVitchcrafts* (London: W. Wilson for Richard Clutterbuck, 1646) 59-60.

of the house, either by the Window, Door, or Chimney, mounted on their Imps in the form of a Goat, Shepp, or Dragon, til they arrive at their meeting place, whither all the other Wizards and Witches, each one upon his Imps, are also brought.[32]

Nature

Then there were the much more elaborate altars made possible by nature. In the Pocono Mountains, Pennsylvania, probably around 1994, I was surely playing the unconscious role of a little tree worshipper. In 1994 my whole identity was the Pocono Mountains: it was the only place I wanted to be, and whenever I wasn't there, I was planning on being there, playing at it, imagining it. This mostly consisted of collecting outdoor survival gear, packing it into a backpack, and then unpacking it again to lay out in formations that were pleasing to my eye. I was a baby prepper. The goal was to fit everything I'd need to survive in the wilderness into one bag I could carry on my little six-year-old shoulders, plus a blank sketchbook so I could record my experience. I loved everything you could do "Up the Poconos," as we said: pitching my tent, fishing at Bear Creek Dam, climbing up the stones of the dam to meet my grandpa in the parking lot, gathering wood to make a fire so an adult would cook me Dinty Moore Beef Stew in my army-grade mess kit. Sitting very still with my grandma to wait for wildlife to walk by—deer, skunks, chipmunks. Wandering around the edge of the woods near the little house my grandpa built just off the highway. Up the Poconos you could ride go karts. Up the Poconos you could save all of your money and go to the Deer Track Trading Post to buy little carved wooden animals—bears, wolves, bobcats. At Split Rock you could go bowling. At Hickory Run you could go swimming. But most of all, my mom didn't really like going up the Poconos and would stay

32 Anonymous, *A Pleasant TREATISE of Witches.* (London: H.B. for c. Wilkinson, 1673) 4.

home; under the care of my dad and uncles and grandparents I didn't have to bathe every day and, for practical reasons, I could wear exclusively boy clothes: hiking boots, jeans, flannel, hair hidden under a baseball cap.

One day up the Poconos I woke up and a tree had fallen over near the house, a huge American Chestnut. This was big news. It was like I had a new playhouse to climb over. I felt true awe at the stones lodged in the roots of the tree, which no one would have held for a hundred years. This tree became my altar of sacrifices to an unknown god I imagined to be a kind of anthropomorphic apex predator, because I'd just learned the word "apex." This was surely the same god my grandpa made offerings to when he would hang slices of lunchmeat—salami, pepperoni, capicola—on a tripod at night in order to "show me a bear," aka tempt a bear out of the woods for us to watch. I left some of my lunchtime sandwich out on the tree, too. I'd fish out the stones from the roots and line them along the trunk, then little by little, I began to use my knife to peel off twigs and whittle them, then I started to carve into the trunk itself, strange figures and characters like my favorite wild animals (bears, wolves, bobcats) and my favorite cartoon characters (the Ninja Turtles). Instead of carving sometimes I drew with chalk I'd found clumped with dirt in the tree's roots. My goal was to work on it every day until we left later in the week, then leave the assemblage to the elements—I knew winters up there were harsh and imagined them being blown away, decayed, and then I knew my work would be complete, the offering accepted. It made me feel so calm: at the end of the week, I wrote ABCDEFGHIJKLMNOPQRSTUVWXYZ BROOKE GOODBYE

Birds

I didn't learn about meditating until I was a teenager, but as a child two of my favorite games were truly meditative. One was initiated by my grandmother: to sit in silence and whisper the names of as many birds as we could see so as not to startle them. Our knowledge was limited, mostly we spoke with our eyes and maintained total silence: I can still see her, in her jewel-toned mumu with her staff in hand, raising her eyebrows at me, which meant, *Look where I am looking*, and then slowly dragging her brown eyes to fixate on a tree where a barn owl sat in the twilight.

Treesies

When I learned in school that trees give us the oxygen we breathe in exchange for the carbon dioxide we exhale, I got excited. This could be a game! And I called the game *Treesies*. It was essentially a walking meditation: walk slowly and for every tree, exhale deeply, then inhale and thank them. But it could also be done sitting down, looking out at the horizon and counting the trees, an exhale in offering, an inhale in thanks.

Stigmata

All kids are inherently weird, and either they get away with it or they don't. Not getting away with it, having your strangeness stripped of you at a young age, felt like the worst fate to me, even then. The kids that happened to—kids who were more traditionally feminine and pretty, or masculine and athletic, seemed to suffer a particular kind of abuse and policing at such a young age. I didn't want what they had—even kids that fit in seemed to get treated badly. I got to remain a little weirdo under-the-radar, there was nothing anyone could do about it.

What's wrong with me? was one of the earliest questions my baby brain had thought to ask. My earliest interiority. But also, *What's wrong with you?* was a really common expression of anger and deep frustration where I grew up. Shout it with the right level of disgust and you're going to win the argument. It's a question adults ask of children all the time; it closes a discussion, focuses the blame squarely on the person something is supposedly wrong with. It's a question that sinks in with corrosive effects. I can't remember a time my intuition wasn't undermined by the internalized voice of some adult: *What's wrong with you?* I have clear memories of lying in bed at night as a child, and later a teenager, thinking in an obsessive loop: *What's wrong with me What's wrong with me What's wrong with me What's wrong with me.* I never got an answer, just feelings of dread at coming up short—it was something huge and unknowable, and for that reason, worse than anything that ever had come before. I worried I'd have to spend my entire life figuring out what was wrong with me, while everyone else was asleep, so I could keep my search for an answer a secret. I was already instinctively ashamed of the answer.

At one point, part of my wrongness was self-selected and therefore clear to me: we'd learned about St. Francis of Assisi in school who, like me, loved animals. He also, like me, loved God. *You learned about St. Francis of Assisi? Did they tell you about what really happened to him?* My uncle—the one who swore he'd seen a devil once, the one who was most steeped in the Book of Revelation—told me all about it: St. Francis had "the stigmata," which meant he was so good that he was granted the miracle of pain in the form of the wounds that Jesus Christ had at the Crucifixion. The stigmata meant you got bloody wrists and feet, like if someone had driven nails into them, and a gash in the side like someone had stabbed you. No, thank you! Wounds that oozed with blood and pain and never healed and smelled like an "Odor of Sanctity," whatever that was, sounded like the worst gift, worse than the pink tutu I had been given for ballet lessons I didn't want, that I had no choice but to destroy. It didn't sound like a gift at all. It became my greatest fear, and I had to do something about it. I had to make sure God knew I was not *that* good. I had to let a little badness into my life, as a matter of self-protection.

I consulted the Ten Commandments. It became a little inspirational checklist of things I could try to do to avoid getting the stigmata from being too good. But it was hard to practice in reality:

1. *Thou shalt have no other gods before me.* I had no idea (yet) what it would mean to have other gods than God, or what a graven image was.

2. Commandment two I could handle. *Thou shalt not take the name of the Lord thy God in vain.* God damnit! Dad said that all the time. Did I have to say it out loud or in my head? I tried both.

3. *Remember to keep holy the sabbath day.* There's no way I'd miss Church, I loved all of the robes and flowers and incense and singing.

4. *Honor thy father and thy mother.* Also hard. I'd always felt so bad for my parents; they always seemed so stressed, I didn't want to add to their trouble any more than I already did.

5. *Thou shalt not kill.* Did wishing death on someone count? I wanted the paparazzi who killed Princess Diana to die, after I saw how much her death wrecked my mom.

6. *That shalt not steal.* Good, I had stolen my pocketknife from my dad's desk drawer. But then he said I could keep it.

7. *That shalt not commit adultery.* I had no idea what that meant.

8. *Thou shalt not bear false witness against thy neighbor.* I had never been to court. But I watched a lot of *Night Court* at that time. Ultimately, I had no idea what this one meant.

9. *Thou shalt not covet thy neighbor's house.* Bingo! My dream house was my friend Kyle's uncle's trailer on the edge of the Pine Barrens in New Jersey. I remember a boy laughing at school about it—*You Want To Be Trailer Trash?*—and then another boy who lived in a trailer fighting with him. I just thought it was so cool to be able to live in a house you could decorate however you wanted and move as close to the woods as you could.

10. *Thou shalt not covet thy neighbor's wife.* Hmm. I remember thinking hardest about this one, because I did want

a wife at some point, someone like April O'Neil or Dr. Ellie Sattler. But did I want Karen or Norma or Donna or Tammy, who all lived on my block? Maybe I needed to get to know them better first. This could be a sin I had up my sleeve, in case the other ones weren't enough to ensure my protection from the stigmata.

In addition to the cosmology of a wrathful, rule-driven Christian God who punished pretty much everyone who'd worshipped him, my sense of wrongness was embellished with cartoons from the cultural landscape. As a child the worst thing I could think of was *"Man was in the forest"*—how the death of Bambi's mother is accounted for in the 1942 Disney movie. I remember thinking, *That's me! I'm Man!* And crying until I could barely breathe. Maybe that's what was wrong with me—I'd killed Bambi's mother, somehow? And Bambi's mother was also my mother.

The bad feelings increased as I started embracing my darkness and engaging in orphan play. Orphan play is a sinister game of make believe where you pretend to not have a family. All of my games were variations on the same theme: I had to survive in the wilderness with my pocketknife, my backpack, that beef jerky that came in tins like chewing tobacco, my canteen, a compass, and some matches. The reason behind the need to survive was that I was an orphan, no one would come to find me. I was happiest imagining myself alone in the woods, able to roam free and forage. I'd packed my little green Jansport to carry these items with me everywhere I went, convinced that my desire to imagine myself this way meant it would one day happen in reality—and when it did, I'd be ready. All night I'd feel guilty that I'd played all day pretending that my parents were dead. Was *that* what was wrong with me?

Every bad thing I could think of would eventually metabolize into my fantasy life, whipped into a frenzy from the media I was consuming: Pinocchio getting kidnapped and turned part donkey for smoking a cigar on Pleasure Island; the boy crashing his motorcycle and dying in The Shangri-Las song "Leader of the Pack;" the Teenage Mutant Ninja Turtles' melancholy over their mutant identities in *The Secret of the Ooze*. All of these characters had something mysterious wrong with them, that they couldn't fix. They all suffered for it. But at least they did not suffer the stigmata.

Dreams

Then I started lucid dreaming. I'd looked it up in an encyclopedia and found a book that said lucid dreaming was used by physicists to work through complex problems in an alternate dimension of their consciousness. Cool. I could use this. It was an ability I had been given to find out what was wrong with me and fix it or atone. I would come home from school and take a nap right away so I could get to work.

The dreams always started the same way, and that's part of it: you have to develop an awareness of the repeated signs and motifs in your dreams in order to train your mind to recognize it as dreaming, and then take control. The dreams always started with finding and feeling the hem of a deep red velvet curtain between my fingers—because I'm a hugely dramatic person with a Leo stellium?—then drawing the curtain aside and stepping across the threshold into the room of the house I'd been in all along. This part of the house was filled with the kind of crap I love, stuff that looked like it came from a combination of the Discovery Channel store and Natural Wonders, two of my favorite chains in the malls where I grew up. I would walk through this room and rifle through the objects—meteorites, fossils, bones, gems, brass instruments like little telescopes, and, above all, an array of little puzzles made of bent metal and string and wood that were meant to be untangled. A Rubix Cube made out of stone, with no color; those little woven finger traps, trick locks. And—lest we forget to honor the supply chains that somehow led to an Indigenous instrument from southern Chile ending up in strip malls around America—rainsticks.

I believed that the house was my subconscious's way of visualizing my own mind for me to wander around in. I felt worried about that, too, like, wasn't that kind of boring and straightforward? Couldn't my brain come up with something cooler and more complicated? I guess there were some perks, like that it was a somewhat busted haunted house. Ramshackle. There was a room with a maze in it, there was a library that felt cozy. Sometimes there were presences in the house, like ghosts that I could only see out of the corner of my eye, and they truly frightened and filled me with dread. I'd reach a point in the house where I could climb a spiral staircase to the top of a witch's peak—as a child, spiral staircases represented to me the absolute height of luxury for some reason—and be free to leave through a skylight and explore the rest of the world if I wanted. This was the only exit. But no matter how long I wandered around, I was never able to banish the haunted presence or figure out the entry to certain rooms. And, even if I solved one of the little puzzles, it would reset itself too quickly to feel any pleasure from it. It disturbed me that my mind was presenting itself to me as a house, but nothing I did could change the contents and decoration of the house for very long. There was something wrong with me I couldn't change. I'd wake up and think, again, *What's wrong with me?* How could my life be that irrevocably fucked up if I felt like I had barely lived?

All I could do, having reached a dozen years old, was develop a spiritual practice and fandom, which were similar in being really obsessive and dorky. I had wanted to be a witch, or a vampire, or a vampire witch, and had gotten in trouble for it. I was reading Anne Rice novels, and my aunt tipped off my parents that she had seen Anne Rice on the Rosie O'Donnell show "dressed in flowing black robes, Satanic," and this began the close surveillance of my spiritual life. I was banned from wearing black clothing, the only color I wanted to wear. I wasn't allowed to leave the house, so I couldn't spend time with the small fringe of other goths at my school. I wasn't allowed to fully close my bedroom door, so I could never have any privacy to light candles without getting screamed at. But I had headphones, and I had the early internet to look up information about witchcraft and Satanism. I could spend hours reading about self-initiation and spell-casting on lurid, cloud-background Angelfire websites with little flying bats and brooms as cursors, little animated gif candles and flames and fairies. I could make websites like that myself, I could roleplay on neopets.com as a wolf-like mutant wizard named "Hephaestus." The first iteration of the internet was a total mess but hanging out on websites like *Raven Haven, The Den of the Dragon, Decadent Dandies,* and *Fallen Angels* at least beat the feeling of having no friends.

In one of my lucid dream rooms there was an altar and building fan websites on the internet altered one aspect of it in my dreams. The altar was the only thing that changed in the house, and the changes were for me to find, rather than make, over the course of a dream. It was piled with stuff, and each time I visited, it would have more and more clutter on it: crow feathers and owl feathers, candles with beeswax that never burned down but dripped and formed sculptures of wild animals on the floor, strings of repurposed red rosary beads, dog tags and pilgrim badges and pins, pocket knives with carved handles, dowsing rods and tree branches, piles of photographs of people I didn't recognize, CD cases for bands I didn't recognize. I can still see the altar as clearly as if I'd made it in my waking life, except there was something pixelated about the tongues of flame on each candle.

At the time I didn't see lucid dreaming as a gift for it's own sake, but as a tool to solve a problem. Later I realized, since I hadn't been allowed to express my hormonal urges in any way without being punished, the onslaught of puberty presented itself to me as a sudden ability to experience vast, sprawling lucid dreams. My brain was making up for the lack of options my body had: wondrously generous and inversely related to my ability to dissociate in school every day. It wasn't enough: soon I would need additional space to put my imagination through its paces, and the internet would provide it.

CRUSHED VELVET

Between the ages of fourteen and seventeen I ran the second most popular website about the actor Alan Rickman. My obsession cracked open a whole world. My entire personality became dominated by a projection of a projection about who this old British man *was*, embellished by deep research. What did the intensity of my fandom mean? I honestly didn't know. But I always knew I was developing something beyond a celebrity crush. I just followed my feelings and all related compulsions where they led me and waited for meaning to emerge. In the meantime, these years spent in the unconditional faith that the subject of my obsession—Alan Rickman—would think I was *cool*, would *love* me, amounted to a total transformation with deep implications for my future as a witch.

The oldest magical ritual is surrender, the leap of faith. Fandom requires a similar leap, and I took it. Just like today, in that era of the internet, second was best; first place always goes to a middle-of-the-road or simply the most obvious choice. I didn't want to be obvious. My second-most-popular website was a signal to exactly the people I wanted to be: weirdos who weren't out yet as queer or trans, and middle-aged women who flirted and hinted at wanting to have cybersex with me.

When you're a fan of a celebrity, a lot of time is spent consuming their media output, reading interviews with them, looking at a lot of pictures, and from there you extrapolate about what they might be like. You watch the same movies and clips over and over and over. You make fan videos to your favorite clips, so you can watch them over and over and over to music you like. Like when I took the scene from a music video for "In Demand" by the band Texas in which Alan Rickman tangoes at a gas station with lead singer Sharleen Spiteri, and reworked it to Smokey Robinson's "You've Really Got a Hold On Me"—one of my favorite songs since childhood, when I saw him perform it on Sesame Street to introduce the letter U. Being a fan is incredibly creative; like a magpie, I found and gathered up the shiny things that reminded me of the subject of my obsession, and made little piles and collages and art and altars.

I took all the information I could find about Alan Rickman and used it to alter, discipline, and constrain my own behavior until I became a version of myself that I thought would be respected by the celebrity I was imagining in my head. I conducted myself to a standard that I thought Alan Rickman would get along with if he were to meet me. By age eighteen I had fully metabolized everything I thought to be true about a person I had never met, devouring and absorbing him into my own body. Then I, Alan Rickman, got honest with myself, and started having sex with women for real. And *then* I moved to London, and when I had enough money, I started to medically transition into Alan Rickman. He's writing this now, in a way. Especially since the other Alan Rickman died in 2016.

When the obsession first struck I thought: there's work to do. But by age eighteen I was ready—I was certain Alan Rickman would think I was amazing. Like any devotee, I worked hard to be prepared for that eventuality. I was raised Roman Catholic; Protestants believed in salvation by faith alone, but I didn't know any Protestants. I was good at work and I was good at homework. I was so good at homework that I conceived of my desire to be—and be loved by—Alan Rickman as an issue which homework could solve. Doing enough homework was my justification for everything: my likes, my dislikes, my worthiness for love, affection, praise, food, clothing, shelter. If I didn't do homework, I was a disappointment and a disgrace to everyone around me. If I didn't do homework, I was lazy and stupid and selfish and destined for a life of misery. If I did do homework, I was lovable, I was setting myself to make my dreams come true. I applied this worldview to my new interest and learned so much. All of my learning expanded my imagination—the ways I could picture meeting Alan Rickman.

I would imagine meeting Alan Rickman. He would want to talk about Chekhov with me. Why Chekhov? In an interview I'd read, Rickman described something as "Chekhovian," and I had no idea what that meant, so I went to the library and read anything by or about Chekhov that I could get my hands on. I wrote notes about an idea to stage *The Seagull* in the parking lot behind the KFC next to the trolley station, where there were lots of seagulls. In the final scene the characters could play bingo in my grade school cafeteria a few blocks away, which doubled as a bingo hall on weekends where everyone smoked indoors, the smell of smoke got into our uniforms during the week—it was the first place a lot of girls in eighth grade could get a paying job, working the bingo nights. But labor was gendered at that age, and I believe I didn't get that job because I wasn't a girl. I was already making money off tips as an altar server, working the weddings and funerals in the parish. Still, the cafeteria would be the perfect place for my play. And surely the shock of Konstantin blowing his brains out would be less shocking in this setting of parking lots, cafeterias, public transportation—the blue-collar depressive landscape of suburban decay. Alan Rickman would come to this travelling, indoor-outdoor performance and nod his approval: "*Very Chekhovian*," he would say, just like he had said in the interview. In my dreams, I never made Alan Rickman say anything he hadn't already: I just created new scenarios and contexts for him to say the things he'd already said in movies and interviews. Sometimes, while napping, I would dream that I was Alan Rickman, and he was saying these things just before plunging his huge cock deeply inside some hot actress on set: Laura Dern, Diane Lane, Kate Winslet. *Not Very Chekhovian*. I'd wake up and feel guilty.

I read all of Jane Austen's novels because he was in *Sense and Sensibility*, all of Shakespeare's plays and poems because of the long list of productions he'd done with the Royal Shakespeare Company—and, of course, *Les Liaisons Dangereuses* because of his award-winning turn as the libertine Le Vicomte de Valmont. That was sexy, it got me into the libertine novels I could find as Penguin Classics and on Project Gutenberg.org, like Denis Diderot's *Les Bijoux Indiscrets*, aka *The Indiscreet Jewels*. *The Indiscreet Jewels* is about a magic ring that forces women's vaginas to speak, describing everyone they've had sex with. Awesome. And then of course, the Marquis de Sade, a true freak whose work I only half understood, but whose *Justine* made me feel hot and bothered. I was Alan Rickman fucking Justine upon an elaborate chaise lounge, once I learned what a chaise lounge was. I began prognosticating, reading far out to see if I could find anything Alan Rickman might get cast in, so I could say: *I knew it! I knew they would make a movie of* The Indiscreet Jewels*!*

I got into noir because of "Murder, Obliquely," Alan Rickman's episode with Laura Dern and Diane Lane in the series *Fallen Angels*, which I was able to download illegally off of LimeWire. *Fallen Angels* dramatized works by Dashiell Hammett and Raymond Chandler, whom I then read for clues about how I could be more desirable to Alan Rickman. I practiced narrating my life like a noir detective, like Philip Marlowe. Then I read anything I could about *animal magnetism* and the early history of psychiatry, since I had specially ordered a DVD of Rickman as Franz Anton in *Mesmer* (1994) from the Suncoast Video at my local mall. I began to experiment with magnets, carrying them in my pockets. I read a book about hypnosis. I wore more ruffles, I listened to chamber music and fantasized about experiencing the frenzied liberation of people who had taken the magnetic cure.

Alan Rickman also got me into a gay culture outside of the total hatred towards gay people that everyone around me harbored: the first time I ever saw two men kiss was in the startling finale of *Dark Harbor* (1998), and the first time I ever saw two women kiss was in a movie that remains in my top ten, *Blow Dry* (2001), about competitive hair dressing in the UK. And of course, I'd read all of Noël Coward because I'd wanted so badly to be able to afford to see Rickman perform, live in New York City, in Coward's *Private Lives* in 2001. My childhood and teenage years felt like a lot of waiting—just biding my time, is how I thought of it then, essentially trying not to kill myself or get killed. I turned this waiting into waiting for Alan Rickman to make more movies, to be photographed in more photos. The waiting time became time for more research to feed my imagination about what he might be doing, what I could be doing when I was old enough to make my own decisions and live my own life.

This was all painstaking work that started with encyclopedias and card catalogs in the very small local and school libraries, and the Waldenbooks at the mall. I had no money, and *Wikipedia* didn't exist. But then the internet came and was free: at the local CVS I could grab stacks of *America Online—500 Free Hours* CDs, which allowed me to dial up. Each CD required creating a new account, so every few months I would have to change screen names. Sometimes they'd be variants of a name I really liked—there was a series of Magic_Wolf87(s). There was the I_Am_Baroque series, a pun on how "broken" I felt in the emo parlance of the time, and how much I enjoyed the lavishness of Baroque art and sculpture (think Caravaggio, Bernini's *Ecstasy of Saint Teresa*). There was a series of speechless_death(s) after a favorite Shakespeare quote about language and exile. The group of friends I met in AOL chatrooms always knew me, and I kept their screennames in a little address book so I could reach out to them whenever I had to delete one account and start a new one.

Google Image Search was new—usually to find information, you would go to websites like TheFanListings.org, or EliteFanPages.com, search for the person, band, movie, book you were a fan of, and see which websites had been set up as altars to that subject. You could also go to FanFiction.net to search for writing about the celebrity, movie, show, book you loved, and if you didn't find what you wanted, you could write it yourself, either to submit to the archive or collectively in online roleplaying games. Fansites tended to have a biography, a list of the person's work, a gallery of images, maybe some transcribed articles or press, and a guestbook for visitors to sign. Sometimes the guestbook would take on a life of its own and become more like a message board thread, and this was true for the number one website for Alan Rickman, AlanRickman.com, which had an iconic, cloudy blue sky background over the whole site, and no other design effort put into its many pages, pages heaped upon one another with no attempts at organization. What kept it first among Alan Rickman fansites was that guestbook, where hundreds if not thousands of people posted. There were regulars, friendships, rivalries, a whole culture of people who claimed mostly to be women in their thirties and forties, vying with one another to appear as the person Alan Rickman would love the most if he ever descended from upon high to look at a web page. But he was on the record as disinterested in the internet.

I started my own website—CrushedVelvet.net— sometime in 2002, to answer the lack of up-to-date information and analysis within the fandom. I had taught myself how to use Adobe Photoshop and designed all of the graphics myself. I'd learned graphic design and website coding for Alan Rickman. By July 2003, site traffic was significant enough that I bought the domain name Rickman-Fan.com and closed Crushed Velvet. This was a practical decision: I'd initially imagined Crushed Velvet as a personal webpage to bring together my tastes (for example, my taste in velvets, decadence, dandyism, syphilitic poets and writers, deathbed converts to Catholicism), but as Alan Rickman began to dominate them—as I began to become him—it made sense to change names. The popularity of my site meant I was constantly exceeding my bandwidth, and I needed an upgrade. I kept Rickman-Fan.com up until graduating high school, in the middle of 2005, a few months before turning eighteen and moving from the outskirts into West Philadelphia for school.

A crowning artistic achievement: using Adobe Photoshop to collage different images together, I designed the Alan Rickman website to look nothing like the typical fansite styles of the day, with a high-res image and a menu. Instead, my site had "brushes" I had made in Photoshop to look like blots of spilled ink, collaged with an image of an ink well, a fountain pen, and manipulated black and white photographs of Alan Rickman in obscure roles (the Reverend Obadiah Slope in *The Barchester Chronicles*; Hendrik Höfgen in *Mephisto*), making them look like scattered Polaroids. I added a piece of paper where I'd traced out his iconic signature, and used the blotted ink stains over a background of wood grain to make it look like *you were sitting at the writing desk of Alan Rickman, possibly because you yourself were Alan Rickman*. My AOL friends lost their minds, it was so awesome. I accidentally ruined my mom's credit rating ordering more server space because of how popular it was. Unlike more basic fansites, mine was also an archive of my reading—excerpts from plays, poems, philosophical and psychological books I'd taken out of the library, that would let others submerge themselves into the mindscape of Alan Rickman, who was me.

Cobbling together a sexuality and a gender meant stitching together a patchwork quilt from cultural references that were only occasionally expressly queer or trans, but mostly weird and countercultural in some way that read as both queer and trans to me before I had that particular language to describe myself. My cursory search for explicitly queer content consistently failed me: in theology class at school, we were taught that homosexuality was a sin; the news had shown how people like Brandon Teena and Matthew Shephard got killed; kids joked that faggots got AIDS and died. The news was always bad. A story about the corrective rape of lesbians, a story about a father killing his own son when he found out he was gay. Most of the kids in my class called me boys' names and avoided me. I had to build my own algorithm and think myself outside of the cultural and spiritual poverty of this scene. I had to learn how to build a world (a website) that could be beautiful and sprawling and display my tastes for *the finer things*. It felt like having a taste for nice things was the most powerful way I could survive straight hegemony. I could cut open boring, deadly straight culture for my own camp purposes.

This *was* the low camp of Web 1.0, the aesthetics of which—animated gifs and word-art effects on text—have certainly lived on in the art and DIY publishing world and the humor and genius of memes. An iconic feature of this moment in the history of fan culture on the internet was the icon itself: fan websites including mine offered themed bundles of user icons for LiveJournal (100 x 100 pixels) as well as desktop backgrounds (800 x 600, later 1024 x 768). But the tiny icons were the most popular canvas for imaginative forms of idol worship, and I produced new bundles on different themes every week: a creatively cropped black-and-white photo of someone you loved, or a screencap from your favorite movie, with a relevant quote or just some lyrics from a song you loved. Example: an image of Trent Reznor, Photoshopped to look like a young Alan Rickman as Severus Snape in his wizard robes, with a line from Nine Inch Nails's "Closer," written in a minimalist sans serif invoking a bleak industrial landscape: *You Can Have My Isolation*. Or the design I used for the December 2002 edition of Crushed Velvet: an image of Alan Rickman, hunched on a chair in a dressing room, a moment where he's himself and not a character, arms crossed, chin resting on the crook of an elbow, looking right into the camera. Over this image I laid a star map from the early twentieth century—the northern hemisphere. According to my profile at the time, my nickname at the time was Davey, the poem I was most interested in reading was "And Thou art Dead, as Young and Fair," by Lord Byron, the book I was reading was *The Faerie Queen*, I was listening to the NIN side project LP, Tapeworm, and you could contact me at the email address CrucibleofBrooke@aol.com.

Crushed Velvet dot net was my projection, how I wanted people to see me. Who were the people that responded to this calling card? A small group of about six or seven friends with whom I created a private H**** P*****© RPG. I would log into our password-protected message board and crank out long descriptions of the dark, brooding wizard I felt myself to be, a young man with long, lank hair, tattoos, and flowing black robes of crushed velvet. The air of the room in the dungeons where I lived was heavily perfumed with woodsmoke and incense; the bookshelves crammed with old, rare, leatherbound tomes, gilt at the edges and blindstamped on the covers with my monogram. Often my descriptions would begin and end with this character gathering the ingredients to perform some forbidden magical ritual: summoning an obscure demon to do my bidding, reconstituting papyrus scrolls thought to be lost forever when the Library of Alexandria burned, concocting potions to cauterize the cuts and wounds received in sex magic rituals. We would describe virtual visits to one another's virtual living quarters, converse on the nature of existence and reality, and most exciting of all, we would co-write sexual encounters between our characters.

By the time I upgraded to human subjects, I had a lot of experience writing about sex I'd never had. A few years earlier I'd spent time lurking on the message boards of Neopets.

com. Neopets was a website that was designed to look like a whole cartoon world with different locations, landscapes, neighborhoods, amenities and games. You had pets that were variations upon real and fabled animals: cats, dogs, foxes, dragons, gryphons. You fed them and battled with them to advance their powers. You could "paint" their coats with different designs—but the paintbrushes were rare, and hard to come by. My username was neogoddess87 and I played Neopets that way: as a goddess caring for my magical, mortal creatures, which included a gryphon-like, part-lion, part-eagle named Hephaestus, after the god of the forge, and a wolflike creature named Romulus. They worshipped a goddess as part of a religion I made up, whose acolytes aspired to be elevated into constellations upon death. I spent hours inhabiting Romulus, a powerful alpha wolf, stalking the boards for mates to mount and impregnate. I'd definitely been one of those "wolf kids," reading anything about wolves that I could and also having wolves on all of my things: folders, notebooks, light fixtures, hats, T-shirts. There was no sex education at my Catholic School, so with the onslaught of hormones, everything became a matter of wolf sex. I didn't have crushes on any of the awful kids in my grade, and they didn't have crushes on me; the feelings were mutual, I funneled all of my filthy furtive imaginings into the realm of the only pornography I'd seen at the time: nature documentaries about apex predators.

The style of prose for roleplaying these creatures on the message boards was purple and pornographic. You could join someone else's thread or start your own:

> *Eyes of blue fire and sharp fangs glare in the moonlight, all that's visible of the huge beast of ebon-hued pelt that lies crouched in the shadow of a gnarled old oak. Powerful claws flex in the soft earth over muscular haunches, flecks of blood from a kill not long dried—the beast has slaked his thirst, satisfied his hunger. Now, midnight, his nostrils flared,*

he waits patiently to catch the scent of a she-wolf on the westerly wind that blows around him.

I'd refresh the thread until someone responded:

Violet eyes seeing all and fearing none, a lithe female bends to drink from the nearby stream, her soft pink tongue delicately lapping the cool clear water. Her ears dart forward, her eyes flicker toward the shadows of the oak: a descendent of warriors, she is no stranger to the dangers of the forest, to its secrets in the shadows. She leaps quickly to a branch and looks down at the male, a smirk on her maw that shows the twinkle of a fang: Good Evening, Stranger.

We'd get to know each other like that for some time, then meet over chat, off the message board, to mate.

Romulus could smell the blood of Guinevere's heat. He licked his chops absent-mindedly, instinctively, feeling a different kind of hunger grow and pump hot through his veins with his blood. He nuzzled his huge maw into the soft fur of her neck and breathed in the scent of her more deeply, nudging her coaxingly to the ground, ready to mount.

Guinevere whined ever-so-softly. She faced him, looking deeply into his eyes to say: I want this, too. Then nudged and rubbed alongside him, her delicate form against his muscular body, her dainty snout dipping under to sniff and lick at his sheathe almost playfully, her heat rising with anticipation. She crouched and looked back over her haunches at him, invitingly.

Romulus closed his eyes with the pleasure of feeling her body against his, her playfulness, her eagerness. At her coaxing he felt himself start to become stiff and engorged. As he turned to follow her lead he was almost panting with the effort of self-restraint. He mounted her gently at first and then used his paws to hold her down, teasing her with the hardness of his member, rubbing the huge shaft near her soft, warm, wet opening but not entering, not yet.

She whined loudly and reared up against him, arching her back and grinding against his engorged member.

He clenched his paws around her more tightly, grit his teeth, and plunged himself inside of her.

She whimpered as he entered her, panting with the effort of taking all of him as deeply inside her as she could.

He growled and nipped at her neck possessively. He thrust and pumped himself in and out, again and again.

When his teeth sunk into her she threw her head back, howling with delight, bucking up against him, setting a rhythm to their mating.

Her movements, the sound and smell and texture of her pleasure, made him wild—he felt his member get bigger and harder than ever, push further out of its sheathe than ever. He stabbed at her, feeling ready to explode, locking into coupling with her, his member knotted inside.

Her howls pierced through the night, their echoes filled the forest with the rippling infinitude of her mounting pleasure, the rapture of feeling completely filled by him, the visions produced by deep and abiding penetration, her anticipation for the burst and blossom of his seed: the strong young pups she would suckle, the fearsome pack they would raise and rule together as mates. She began to feel the build of intensity release as a rippling, rolling pleasure, then joy, then contentment and completion. She was delighted to feel him locked inside her, almost a hostage to all those different textures and movements of pleasure of hers, she was open and ready for him to explode inside her.

Almost as instantaneously as she began to quiver and quake, Romulus lost total control of his body, clenching her and thrusting wildly, feeling himself spurt and come deeply inside of her, releasing his seed. He came so hard he had to bite deeply into a branch of the oak tree as if to bridle himself, the violence of his orgasm kindling a kind of violence in his very self that he could not control but had to redirect. By the light of the full wolf moon, the gnarls in the tree itself finally appeared as they truly were: not so much signs of growth and old age, but scars from the teeth and claws of generations of wolves who had coupled here.

By 2002 I was ready to really challenge myself as a writer and expand my horizons outside of the animal world, decanting wolf sex into avatars that looked like Alan Rickman playing a wizard, but represented me. Whatever childhood interest in witchcraft I'd had, this next initiation—downplayed because it was purely digital—set the foundation for both my real-world sexual exploits and my life as a witch. As the *Malleus Maleificarum*, a hateful work that spurned on the witch panic beginning in the fifteenth century says, *All witchcraft comes from carnal lust.* I was determined to prove that true and to have a good time doing it.

But as a teenager, my idea of what sex would be like, as someone who was out of my body most of the time and a virgin, was that during sex your whole body was one hugely sensitive nerve. Any way of touching or being touched slowly turned the body, groomed it, into this nerve. It initially looked and felt like static electricity, rubbing a balloon on the carpet and then on your head. I imagined an orgasm was the process by which, through a lot of stroking and petting, every single thing on a person's body would stand to attention, like an erection but including all limbs, hair, gooseflesh. This would bring you closer and closer to orgasm, which I imagined looked and felt like an explosive seizure. My character would spend a lot of time tracing his long pale fingers across the chins of the women he was going to bed, and they'd moan and moan as if their jawlines were sexual organs. This kind of slow teasing could go on for hours. In one session, my character had such an intense orgasm that he ejaculated all over the ceiling of the crypt—except the cause of this was another character using a straight-edged razor to merely shave his five o'clock shadow. In a later scene, a different character happened upon the ceiling jizz and scraped it off to use in a potion to bind him to her. It took months for the potion to wear off, but months were all she'd needed to get her fill of using his body however she pleased.

We were often speaking on two different platforms at once: chatting as ourselves on AOL Instant Messenger, and narrating as our characters within the message board. *Tonight's the night, are you ready?* As in, tonight the build-up of longing between our two characters reaches a fever pitch and we're going to describe them having sex, we who have never had sex! *Actually I think they have to have one more chance meeting in the forest, one more argument, before they get annoyed with one another enough to actually need to fuck.*

Oh, okay.

Trust me, it's gonna be fun.

Cool.

The adults around me and my fellow teenagers were all mystified: Why Alan Rickman? I remember the girls at my school, their perplexed-and-a-little-scared faces: everyone was crazy about James Van Der Beek in *Dawson's Creek*, and Josh Hartnett. I was into lifting weights in my neighbor's shed while listening to Nelly and playing roller hockey, but my eyes lit up at the name of a man who had just turned fifty-eight: Alan Rickman. No one really knew who he was except the older male teachers at school: *You mean the bad guy from Die Hard and Robin Hood?* Yes, I was actually queer-coding myself as a villain, it was so complicated. *But why do you like him so much?* What was legible to people was that I seemed to have a crush on a man, which they accepted. "Oh, you're just like Jo from Little Women," my mom said, "she married a much older professor. You just need to meet someone mature, like you are."

I knew that wasn't it. But, why Alan Rickman? The fervor of my devotion has erased any memories of how I came upon him—I acted like I'd always known. It was probably as a fly on the wall watching my dad watch action movies, and since that wasn't an interesting origin story to me I buried it. But the how and why didn't have to be clear to me in order to indulge a voracious appetite of reading anything remotely connected to his career, which turned out to be the whole of literature, history, philosophy. I could connect two thousand years of culture to Alan Rickman. To understand Alan Rickman, I had to read everything related to him; but then, to continue to *live* as Alan Rickman, I had to pre-empt his every move. Because I played Severus Snape in a closed roleplaying forum; in order to perfect my backstory for the role of the Potions Master I got deeper into witchcraft, hermeticism, alchemy, and Frances Yates's writing on memory and Rosicrucianism. After childhood, this was my second great initiation into witchcraft: this time, using a Sharpie to draw the sigil of Lucifer into my inner left thigh, and using my old pocketknife to cut into my right thigh and spill blood in the name of the Devil while reciting the Our Father backwards. Satanism felt like the perfect real-world religion to dabble in: it was clearly what Severus Snape's own *dark mark* was based off of, and for me, a fully confirmed Catholic, the ultimate acceptance of my fate as a fallen, banished member of my congregation.

Hence, TheCrucibleofBrooke@aol.com: I had reached my boiling point, and the crucible is the open vessel in which the impurities of substances are burned away in the earliest stages of alchemical transmutation from base metal to gold. Our bodies are crucibles, open-mouthed containers that collect the sum of our experiences, a heady brew that seeps into and colors our souls; how we fill and burn off the contents of the crucible is how we achieve spiritual perfection. The word 'Crucible' also just sounds intense, mysterious, and cool.

But part of me—my raging, surging hormones, so incredibly constrained by having no money, no close friends, no freedom to move around, and no privacy outside my password-protected email (even the door to my bedroom didn't close all the way)—knew I was up to something beyond a crush, still going on gut instinct and hoping the meaning would follow. And my instincts had grown darker, more evil: every night when my parents were asleep, I would log onto my computer and enter an AOL chatroom with a secret screenname I kept and told no one about: Piscean_Alan.

Alan Rickman said once in an interview that he really identified with being a Pisces, that he felt duality—like the water sign emblematized by two fish swimming in opposite directions—between a desire for intense privacy to replenish his psychic wellbeing, and the need for nourishment in the form of public attention, especially stage performance. He said, in general, he'd felt pulled asunder by life's dualities. I loved that he loved astrology, and I started to get into it, too—but his stars, not my own. I felt that if Alan Rickman did have an AOL screenname it would refer to his sign; he'd have the same ambivalence toward socializing on the web as he described feeling as an artist. To prepare to enter into the mind of Alan Rickman, I would light a little tea light, sometimes burn a cedarwood joss stick I'd managed to sneak into the house. I'd breathe deep and meditate in the lotus position like I'd read about, counting one to ten, up and down again, focusing on my breath, for ten or twenty minutes. Then I would log in as Piscean_Alan and imagine what it would be like to have a life rich and social enough that you wouldn't need the internet to connect with people—on the one hand—but on the other, fame might make it hard to connect *deeply* with people who couldn't see beyond your stardom. How Alan might feel lonely and want to talk about opera, classical music, or visual art, when he was sequestered away on set. I, too, felt lonely, because I didn't know anyone who wanted to talk about these things with me, which also meant I could relate to being famous.

Because I was Alan Rickman, I was also an actor. And because I'd read all of Chekhov, I of course had to read all I could find of Chekhov's friend and collaborator, the director Konstantin Stanislavski, who wrote a three-volume guide to his famous method of acting, translated as *An Actor Prepares, Building a Character*, and *Creating a Role*—his ABCs of acting. I could apply these intensely soulful principles of empathy and immersion to become the character of Alan Rickman on America Online. Alan Rickman's super-objective was to keep his acting abilities fresh and grounded—thus preparing him for future roles—by connecting with how real people were learning to connect within the brave new world of home computing. Lingering in the chat rooms, making occasionally "high brow" references and snarky remarks in outdated English—what I thought could be British English, words like "alas" and "methinks"—occasionally I would get individual message requests from people in the chat: *Hi, I have to ask…are you Alan Rickman? You seem like you could be him!* After some flirtatious banter to avoid the question, I would circle back around to reveal my secret to them: *Indeed, I am*—wouldn't an old British man say "indeed" a lot?—*But please, please do not share this screenname with anyone, I am quite private, you know.*

This is how I met Diane, aka Mad4Rikman@aol.com, for the second time. Diane was a divorcée in her forties who found me first through Crushed Velvet dot Net. She was convinced, when she spoke to me as me—CrucibleofBrooke—that we had been lovers in a past life, that I had been her boyfriend or husband and that we needed to do past life regression to get to the bottom of it. We talked all the time. She knew I was living as a teenager, attending an "All-Girls" Catholic High School. We'd talk about our days, what we were up to, what we were reading. She told me a lot about her troubles as a single mother, especially with finding childcare. I told her about my ambition to move to a place in England called Cumbria to apprentice as a tailor with someone whose blog on men's fashion I read; I wanted to learn to make my own three-piece velvet suits for the winter, linen for the summer. I had an idea I could transform my interest in the "dandyism" of Beau Brummell into a trade in bespoke suiting, maybe aspire to work on Jermyn Street one day. She thought that was so "cute." When she found me as Piscean_Alan, she believed that I really was Alan Rickman—so familiar to her!—and that she had known Alan in a past life. It was both me. I was sixteen years old. The word "catfishing" didn't exist at the time, and in the wild, wild west of the early internet, everyone assumed as a matter of basic etiquette that the person they were chatting to was a perverted old man, that they were taking their lives into their own hands by sharing any information with this potential serial killer. I was doing the opposite—seemingly a sixteen year old girl, pretending to be a fifty-eight year old man. That made it okay. Eventually, Diane met a man at the Pennsylvania Renaissance Faire named Wayne. They started dating. *I bet you'd love him! I hope you can meet some day!* She came online less and less.

I finally graduated from high school, moved to Philadelphia for college, and met people my age who actually wanted to be my friends and teachers who actually said encouraging things to me. There was a world to inhabit and explore, something to speak into other than a void. I shut down the website without an afterthought. Alan Rickman didn't come up at all in my studies, my reading, the movies I was watching, the conversations I was having. But often the knowledge I had consumed to feed the version of him in my head would come in handy in class; teachers would be surprised at some obscure text I knew, or I'd get a laugh from an odd turn of phrase I'd mimicked from one of his movies or interviews. *Transition complete.* Now that I was Alan Rickman, I didn't have to talk about it. And because I'd moved to the city, I was stealth. The ultimate triumph lies in the fact that nothing further had to be said; it had all been done, a spell of habits gave way to a becoming that had changed me down to the level of my DNA.

When the other Alan Rickman died in 2016, I received the most bizarre condolences—from my parents, from someone I went to high school with, from a few friends I had told about "the website." It had been over a decade since I'd thought of him. But I had to say: Thanks, Alan Rickman, for what your masculinity gave me as a teenager. Becoming you made all of my dreams come true. I did move to England. I did trace my long pale finger down the spines of ancient books at Oxford. I did end up practicing witchcraft. I did end up wearing nice men's clothes. And I did, incidentally, encounter the other Alan Rickman, twice, at the theatre. Our tastes matched up. I'd waved and nodded to him, raised a glass of champagne in his direction; he'd raised his back. Cheers. He was just being a friendly actor. It was cool. *If only you knew!* I thought.

In time, I'd find other ways of honoring his death, through a singular kind of grief: the grief of letting go a of a dissociative experience used to survive a lot of pain. The relief of shedding an old habit that no longer served me. Sitting down to fill out the paperwork to prove I had gender dysphoria, to access the hormones I needed, a lot of it came back to me: *What is your relationship to the gender you were assigned at birth? How long have you lived as your chosen gender identity?* Let me tell you how I survived the near-death experience of being assigned female at birth by remaking myself into an old British thespian. Let me tell you about a dissociation I clung to so defiantly that it all came true, from the leather-bound books to the crushed velvet and, maybe most importantly, to the fucking like wolves.

EROS AND MAGIC IN THE RENAISSANCE (1987)

Eros and Magic in the Renaissance by the Romanian religious historian Ioan P. Couliano, is one of the most bizarre and compelling books about ceremonial magic I have ever read. It grabbed me and deeply influenced my own worldview as a young witch and scholar, and yet I had trouble recommending it to Treadwell's visitors owing to its density. Stick with it, I would say to potential customers. *There's a lot of philosophical jargon and incredibly obscure references . . . but if you are able to let them flow over you, you'll get to the gold.* At least, letting what I don't totally understand flow over me in an almost psychedelic swirl of words in hopes that it may sink in and accrue meaning over time is the only way I can describe how I must have taken this book in, as an ignorant but eager nineteen-year-old.

My university library, where I worked, had a special room of scholarly books related only to the study of Shakespeare and the cultural context that informed his plays. That was a specialty of the English Department, and it was my chosen field. These books couldn't be checked out, only read in situ. On my lunch breaks, in an exercise in bibliomancy, I would go into this specialist library and pick books at random to read through. But a book with the words *Eros* and *Magic* on the cover appealed to my tastes and so the choice was less random. I kept a bookmark in it and revisited the book over a period of a few weeks until I got through it. In one way, the book is very gay and helped me make sense of my then un-acted upon gay longings: Eros, Couliano tells us, is passionate erotic desire separated from sexual reproduction: "Magic is merely eroticism applied, directed, and aroused by its performer." According to one of the book's major figures Marsilio Ficino, Eros is the foundation of magic:

> The whole power of Magic is founded on Eros. The way Magic works is to bring things together through their inherent similarity. The parts of this world, like the limbs of the same animal, all depend on Eros, which is one; they relate to each other because of their common nature. Similarly, in our body the brain, the lungs, the heart, liver, and other organs interact, favor each other, intercommunicate and feel reciprocal pain. From this relationship is born Eros, which is common to them all, from this Eros is born their mutual rapprochement, wherein resides true Magic.[33]

I encountered Marsilio Ficino during my research into wizardry as a teenager, on websites about Hermeticism, astrology, and alchemy. In the Italian Renaissance of the fifteenth century, Ficino elevated these branches of knowledge through his own writing, teaching, and extensive translations, including Plato's complete works, and the *Hermetica*. A collection of texts attributed to Hermes Trismegistus, a legendary blend of the Greek god Hermes and his Egyptian counterpart Thoth, the *Hermetica* contains a wealth of magical philosophy from Mediterranean, North African, and Arabic sources. These texts discuss astrology, medicine, alchemy, and magic, most famously, in "The Emerald Tablet," from which has been lifted the adage: *As above, so below*.

I couldn't believe my luck: it felt magical to finally entera world where libraries had books like this, where I could encounter Ficino in print for the first time, with translations

33 Ioan P. Couliano, *Eros and Magic in the Renaissance* (Chicago: University of Chicago Press, 1987) 87.

of his writing about love and magic. These writings allowed me to approach my fragmented witchcraft from the opposite direction: a well-documented and elite intellectual tradition grounded in rich philosophical heritage. These were the esoteric source texts that were used, in part, to plug the gaps and folklore of witchery, cunning, and faith healing. I wanted it all: a vulgar craft in which my nails were always dirty from working from the soil, a practice covered in sweat and piss and blood and cum, and the elevated writings of a Ficino who linked these grubby spells and superstitions to the heavens: *As below, so above.*

Couliano's book made a philosopher of me in the etymological sense of the word, a lover of wisdom. No one talked about philosophy where I'd come from. Taking a class in the Philosophy Department was not an option, it was too macho. I didn't know I could claim the word for myself before I saw it laid out: "The supreme lover is the *philosophos*." I wanted to be that! And, "The body is just an instrument, whereas love, even the kind with a sexual goal, stems from the powers of the soul."

In Ficino's writing, drawing thousands of years back from Plato, "all is reduced to a question of communication: body and soul speak two languages, which are not only different, even inconsistent, but also *inaudible* to each other." This disjunction is only mended through human imagination, which produces "phantasies." "The inner sense alone is able to hear and comprehend them both, also having the role of translating one into the other. But considering the words of the soul's language are phantasms, everything that reaches it from the body—including distinct utterances—will have to be transposed into a phantasmic sequence." To see the faculties of imagination elevated to such a high place of significance was earth shattering to me, who had always felt punished or at least guilty on account of the places my imagination had taken me. It would take a long time to undo this dissociative rupture, to fully use my imagination and inner sense to harmonize what was going on in my soul and my body.

At least that message from the book washed over me and took longer to sink in than some of its more immediate arguments. In addition to understanding the work of the magician or witch as the work of the lover, and part of a rich philosophical heritage, Couliano focuses on a dark outcome of theories of Renaissance magic, especially as they survive in the writings of Giordano Bruno, a student of Ficino's writings.

Bruno is most infamously known as a heretic, burnt alive on February 17, 1600 by the Catholic Inquisition for his beliefs. This brutal death is often attributed to his most famous belief—that of infinite worlds in an infinite cosmos with no center—although that incredible argument did not lead to his condemnation so much as his refusal to accept the divinity of Christ and the virginity of Mary. Couliano's deep dive into Bruno's writings considers the Neapolitan upstart in his own context, without the backwards glance and scientific understanding we bring to bear upon him today. And this is where the book gets creepy, tracing Bruno's writings that argue for the use of magic and Eros for the purpose of mass control. Bruno takes the idea that love is at the heart of everything, and therefore rules all, and turns it into a tool for manipulation, a trajectory which Couliano follows to the present:

> Nowadays the magician busies himself with public relations, propaganda, market research, sociological surveys, publicity, information, counter-information and misinformation, censorship, espionage, and even cryptography—a science which in the sixteenth century was a branch of magic. This key figure of our society is simply an extension of Bruno's manipulator, continuing to follow his principles and taking care to give them a technical and impersonal turn of phrase. Historians have been wrong in concluding that magic

> disappeared with the advent of "quantitative science." The latter has simply substituted itself for a part of magic while extending its dreams and its goals by means of technology.
>
> . . . Is the Western State, in our time, a true magician, or is it a sorcerer's apprentice who sets in motion dark and uncontrollable forces? That is very hard to say. In any case, the magician State—unless it involves vulgar conjurers—is vastly preferable to the police State, to the State which, in order to defend its own out-of-date "culture," does not hesitate to repress all liberties and the illusion of liberties, changing itself into a prison where all hope is lost.[34]

Bruno wrote with extreme caution about the care that must be taken with magical erotic manipulation, in a sense coming to the conclusion that the level of impartiality and desire to create a common good is so extreme as to be impossible for a human to attain. Bruno's writings are an extreme thought experiment which Couliano sees alive in contemporary culture. In the end, Couliano imagines a utopian magical State that works out "a long-term magic to neutralize the hypnosis induced by the advancing cohorts of police," and a future without police in which "coercion by the use of force will have to yield to the subtle processes of magic, science of the past, of the present and of the future."[35]

From this vision, Couliano surveys its opposite, what he calls an intrasubjective magic in which the magician invokes, works with, and manipulates corresponding dates, spirits, demons, planetary influences, and ingredients to put forth their will in the world, based on the imagination generated by what we love and desire. He also traces this erotic magic as it was condemned and dispensed with by ultraconservative Puritans,

34 Couliano, *Eros and Magic in the Renaissance*, 104-5.
35 Couliano, Eros and Magic in the Renaissance, 106

and driven underground, alongside the rise of the witch craze: "In a sense, the witch craze was the social counterpart to the destruction of religious images, in both cases, the victim was human fantasy. The idea behind the *Malleus* is to stop the social disorder caused by the exercise of magic." From there, "the Reformation" expands its hunt, finding "the great culprit guilty of all the evils of individual and social existence: sinning Nature."[36]

Couliano concludes with one sweet "hope that may be utopian: that a new Renaissance, a rebirth of the world, may overcome all our neuroses, all conflicts, and all divisions existing between us."[37] This epic book tracing centuries of entanglement between desire, fantasy, magic, religion, science, and politics changed the way I considered my impulses and the magical Renaissance in which I was participating forever. And for their author, their implications for understanding modern conservatism, totalitarianism, and the police state, were not merely historical: in 1991, he was killed in a bathroom on the campus of the University of Chicago where he worked. The case remains cold, the murderer unknown, but his writings against the Romanian police State, as well as other far right groups, support theories of a political motive.

---

36 Couliano, *Eros and Magic in the Renaissance*, 191, 208.

37 Couliano, *Eros and Magic in the Renaissance*, 223.

MULES AND MEN (1935)

I truly came to accept and appreciate the intellectual and emotional pitfalls of the distant historic record I was attracted to—polemical pamphlets, collections of folklore, records of the trials of witches and heretics—by reading Zora Neale Hurston describe her work collecting folktales in the deep south in the early twentieth century. The book is a methodological goldmine for a witch, in addition to offering a wealth of information about Black syncretic spirituality, culminating in a breathtaking description of Hurston's own initiation into hoodoo. The tension between Hurston's combination of experience, desire, and anthropological training both propel her on her travels, and causes trust issues with the people she meets, whose stories she wants to record.

> Folklore is not as easy to collect as it sounds. The best source is where there are the least outside influences and these people, being usually under-privileged, are the shyest. They are most reluctant at times to reveal that which the soul lives by.[38]

This is especially true, she writes, when race is a factor, as well as gender and class, and her confessional tone is something I have found lacking in a lot of the collected folklore that survives from other places and times. White people cannot

38 Zora Neale Hurston, *Mules and Men* (New York: Perennial Library, 1990) 2.

be trusted in a society built on white supremacy, nor can the records they keep, to document that society. In understanding the validity of any source—spiritual, magical, or otherwise—we must take into account who is speaking, who is being spoken to, how it is being recorded, and how the social and political context create constraints on our understanding. This is true for understanding the shortcomings of witch trials of the fifteenth to seventeenth centuries, as it is for studying the cosmologies and spiritualities of Indigenous people and People of Color. Even Zora Neale Hurston cannot escape it. She decides to begin her journey collecting folk tales in her hometown of Eatonville, Florida, with the idea that her familiarity will allow her easy access. She is initially met with some reticence from her old neighbors on account of having gone up north to college, but eases back into society after attending a wild party and records a treasure trove of stories, songs, games, and tall tales called "lies." The trust she rebuilds pretty much disappears when she crosses the county line, and in each place she travels from Florida to Louisiana, she must start afresh. In Polk County, Hurston is received with coldness and finally learns the reason:

> They all thought I must be a revenue officer or a detective of some kind. They were accustomed to strange women dropping into the quarters, but not in shiny gray Chevrolets. . .
>
> The car made me look too prosperous. So they set me aside as different. And since most of them were fugitives from justice or had done plenty time, a detective was just the last thing they felt they needed on that "job."[39]

She lies and tells them that she is on the run and wanted in Miami for bootlegging, and it works; the stories begin to flow freely.

39 Hurston, *Mules and Men*, 60-1.

Whereas in the first half of the book, Hurston's personality and willingness to drink, dance, and have a good time allow her to genuinely connect and build trust among her informants, the most compelling part for me is when Hurston reaches New Orleans to undergo an initiation in order to get access to hoodoo rituals.

> Belief in magic is older than writing. So nobody knows how it started.
>
> The way we tell it, hoodoo started way back there before everything. Six days of magic spells and mighty word and the world with its elements above and below was made. And now, God is leaning back taking a seventh day rest.[40]

Hurston spends around five months looking for a reliable informant in Luke Turner, who claimed to be the nephew of Marie Laveau, Hoodoo Queen.

It takes her repeated trips to him, putting up with silence and then rudeness, before he will speak with her and tell the story of Marie Laveau, whose legendary healing and magical powers were such at that point that she was worshipped as a god. Turner recites descriptions of Laveau's rituals, of the words she spoke to affect her magic, often ending with, "So be it!" I remember this every time somebody posts a picture of Octavia Butler's notebook on social media—"So be it! See to it!"—and I hope it means the poster is engaged in deep ritual preparation, purification, fasting, initiation. For, when Hurston asks how Laveau worked these spells, so be them, Turner tells her: through her great Altar of power, which allowed her to become one with Spirit.

> The next day he began to prepare me for my initiation ceremony, for rest assured that no one may approach

40 Hurston, *Mules and Men*, 183.

> the Altar without the crown, and none may wear the crown of power without preparation. It must be earned. And what is this crown of power? Nothing definite in material. Turner crowned me wit ha consecrated snake skin. I have been crowned in other places with flowers, with ornamental paper, with cloth, with sycamore bark, with egg-shells. It is the meaning, not the material that counts. The crown without the preparation means no more than a college diploma without the four years' work.
>
> This preparation period is akin to that of all mystics. Clean living, even to clean thoughts.[41]

The intense initiation that follows is the first of several—each practitioner Hurston found insisted on initiation to build trust in order to share rituals whom none but the initiated are permitted to know. So not only is *Mules and Men* an invaluable compendium of Black history and spirituality, but an exemplar of extreme commitment to the spiritual and miraculous: if our magic is to work, it demands preparation and discipline. Dabbling will not yield the most satisfying results, we must dedicate our lives to it and make of it a priority to experience the highest highs. Throughout Hurston's determined book, she remains an exemplary student of mysteries both human and divine, because she is willing to put in the time.

41 Hurston, *Mules and Men*, 198.

A SOUND MAGICIAN

The place this ritual happened was Deptford High Street, where I had a one-bedroom apartment. It was May 30, 2017. I was a few months shy of turning thirty, which means I was the same age Christopher Marlowe was when he was murdered under very mysterious circumstances on the very street that I live on, four hundred and twenty-four years ago this night. Usually I prefer birthdays of the dead, but the place I am in is so powerfully linked to an untimely death, it would be a shame not to do something about it. Christopher Marlowe, affectionately Kit Marlowe, was a major playwright at this point, infamous—Shakespeare was a fan and contemporary. His death is a flashpoint for conspiracy theories: was it a drunken brawl or a premeditated hit? The conspiracies spin further out: was his death a blood sacrifice in the aftermath of one of John Dee's rituals? Or did Christopher Marlowe fake his death and leave England in exile?

What's agreed upon is: there was a warrant issued for Marlowe's arrest for heresy on May 18th. He was arrested but granted bail on May 20th. He spent his last day on earth with three men known to be involved in espionage and other stately dirty work, in a room hired for a private meeting. A month after he was killed, his murderer, Ingram Frizer, was pardoned. The Coroner's report—which renders the name "Marlowe" as "Morley"—described that "malicious" words were exchanged between Marlowe and Frizer over payment ("recknynge") of the bill, that Marlowe drew Frizer's own dagger and stabbed him twice in his head, and then Frizer "in his own defence & for the saving of his life, then & there struggled with the said Christopher Morley to get back from him his dagger aforesaid; in which affray the same Ingram could not get away from the said Christopher Morley; & so it befell in that affray that the said Ingram, in defence of his life, with the dagger aforesaid to the value of 12d, gave the said Christopher then & there a mortal wound over his right eye of the depth of two inches & of the width of one inch; of which mortal wound the aforesaid Christopher Morley then & there instantly died."[42]

Most of what we know about Marlowe prior to his death relates to his lawbreaking: an arrest for homicide in 1589, for counterfeiting money in 1592, and of course, in 1593 just before he died. The gaps in the story get filled in with the content of his notorious plays, art forced to imitate life, many of which feature bloody-minded, heretical men obsessed with power and personal gain (*Doctor Faustus, The Jew of Malta, Tamburlaine, The Massacre at Paris*); rulers whose obsessions lead to their death (*Dido, Edward II*). The main characters of Marlowe's plays all worship at the altar of maximalism: their excesses of extreme emotion lead to outpourings of violence, and violent ends, accompanied by frantic speeches. Marlowe's blank verses describing sex and violence, magic and power, became the height of theatrical fashion, and then fell out fast after his death amidst a new generation of Puritanical audiences, and new theories of "good" writing took hold, such as is found in George Puttenham's *The Arte of English Poesie*.

Published in 1589, Puttenham includes a whole cast of elaborately name characters—"figures" of speech and literary

---

42 "Death in Deptford." *The Marlowe Society*, Accessed April 19, 2024. https://www.marlowe-society.org/christopher-marlowe/life/death-in-deptford/.

modes—described often in order to banish. The book is basically a compendium of dos and don'ts for writers, listing rhetorical strategies, defining and often dismissing them. These figures became my angels and demons. Forget the *Key of Solomon* and its princes of hell, I invoke Puttenham's figures to enhance their attributes in my art, I incorporate them into my spells. The England of the 1580s was a time of high necromancy and ceremonial magic, on stage and among the elites, its potential oozing out of every old book with strange, unstandardized spellings. And I am an adept at bending books to my own purposes, whatever they are. One of my favorite aspects of working in an occult bookshop isn't just selling expressly magical books—*The ABCs of Witchcraft, Seventy-Eight Degrees of Wisdom, An Encyclopedia of Magical Herbs*—but leading customers into our used book section and egging them on to repurpose unsuspecting novels and theory: "*Read Jean Genet for love spells, check out Sylvia Wynter for earth magic.* Anything can be a grimoire!" The *Key of Solomon* freaks me out not because I'm afraid, but because I hate the idea of working from the same books as the most fucked up Olde Englishe men—one-handed readers like John Dee and Humphrey Gilbert who'd meticulously plotted the chokehold of empire with their other hand.

According to George Puttenham's *Art of English Poesie,* the figure of Sinathrismus is a big *don't,* and that piques my interest. The name Sinathrismus comes from the Latin: "to heap up, to amass." Puttenham writes: "we lay on such load and so go to it by heapes as if we would winne the game by multitude of words & speaches." In other words: it's your game to lose, and you blow it by overstating your case. Of course, queers know all about the crime of being extra, how it's all to blame for the violence against us. Sinathrismus is extra and I love him. Puttenham gives a few literary examples of Sinathrismus incarnate and they're all passionate outbursts torn between the extremes of hate and love that he frowns upon. He's so judgmental, like he thinks that only crazy people would be so repetitive and maximalist. As a reader, I am choosing to take it very personally—this describes me exactly, at this point in my life and most of the others, an emotional maximalist with heaps of feelings and desires. Heaping is how I deal: I splurged on the opera again and again to mourn my dead mentor; in the weeks and months following my divorce, I wept openly in the old church where Thomas Tallis was buried at a live performances of the *Lamentations of Jeremiah*. I meditated daily in the basement of the British Museum surrounded by Assyrian frescoes of men hunting lions—beast after beast rent through with arrows. *I surround myself with these lions until I no longer feel like these lions.* The only way out is through, sure, but I like to amplify the process with the art and articles of clothing I adorn myself with, a heaping figure through and through. And besides, how am I to fight back against the overwhelming legacies of capitalism and colonialism if I don't at least try to reframe my excess of emotions as a resource plentiful enough to change the world?

Puttenhem was influential, a gold standard really, and later Angel Day agreed with him about Sinathrismus in *The English Secretary* (1599). There, Sinathrismus is described as "a heaping of words diversly signifying togithers, as to say, Hee was a man wholie malicious, exceedinglie proude, utterlie arrogant, altogither subtill, by nature cruell, and in speeches contentious." Day includes an example of a letter that commits the sins of Sinathrismus:

> There was no rake-hell, no ruffian, no knave, no villaine, no cogging raskall, no hatefull companion, no robber on high waies, no privy pilferer, but his hande was in with him, and that he was a copesmate for him, no brothell house but he haunted, no odde corner but hee knewe, no cutter, but hee was a sharer with, no person

> so lasivious, abject, vilde, or dissolute, but hee would be a copartner with.[43]

All of these citations of Sinathrismus feel a little like gay bashing, right? Am I reading too much into the faggy sibilance of the name, Sinathrismus? I chant it a few times. *Sinathrismus Sinathrismus.* It's a name that sends one hand to my hip as I say it, the wrist of the other goes limp. Sinathrismus is kind of a scapegoat that lets men like Puttenham and Day—men writing for other men to read in a time of extremely passionate friendships among them, shared beds and all—have it both ways, citing at great length the descriptions of lust, rage, lasciviousness, wildness, that they supposedly disapprove of. That's typical of the time, authors publishing catalogues of heresies and scandalous news from the supposed position of a critic. If you say it with clutched pearls, does that really make much of a difference? The knowledge is still *there*, set in ink, a lifeline for those who need it to read against the grain. Anyway, all I want to do is feel, think, act in heaping ways, amassing all of my loves and hates into their separate and sometimes not-so-separate piles. Sinathrismus is a camp literary strategy for a magic of correspondences, heaping up as many sympathetic words as possible to work the spell. Sinathrismus is one of my household gods.

I have no money, but the heart of a maximalist, so what I can heap up, pretty much, is language and trash—words I find on pages and in people's mouths, books people left out in the rain, stones and sea glass I find on the beach, free things and thrifted things and things sold for cheap because they've recently been free or thrifted. There's a Salvation Army up the street, I drop off some things I don't need, I acquire others, give and take, the Six of Pentacles. I can decorate my whole apartment that way. George Puttenham would have retched

43 Angel Day, *The English Secretary, or Methode of writing of Epistles and Letters* (London: P.S. for c. Burbie, 1599) 45.

with distaste at the latticework of wires that probably belonged to a bed frame I dragged in from the street and propped up against my bedroom wall to hang all of my little baubles and plant clippings. I have wedged in some books, some folded up papers I've written on with intentions, good and bad. One hundred percent trashy heapings I've imbued with meanings and magical correspondences, my altar to Sinathrismus.

O Sinathrismus, Heaping figure, O wild excess, O abundant abandon, I'll bury myself alive in you.

As I sleep, I absorb the influence of its assembled parts and infuse it with every level of my consciousness. I am ready to dedicate my life to maximalism as witchcraft, an accumulation of charged objects that remind me that everything has a soul and every soul is divine. In other words, God is Everywhere, but not in the way Christians imagine, like an eternal surveillance state, but as an eternal source of discovery and delight, gnosis, and revelation.

I climb out of my bedroom onto the roof to preside over Deptford, to open the ritual for Christopher Marlowe, certainly one who wrote into the excesses presided over by Sinathrismus. I call the corners and banish any malefic spirits from the circle, I call to the planetary intelligences and to Hermes in particular, the god whom Marlowe invoked to represent himself in plays; I call to Apollo and Bacchus, also present in his plays. I thread four hundred and twenty-four beads I found in a box for sale for £4 at a thrift store, then they are undone and I cast them over my shoulder, counting backward four hundred and twenty-four years. I use the beads to make a trail into my apartment, chanting one Marlowe's most famous poems, inviting him to my altar where there is a bouquet of roses, myrtle, ivy:

Come live with me and be my love,
And we will all the pleasures prove,
That Valleys, groves, hills, and fields,
Woods, or steepy mountain yields.

And we will sit upon the Rocks,
Seeing the Shepherds feed their flocks,
By shallow Rivers to whose falls
Melodious birds sing Madrigals.

And I will make thee beds of Roses
And a thousand fragrant posies,
A cap of flowers, and a kirtle
Embroidered all with leaves of Myrtle;

A gown made of the finest wool
Which from our pretty Lambs we pull;
Fair lined slippers for the cold,
With buckles of the purest gold;

A belt of straw and Ivy buds,
With Coral clasps and Amber studs:
And if these pleasures may thee move,
Come live with me, and be my love.

The Shepherds' Swains shall dance and sing
For thy delight each May-morning:
If these delights thy mind may move,
Then live with me, and be my love.[44]

The next two days will be spent mostly at home, not traveling beyond the boundaries of Deptford High Street, on

44 Patricia Hoda, "The Passionate Shepherd to His Love." *Marlowepedia.* May 27, 2024. https://christopher.marlowe.at/the-passionate-shepherd-to-his-love/.

a strict dict of Marlowe's writing. The only known remnant of Marlowe's handwriting comes from the reading of Katherine Benchkin's last will and testament, which he witnessed in 1585, signing his name: *Cristofer Marley*. He would have been twenty-one at the time. Above the signature, his father John had signed too. I practice forging his signature.

It wasn't the first time I'd forged a 16th-century hand. Paleography is the word for the study of handwriting—in my case, different styles of handwriting in England from the fifteenth to the seventeenth centuries. There's a knack to deciphering this style of writing—called secretarial—that slowly transitions into a more legible italic over the course of those centuries. The best way to decipher the harder-to-read letters—e's, s's, o's, and any capital letter—is to learn through doing it yourself, essentially through forgery. I learned this better with others when I was a student: one beloved professor would have us read aloud from lewd sixteenth-century poems in a circle, going word by word, laughing when we finally recognized the word "dildo." My friend Rudolph and I used to write out Britney Spears and Madonna lyrics in secretarial hand in the paleography class we took together. It was a fascinating subject presided over by a bad teacher; we had to do something to keep it lighthearted for ourselves otherwise our anger would prevent us from learning anything. And now I had this memory to draw from, was initiating contact with the spirit world by writing to Christopher Marlowe in an approximation of his own handwriting, writing out his name, and then writing out his poetry.

On June 1st the ritual culminated in St. Nicholas's churchyard, four hundred and twenty-four years to the day when Marlowe's remains were dumped in an unmarked grave. There is a headstone in the churchyard placed there a few decades ago that infuriates me, reading: "NEAR THIS SPOT LIE THE MORTAL REMAINS OF / CHRISTOPHER MARLOWE / WHO MET HIS UNTIMELY DEATH / IN

DEPTFORD ON MAY 30TH 1593 / Cut is the branch that might have grown full straight. / Doctor Faustus."

Of all his poetry and plays, the quote chosen comes from the end of Doctor Faustus. The line is spoken by the Chorus in the final scene, just after the doomed magician has been dragged offstage by demons to hell:

Cut is the branch that might have grown full straight, and continues:

> And burned is Apollo's laurel-bough,
> That sometime grew within this learned man.
> Faustus is gone: regard his hellish fall,
> Whose fiendful fortune may exhort the wise,
> Only to wonder at unlawful things,
> Whose deepness doth entice such forward wits
> To practice more than heavenly power permits.
> [Exit.]
> Terminat hora diem; terminat auctor opus.
> ["The hour finishes the day; the author finishes the work."][45]

How rude to cut into stone such a moralizing judgement and turn an artist's own words against him that way! And of course the insult, the condemnation, only feels harsher in the fullness of its twentieth-century meaning—when the memorial was actually chosen, made, and placed in the cemetery—straight as in not a fag, not a criminal, or an outlaw. As if Marlowe, as infamous for his writing as for his debauchery, his accusations of treason, his company of ne'er do wells, his association with and as a sodomite, a protogay icon, would have straightened

45 Christopher Marlowe, *THE TRAGICALL History of D. Faustus* (London: by V.S. for Thomas Bushell, 1604) sig. F3r. A Digital Anthology of Early Modern English Drama, Meaghan Brown, Michael Poston, and Elizabeth Williamson, eds. Folger Shakespeare Library, http://emed.folger.edu

himself out and grown up to be respectable. Well, times change, I was making a whole life out of worshipping unlawful things, moving way beyond the drab, limited imagination of the heaven I'd inherited from Christianity. Kit Marlowe would want to know.

It's late but it's not midnight, it's important the day is still June 1st. There's a tree growing by the wall into the churchyard I can use to aid in my climb. I have made a laurel crown and I'm wearing it. I light candles and sit in the circle, it feels so iconic to be working magic in a graveyard! I am here to continue to seduce Marlowe to my altar with his own words. I have brought tracing paper to make and edit a rubbing of the memorial; I tape the paper to the slab and make the rubbing with light green wax, then take black charcoal and cross out, "Cut is the branch that might have grown full straight," writing out a better line, from the opening of Faustus:

A sound magician is a mighty god

But the main event is to perform from Marlowe's gayest play, Edward II, reciting a speech by Gaveston. The play opens with Gaveston in exile, receiving a letter from the newly crowned Edward II inviting him back to England: My dad is dead, Edward basically says, so now you can come back! "And share the kingdom with thy dearest friend." It was speculated upon, even by near contemporaries, that Gaveston had been exiled by King Edward I because of his closeness to the young prince, their passionate love for one another. Marlowe runs with this in the propagandistic play, the script oozing with sexual innuendo and erotic mythical references, Sinathrismus on poppers.

Gaveston's desires for their reunion are over-the-top, he describes his fantasy for their shared gay life of art and hedonism, of hot young male servants dressed like nymphs—aka women—acting like satyrs, the horniest mythical beasts:

I must have wanton poets, pleasant wits,

Musicians, that with the touching of a string
May draw the pliant king which way I please.
Music and poetry is his delight;
Therefore I'll have Italian masques by night,
Sweet Speeches, comedies, and pleasing shows;
And in the day, when he shall walk abroad,
Like sylvan nymphs my pages shall be clad;
My men, like satyrs grazing on the lawns,
Shall with their goat-feet dance the antic hay,
Sometime a lovely boy in Dian's shape,
With hair that gilds the water as it glides,
Crownets of pearl about his naked arms,
And in his sportful hands an olive-tree,
To hide those parts which men delight to see,
Shall bathe him in a spring and there hard by,
One like Actaeon peeping through the grove,
Shall by the angry goddess be transformed,
And running in the likeness of an hart
By yelping hounds pulled down, and seem to die—
Such things as these best please his majesty.[46]

This is the life I have, this is the life I want to maintain, this is the life I can share with Marlowe. I add my own prayer, written out in a forgery of his handwriting and read aloud:

O Christopher Marlowe, unruly soul,
That burnt too bright, too hot, too hard, too fast,
I hail and call your spirit here tonight
To feed that flame, so your great fame will last,
And here, Apollo's laurel-bough made new—

---

46 Christopher Marlowe, The troublesome reign and lamentable death of Edward the second, King of England (London: William Jones, 1594) sig. A3r. A Digital Anthology of Early Modern English Drama, Meaghan Brown, Michael Poston, and Elizabeth Williamson, eds. Folger Shakespeare Library, http://emed.folger.edu

I remove the laurel crown to place at his grave.
I wed it here with the finest vintage
Your poor servant can afford—Hail Bacchus!

I uncork and begin to pour a bottle of red wine into the soil.

And Hail Kit Marlowe, whose art and poesy
joined the lithe lyrical Sun God to the
Mad God raised as a girl; strange weddings!
strange ecstasies! what alchemy! what gold!

I'm interrupted by a high-pitched scream just behind me. It is so startling that I shout involuntarily. I understand the idea of the heart jumping out of the throat, of being scared out of your skin—they're actual feelings that language veils into what looks like metaphor. My heart is racing as I look around the churchyard, the only light coming from my little candles and streetlamps in the distance. I hear running, scampering. *Shit.* I think of the Cookie Mueller short story where she ends up on a mountain outside of San Francisco with a man invoking a demon; when she hears the sound of footfalls, she gets the hell out of there. But it's okay, I'm okay, I'm not invoking demons. The source of the scream was not a child, or a woman, or either of those people being murdered, but a fox. If you've never heard a fox scream, search "fox scream" online, it's unlike anything you will hear, so close to a human voice and yet upsetting for the ways in which it is not a human voice, the ways in which the brain will try in a panic to reconcile it into a "human" category, how that will only make it more eerie. Everywhere I've lived in London has its own local foxes, but the sound is never something I've gotten over—and this time it was so close I could practically feel its breath on my neck. I'm squinting in the darkness to see where the fox is coming from and it comes closer—bold—but then I realize it's so bold because it's not an adult fox, but a young one. There are a few of them, they're playing—babies. They're bold because they don't know any better. One little fox comes right up to me, technically into the bounds of the magic circle. A *kit* fox. *Kit. Kit. Kit!* I remain very still, it is so close I can smell it. It smells bad. It makes for the laurel crown. I thank the goddesses, I thank the gods, I thank Kit Marlowe, I thank the kit foxes, I pack up and run home.

I'm in a new magical Renaissance and re-appraising my love of Renaissance magic. It's amazing what you can accomplish when you're not living in total fear and misery. The pressure valve lets up a little and suddenly there's time to think. Ever since I moved to Deptford in April I'm feeling prolific, more Sinathrismus than ever. Before that time, all of my spiritual energy was invested in surviving the experience of living in a haunted house; haunted by my own breakup, my regrets, my need to forgive myself and move on. My ex had moved out and I'd stayed put with my dog, switched bedrooms, taken on a string of roommates, saged the shit out of everything. It was a heartbreaking place to be, suffused with sad memories and even harder, the happy memories.

Working with Kit Marlowe returned me to some of the reasons I'd made my life in the UK to begin with, which at best I'd lost sight of, at worst actively avoided. My ex-wife and I met at Oxford, but I'd grown ashamed of ever going to Oxford. Falling in love with her there had made a difficult year much sweeter, much more balanced with moments of excitement and joy. I'd held that alongside the pain of leaving all of my friends back in Philadelphia, in New York. And then, the disappointment and heartache of being far enough away from my blood family to see how estranged we'd always been, to mourn the reality that they'd never really come looking for me, that I wasn't real to the people who raised me, whose gestures and turns of phrase and sense of humor I shared. Even the scholarship I'd gotten to Oxford, which felt on one side of the ocean like a miracle in a global financial crisis, something to celebrate, was totally different in its experience on the ground there. One student had called me a charity case, another had loudly suggested in front of everybody after a seminar that to come as highly recommended as I did, I surely had fucked the professor who'd vouched for me. This was from the kind of Gay Man who got drinks in the Oscar Wilde Room at Merton College and did not really approve of dykes. The nicknamed of people who went to my college, St. Hilda's, which had been a historic women's college but had just gone co-ed: Hildebeasts. I didn't know anything about the college system but was judged for that for that too. Oxford was one of those places that was Gay but not at all Queer. Me and Rudolph stuck out and stuck together.

Free and free-flowing alcohol at every departmental event suffused all social interactions. It was a bad scene, and to make the most of it I focused on my favorite things: drinking too much free booze, fucking my girlfriend for hours every day in either her single bed or mine, and reading as many early modern books and manuscripts as possible in their rarest forms. I'd spend day after day in the Duke Humfrey's Library, restored from its fifteenth-century origins in 1598 and containing the oldest shelves of the Bodleian Library. In spite of the loneliness and general antagonism of wealthy British people, day by day I could speak to my teenage self, working through Robert Burton's *Anatomy of Melancholy*, poetry by John Donne, plays by Christopher Marlowe, early English translations of Marsilio Ficino and Giordano Bruno, works of the Rosicrucian Enlightenment, works of alchemy, works of early folklore and myth, like William Camden's *Britannia* and Michael Drayton's versified adaptation of it, *Poly-Olbion*.

I was reading with the tastes of the teenage self for whom this was the literal dream come true. It was how I kept a positive outlook: I was looking at books that were restricted, one-of-a-kind, some of them researched and written among the very shelves I sat centuries ago, and many of them related to magic and divination. I was every character I'd ever roleplayed on AOL, and I was Marlowe's Faustus in the making, tired of the fields of knowledge people around me were pursuing, and interested in getting weirder. Doctor Faustus opens with the title character saying goodbye to law, medicine, and religion, the major academic disciplines of the day, embracing the occult out of boredom and cursed ambition:

> ...Divinity, adieu!
> These metaphysics of magicians,
> And necromantic books are heavenly;
> Lines, circles, scenes, letters, and characters;
> Ay, these are those that Faustus most desires.
> O, what a world of profit and delight,
> Of power, of honour, of omnipotence,
> Is promis'd to the studious artizan!
> All things that move between the quiet poles
> Shall be at my command: emperors and kings
> Are but obeyed in their several provinces,
> Nor can they raise the wind, or rend the clouds;
> But his dominion that exceeds in this,
> Stretcheth as far as doth the mind of man;
> A sound magician is a mighty god[47]

I'd always been interested in this strange time period in English history from the fifteenth to the seventeenth centuries—the art and poetry of it, the bawdiness and sex, the gender-bending theater, the heresy and bloody upheaval. The eventual overthrow of kings, the apocalypticism and urgency. On AOL, Diane aka Mad4Rikman@aol.com had said again and again it had to do with past karma, and past lives. Either way, it had always grabbed me, obsessed me, kept me coming

47 Marlowe, *THE TRAGICALL History of D. Faustus*, sig. A3r.

back. I could return and find something new and exciting every time, it was a swath of time that held me fast, and here I was in the thick of it. But the present day experience I'd had was so negative, I'd let go of it; I got accepted to do a PhD, but decided to move to London instead. Sinathrismas was front and center in the PhD proposal, titled: "The Heaping Figure: Literary Copiousness and the Emergence of the Disciplines in Early Modern England." But I needed to be among living people who loved me, I needed to be somewhere with a queer scene; the dead who fascinated me weren't enough to take the edge off such a hostile environment. This god did not want to be worshipped from within the walls of an institution.

I left for London feeling mostly sad about the experience, and then as the years went on, everything that had made the memories worthwhile disappeared; my friendship with Rudolph who'd died, my apprenticeship to Lisa who'd died, my marriage that had dissolved. The last time I'd visited Oxford was for Rudolph's memorial; laughing and crying in an old college chapel as friends related memories of him and played his favorite songs by Björk, Madonna, Lana Del Rey. It was the perfect way to remember him, in a gothic chapel with amazing acoustics for the pop music we were listening to. When I left I thought: *I don't think I ever need to come back here in this lifetime.*

But maybe I'd left too much behind. The little kit fox by Kit Marlowe's grave connected me to my own past, and to a past I'd always taken real pleasure in exploring. Invoking infamous ne'er-do-well genius homosocial Kit Marlowe initiated a process of reuniting my obsessions across witchcraft and occult history and reincorporating them into spiritual practice. This spiritual practice also involved looking carefully at the source material from a fraught time in the history of witch persecution on the one hand and elite magical practice on the other. The desires that led to obsession, deep focus, and long term commitments are powerful spiritual resources to channel into a magical life. My interest in witchcraft and how it had turned me on to

Renaissance magic had been one of the longest relationships in my life, it was time to tend to it with more discipline. On my roof and in the cemetery I'd felt a strong sense: *There's something here for you.* Combining academic knowledge of Renaissance ceremonial magic and witchcraft as I'd encountered it in my job at the occult bookshop opened a path into my spiritual future.

TEMPORARY COVEN

Most of my rituals begin with vacuuming. In ancient Greece, you'd ceremonially sweep the dirt out of your house at the dark of the moon before preparing and leaving a feast for Hekate, the triple moon goddess and Titan presiding over heaven, earth, and the sea, highly respected by the younger gods. Sweep out the old dirt and the bad vibes that go with it, prepare a cleansed space to concentrate on worship. I tried to imagine what it would feel like doing that—living in the time of the *deipnon*, the word for Hekate's rites at each dark moon—while vacuuming the bookshop, to imbue it with that intention and holy continuity. We had an old broom, but sweeping with it felt like a gimmick—it would kick up and redistribute the dust and dog hair, swirl it around a little rather than collect it, to make as an offering to the underworld, which is what the goddess of the witches demanded. A lot of people think witchcraft is about having the look, looking sexy and using your looks to bewitch, and that's great, but more often I think it involves feeling embarrassed and awkward and unsexy and clumsy—gateway emotions to getting totally out of control. Modern emotions that create high-vibrational shakiness and anxiety prime the mind to fall into a more primal array of emotions, from out of control to total surrender, upon entrance into a sacred space. One high priestess put it this way to me: *I love to see a witch fumbling for her reading glasses by candlelight. How auspicious.*

Opening up the bookshop in the morning involved vacuuming and cleaning the toilet before anything else.

Vacuuming was essential because we burnt so much incense, and people trailed in so many things from the outside world—it was a way to appease the many deities worshiped in the space and start each day fresh. Cleaning the toilet was essential because we were one of the few places you could come in to use the toilet without buying anything, and that was important. Not just for trans people but for anyone. I'd been there, stared at or harassed by women in the bathroom, or at a pub, followed in by the bartender and told to *get out.* People should be able to be comfortable in public, and that requires having clean facilities. This was London in the stranglehold of right-wing austerity and gentrification; most of the public toilets installed in the nineteenth century had been left to decay until they were turned into cocktail bars. It only took a few minutes to bleach the toilet bowl, the seat, and the sink and faucets, and make sure there was enough toilet paper in stock. It was probably one of the most important things I could do to maintain the space of the bookshop as a sanctuary, which was ultimately how I defined my job.

Only once did cleaning a toilet feel like an explicit act of magic: an exorcism. One Sunday morning, I had to open up early for a scrying workshop run by a sinewy witch with long blond hair, and, honestly, an Iggy Pop vibe. I started vacuuming while he went down into the basement to set up. When I went downstairs to clean the bathroom I was hit by a wave of the most noxious smell of shit I had ever smelt in all of my years of daily shitting, cleaning up dogshit, and going to gigs at punk houses. *Holy shit.* Had this witch eaten and excreted a literal demon? The stench was so strong it came with feelings, tactility, breadth, and depth. I retreated upstairs to regroup and grab some Dragon's Blood incense—this job was gonna take more than bleach—and smoked out the little bathroom before attacking it with the usual array of products. Ticking the "Clean Toilet" box off the daily checklist felt like closing a portal to an evil dimension. Iggy Pop acted like nothing had happened—was *he* the demon?

I wanted to create the right atmosphere for a book club I was running at the shop, so of course it started with a thorough vacuuming of the basement room that night and a double cleaning of the bathroom. It was one of the first things I was planning as a new employee; I hoped the book club would naturally evolve into a coven. Historically, book clubs were my covens, and the books I read in those contexts were the blueprints of repeated acts of self-initiation, way back to my two-person *Goosebumps* book club where I first encountered the idea that books could contain information for magic, ritual, and self-initiation, that books themselves were magic.

I wondered what would happen if I took that magical book club experience and made it more explicit this time around. When I'd first moved to London, as a way to make friends, I co-founded a queer book club that met one Sunday per month in a gay pub called the Royal George that was ailing due to its location behind a major construction site. We met for years, "supported a queer business" reading and working our way through iconic books like *Stone Butch Blues, Carol or The Price of Salt, The Well of Loneliness*. We made best friends and learned as much as we could about one another. I had never taken classes in queer theory because learning collectively, laden with gossip and irreverence and drinks and greasy food, felt better. It felt correct to talk about literature all afternoon and then go to a lesbian strip club after; I'm glad I held out. But, at the time I was happily married, and so I didn't get involved in the other significant service my book club provided: a lesbian dating service. I only partook of the drama as a spectator.

I wondered if this book club would become a witch dating service? It felt possible. I had a massive crush on one of the people coming, so one facet of the book club was an *elaborate mating ritual.* I had named it *Paranormal Feminisms*. We'd discuss books on witchcraft, apparitions, the weird the wild and the unwieldy, through a feminist lens. We'd contribute to the legacy of Silvia Federici's *Caliban and the Witch* with a collectively managed syllabus of books that amounted to our own view of anti-capitalist witchcraft. We'd sit in a circle around the altar by candlelight—ideal conditions for world-building and flirtation, everyone looks *amazing* by candlelight—and construct a common critical lens of analysis shaped by our feelings as well as our spiritual needs. In the mail-out advertising the first meeting, held ten days before Halloween 2016, I wrote something Very Fancy to drum up interest:

> **Why 'Paranormal Feminisms'?**
> The paranormal is already feminist—falling before, between, beyond the explained occurrences of day to day life, paranormal phenomena resists categorization into ways of normative thinking and living that are at their root patriarchal. The paranormal is the logical extremity that feminism must embrace and celebrate if it is to reach the outermost limits of intersectionality. While the paranormal is by definition inexplicable, it is at its most powerful when interpreted in terms of feminist approaches, which offer clear ways of understanding otherness, inequality, and dismantling biased ways of thinking.
>
> Finally, the paranormal denies distinctions between highbrow and lowbrow reading—comprised of folklore and fairy tales, hearsay and heresy, popular fiction and automatic writing, the tales and their tellers over the centuries who have documented the paranormal are unconventional, other, and often, identified as women.

> The emphasis of the book club is not just about using feminism and the paranormal to upset the order of things, but to consider a new canon of what, and who, is worth reading in order to cause the most upset to that order in the first place.

Pam Grossman had just published *What is a Witch?*, a thirty-six-page graphic manifesto issued by a small publisher in Canada. We bought up as many copies as we could, and for the first meeting we read the whole of the book out loud, together, first a sentence per person, then blending into a chorus of all our voices at once, then opening up to discussion. I had learned from my queer book group that a) preparing for discussion was *work*, and b) in order for the discussion to be lively, people had to hear their own voices speaking right away to banish any shyness or nerves. Usually this meant we'd open by going around the circle and answering one question I prepared something light but on topic. In this case I wanted to start with strong, double-bubble energy, so we read the lyrical little book, and the discussion gave way to a shared reality.

Most readers had only practiced magic in solitude, or hadn't since their teenage years. Some members were more aesthetically witchy with no set spiritual practice. Some were just curious. There was a real range. One member was an older woman who'd come of age in feminist squats, one-third of the throuple that founded the Gay Liberation Front chapter in Aberystwyth, a small town in Wales. Several of the members were younger artists who would come out, change their names and pronouns over the course of the eight months we'd meet. We chanted:

> *I mix potions of cloud and sea and soil.*
> *I mix metals and metaphors.*
> *I'm a mixed-up pan-aged polymorph,*
> *swapping genders and tales.*

For each meeting I'd build an altar in the middle of the room with items on it related to the book; we sat on pillows around the altar and chanted, then discussed. On the altar of the first meeting, for a book about the figure of the witch, I went classic: an altar cloth of powder blue silk, seven green candles to call in some Venusian love and abundance, eight orange candles to Mercury to facilitate open and direct communication, purple irises (the flowers I always brought when visiting witches in their homes to express my admiration), a crystal goblet with water, the jawbone of a sheep I found hiking in the mountains of the Lake District, selenite and citrine and rose quartz for love, some black tourmaline to protect from any bad vibes. I positioned myself opposite the altar from my crush, so I would be framed in part by flowers and two large pillar candles on either side, like the high priestess between her pillars marked B + J (Boaz and Jachin, the pillars at the entrance to King Solomon's Temple, but they'd always read as *Blow Job* to me). On a side table were grapes and figs and cheese and hummus and bread, wine and sparkling water. We chanted:

Eyeteeth, nails, a lock of hair. Cinnamon, beeswax.
A whisker. A stone. Salt. A subway penny. A bronze
rhombus. A wing. A piece of string. Flower petals.
Blood and honey and bone.

Reading aloud together creates a powerful charge—it was a moving experience to be introduced to strangers this way and reintroduced to those I already knew. Most rituals I'd participated in ran that way: scripts were passed out, sometimes lots, or Tarot cards would be drawn to determine who read what part, but there was always group chanting or responses. The witches who came were moved. I remembered what I liked about going to church as a child: the moments when we'd pray aloud together, and then have silence for our individual prayers;

the mix of collective consciousness and personal expression amidst incense, flowers, pageantry.

As a kid, going to church was my way to access luxury and beauty like I'd never seen before, it was heaven and an art museum all in one. The priests had *nice* shoes and smelled like *expensive* cologne, the altar was adorned with beautiful flower arrangements, the books of scripture and song were finely bound and gilt on their covers and fore edges. The light refracted through stained glass windows depicting Jesus, his parents, his disciples, angels and saints, figures who made pain look beautiful. I had never seen so many nice things outside of movies and cartoons. Later it was a scandal that some of the priests turned out to be wearing designer shoes and fragrances purchased through donations from parishioners. *So much for a vow of poverty.* But my essential identity was and is: peasant with airs above my station, broke but always unconsciously liking the most expensive thing. In this lifetime, luxury and finery in a corrupt Church was my introduction to the idea that everyone deserved a beautiful environment in which to contemplate their spiritual truths. I didn't visit an art gallery until I was seventeen, but I was in that church every week, sometimes every morning, soaking up a gorgeous environment where I felt at ease amidst an otherwise bleak, depressing landscape. Spring was my favorite time of year, when the altar would be overwhelmed with stargazer lilies giving off an intoxicating aroma as they opened one by one. I loved the huge bronze candlesticks and crosses, the purple of the priest's vestments during Lent, which he swapped for blood red on Palm Sunday and Good Friday.

As an altar server, the cord tied around the white robe I had to wear, color-coded with the priest's. "Backstage" in a little room to the right of the altar, there was a huge chest of drawers that contained cords of different colors. Everything smelled like incense. There was a little refrigerator where white and holy wafers were kept before they had been consecrated—I remember trying one of the wafers to see if it tasted different before it was transubstantiated into the Body of Christ. I loved arriving early to watch the priest prepare for mass and dress in his vestments, kiss the back of his chasuble, and put it over his neck and shoulders, and smile if I'd correctly predicted the color he was wearing and matched it with my cord. It became my first job: I was so attentive and focused, I was the requested server for the 7:00 AM weekly masses, and high masses alike. And then weddings and funerals—which is how I got paid. After the service, either the best man or the undertaker would tip me anywhere from ten to twenty dollars. I only fainted once, in the heat of the summer (there was no air conditioning), holding the incense thurible for a high mass. The power of the scent made me lightheaded, but to the congregation it looked like I had only bowed lower to the ground, prostrate before the True Presence of God. When I began to realize in my teens how profoundly I did not belong in this church, it was a deep cause for sorrow. I tried writing a letter about it to my parents—*I am in agony, I feel like I am becoming a danger to myself*—but they tore it up in anger before reading it. I got really into Satanism after finding an old copy of John Milton's *Paradise Lost* because Lucifer's agony at being separated from heaven felt dramatic enough to describe my own falling away:

> ...Farewel happy Fields
> Where Joy for ever dwells: Hail horrours, hail
> Infernal world, and thou profoundest Hell
> Receive thy new Possessor: One who brings
> A mind not to be chang'd by Place or Time.
> The mind is its own place, and in it self
> Can make a Heav'n of Hell, a Hell of Heav'n.
> What matter where, if I be still the same,

> And what I should be, all but less then he
> Whom Thunder hath made greater? Here at least
> We shall be free . . . [48]

I had started to grasp how corrosive and deadly the church's teachings were about people like me; it was making me feel crazy. I would read the trolley schedule on the way to school, plan a train to take furthest from my stop in the opposite direction. I would ride and scout for abandoned buildings to kill myself in. I would try to plan the way to maximize my time alone and minimize my chances of being found. Whenever I would snap out of that frame of mind, I heard a voice in my head: *You're Just Biding Your Time. You'll Get Out Of Here. Just keep biding your time.* I'd try to consider how in the world I might create my own environment in which to bide my time, how to cultivate beauty, luxury, community—the prime conditions for spiritual development I'd had in church.

Not to make a big deal out of it, but I wanted the same prime conditions for Paranormal Feminisms, and we'd gotten off to a good start. Even my crush turned out to like me back in just the ways I wanted to be liked: *When I first saw you, I didn't know if you were a boy or a girl, she said. I'm really glad you started this book club.*

Tonight we were reading *The Hearing Trumpet* (1974) by Leonora Carrington, one of my favorite novels, a book about magical friendship and deep crone wisdom, a book about dancing and alchemy and climate catastrophe. I am willing to drop everything to sit down and re-read *The Hearing Trumpet* at any point in time, it always recalibrates my appreciation for life. It felt like a great gift that the book could exist to read, re-read,

48 John Milton, *Paradise Lost* (London and New York: Penguin Books, 2000) Book 1, lines 228-238.

and now read in harmony with whoever showed up to the book club—always a mix of a few core regulars and wild cards.

I vacuumed and started to set up my Leonora Carrington Memorial Altar: there were copper chalices filled with water and red roses for Venus, a prominent force in the book, yellow roses for the friendship of Carmella and Marian, a cauldron filled with chocolate coins to represent Marian's transformation, honey for Zum Pallum, lavender candies, scraps of paper with drawings of wolves and hyenas, a hen's egg, a black egg of obsidian, a snowglobe with a lighthouse in it, and Tarot cards: the Ace of Cups, the Three of Cups, the High Priestess, the Star.

If the author of the book we were reading was dead, I'd write a prayer or invocation to her before others entered the space. For example, when we read Dion Fortune's last, unfinished and posthumously published novel *Moon Magic* (1956), I asked the spirit of Fortune to leave us in peace to discuss her work. I didn't want her notoriously drab energy (unforgiving, conservative, Christianity-infused, r-e-p-r-e-s-s-e-d) to tamper with what I thought would be a lively discussion about her very Pagan and very horny novel about re-consecrating an abandoned church in London to the goddess Isis. I think it worked, she stayed away. Or perhaps her spirit was already too busy: her Society of the Inner Light was still in operation an hour west, in Hampstead. When we'd read a biography of Doreen Valiente, it was quite the opposite: my invocation to her was in hope that she might guide the discussion and add her deep knowledge of the goddess and the gossip of magic to our conversation. I'm not sure it worked; barely anyone showed up, there was a heated debate totally unrelated to the book. Maybe Valiente didn't appreciate a biography that divulged her secrets beyond what she had already agreed to in her lifetime. Or maybe she knew that I didn't finish the entire book in time for the meeting and was annoyed that I wasn't well prepared.

Either way, the offerings of dandelion wine I'd placed on the altar—her favorite—was simply not enough.

That night I prayed to the spirit of Leonora Carrington, thanking her for art, *The Hearing Trumpet*, beseeching her friendship and sense of humor and eye for detail, asking her to expand our vision, and abilities. The opening question was: what's one of the most prominent animals of your inner bestiary? Carrington had once said, "In everybody there is an inner bestiary," and her work was filled with fantastic critters, like her self-portrait beside a hyena, *Inn of the Dawn Horse* (1937). I talked about how I was a real wolf lover as a kid, drew them obsessively, had notebooks and folders and pictures of wolves, read *White Fang, The Call of the Wild, Julie of the Wolves*, whatever I could get my hands on. I also love beavers and burrowing owls and bumblebees and frogs and snails and salamanders. We went around the circle calling out the members of our inner bestiaries, enjoying their distinctions and overlaps, nodding appreciatively, suggesting new additions. We were riled up, ready to talk about the book. What I loved about *The Hearing Trumpet* was the balance it struck between making fun of the pompousness of esoteric orders, piety, religiosity, while maintaining a deep belief in magic. How it made attempts to gatekeep surrealism look ridiculous, and assembled the surreal elements of everyday life into a road to enlightenment by way of hilarity. Again and again I will say: I don't trust witches who cannot laugh. The number of witch memoirs that describe the most ridiculous, hilarious scenarios without cracking a smile or seeing the humor in faith is appalling, and I don't trust them. If your god can't laugh at you, you're not listening. If you can't laugh at yourself, you can't learn. If you can't laugh at your god, your god is not all-powerful.

We spoke about that historic tension between humor and magic, its relationship to Carrington's own life and times as a surrealist artist and escapee from institutionalization for madness. We talked about the big crone energy of the book, how amazing it was to see old women solving mysteries, having adventures. We talked about the figure of the crone as feminist, as queer, as trans. We talked about the elements of gender transition and transformation, the crossdressing in the book, its existence without cruelty or malice, an accepted aspect of devotion and alchemy dating back thousands of years.

There was a recurring theme that emerged from the group consciousness: a lot of participants talked about the kind of crones they wanted to be someday. I started to realize that night, in the safety of a convivial group consciousness, that in addition to worshipping a crone on my altar and where I found her in nature, that maybe in my longing to connect with a divine wisdom embodied by old age, I, too, wanted to grow old someday. I wanted to know how to live that long. It hadn't occurred to me that I would or could. I hadn't planned for it at all. I was twenty-nine and I didn't really picture myself beyond my thirties. When I had been young and depressed and suicidal, the decade felt impossible, and now here I was about to cross the threshold. I had no vision, and that was a bad thing. The most world-bending thing I could think was: I want to grow old. I had to turn the lack of vision into a good thing, a blank check to write myself, to become who I wanted and needed to be. The thought alone required a major shift, major changes I would have to make to pave a road into that horizon.

I'd have to learn about pensions. I'd have to register with a dentist, I'd have to register with a doctor. I'd have to initiate a sex change. I'd grow a beard, like Marian in *The Hearing Trumpet*, but also not at all like Marian. I'd cross dress, like the winking nun, but also unlike the winking nun. I would have to believe that I deserved the things I needed. I would have to face the grief of self-abnegation, I would have to face the grief of how long my reality was denied by the people who were supposed to take care of me. I'd have to spend money I didn't have and fill out paperwork I didn't know how to. I'd have to learn to ask other people for help and rely on them in new ways, take new leaps of faith. Many of the people in the book club would come to take on key roles in this process, including my crush. The book club that didn't quite become a coven gave me the kind of profound insights I'd imagined a coven would, anyway. *Coven*: a gathering, assembly, from covent as in convent, a religious community, referring specifically to witches since the seventeenth century. Not the coven I'd envisioned but the coven I needed, which lasted exactly as long as it needed to. We met till we didn't. The immediate benefit was that the book club did get me a girlfriend, and by the time it was over I saw before me everything I had to do and entered into a covenant with myself. Those few months energized me for the years of effort that would follow.

PIXIE'S PARTY

Throwing a birthday party for a person you love is a fun and effective form of magic! A (mostly) annual tradition at Treadwell's was to celebrate Pamela Colman Smith's birthday—Pixie Smith to her friends—as close to February 16th as possible. I'd go to the grocery store across the street and buy: roses, baguettes and dips, grapes and cheese, a birthday cake of some kind, sparkling water, wine. We'd dress an altar for Pixie: the roses, a cup of water, a plate of food, candles, a scattering of the Tarot cards she designed in collaboration with A. E. Waite, first published in 1909. We'd tape up larger images of her tarot around us on the walls, printed from the office inkjet: The High Priestess, the Queens of each suit, Strength, The Star, The World. But the highlight of the birthday party, and the most powerful part of the evening, was hung up front and center and covered with a silk scarf for most of the night: a small watercolor painting by Pixie herself, that one of the witches in attendance had acquired. After lighting the candles and reading about Pixie for a while—from her writings, from descriptions of her life, stories and lore passed down from friends-of-friends who knew her personally—the witch who had brought the painting would tell the story of its origins, and then uncover it for us to behold.

The culmination of the evening was sitting together in silent contemplation of the painting, its prominent blues and purples, the landscape blending into sky above and dissolving into ocean below, with hints of faces moving through the wind, the trees, the waves. The painting was a remnant of Pixie's practice of playing music and painting what she heard. It was her striking translation of sound to image that had caught the attention of Alfred Stieglitz, who gave Smith a solo show in 1907. She was the only painter featured in his gallery dedicated to photography. I could never stare enough at this painting, small but deeply engrossing, then engulfing, consuming. One year while sitting with the painting, one of the witches was moved to song, wanting to recover for us the lost notes that had inspired the piece in the first place.

My contribution was to read a transcription I'd made from Pixie's letters. Years before, while visiting home in Philadelphia, I'd heard that Bryn Mawr college had a box of seventeen letters written between 1896 and 1900 by Pamela Colman Smith to her cousin Mary Reed, nicknamed Bobby. Shocked that they would survive and be so close to where I grew up, yet practically on another planet, I scheduled a pilgrimage to look at them. I emailed: *I am an academic co-authoring a monograph on Pamela Colman Smith's early work.* I lied, because I couldn't be sure if the librarian on the other end of my inquiry would be excited by my excitement—*I want to use these letters to channel the spirit of the illustrator of the Tarot cards I use!*—or more traditional about access. My lie was unnecessary, I was totally welcome. And so, I ran for the train and got to spend six hours transfixed by the vibrance of letters written by Smith between the ages of eighteen and twenty-two.

Although she was years away from illustrating the Tarot, and they would not enjoy the popularity in her lifetime that they have since, the first thing you encounter when you open the box of her letters is a set of the Tarot cards she illustrated, an edition from the 1970s. It is a wise inclusion: alongside her letters, filled with line drawings of characters, people in her daily life, set designs, and doodles, you can see just how distinct her style is, and how consistent with her visualization of the centuries-old divination tool. However child-like she was (hence the nickname Pixie), A. E. Waite commissioned a confident illustrator whose long-term interest in literature and the occult, ritual, and drama, made for a powerful collaboration. She brought much to the table without his need for instruction.

The letters are filled with references to her reading; her amateur theatrical creations with magical subjects: *Henry Morgan, The Magic Carbuncle, Herne the Hunter*; her adventures in Jamaica with her horse Grag, who frightened easily and was always dragging her into ditches; her travels to New York and London; her burgeoning career as a stage designer and illustrator, with newspaper clippings about theatrical productions she worked on, and an advertisement for a shop she opened in London to sell prints and illustrations. The letters are filled with close female friendships and an eye for the girls: she sees "quite a good deal" of Gwen Hawthorne, who spends the night, she has a good time with Marguerite Beckford, daughter of the U.S. Consul, and takes Marguerite and her little sister Julia out in her buggy with Grag, she paints a portrait of Magdalen Goldie, "she is very pretty! with big blue eyes + with yellow hair—she plays very well on the piano—but is rather stupid in other ways!". She writes at length about Jane Harvey, is sure Jane will be a great tragic actress someday, is mesmerized by her and writes a role for her in every play. Together they write silly poetry, according to a letter written October 5, 1896:

> Yesterday Jane and myself wrote stories in the old way. You know each write a few lines—and we each wrote one—mind was a "little snow flake" hers "the little Green chair—and both were very funny! And then I said lets write ballads each two lines in a ballad form and tell the rhyming words of them and so we did and here are the results—we just screamed over them!
> I don't know if you will think them so very funny but I do hope you will if you have any kindof blues!

The ballad of a Faire Ladie (with nothing about her)
This is my beginning

Janes: "The sun was setting in the west—
A ball of gold was he
He stole a little blackbirds nest
From off the cotton tree!

I thinks thats just lovely! don't you—

2. Within the cave the old witch sat
And she was old and thin— } Mine
I think the cat has eaten it—
It really is a sin—! } Janes

3. The maiden sat on charger white
And many a smile gave she } mine
She gave the bird a dreadful bite
Before she let it free! } Janes

4. Oh! after this terrible fight
Who died? Oh my—Oh me! } Mine
And home they hurried through the night
their grandmamma to see! } Janes

5. Away and away for a year and a day
Over the rolling blue } Mine
And birdie'll always with me stay
In a nice cage so new! } Janes

I think it is quite fun—a little newer than writing stories. Do try it Bobby and send me some of the funny ones![49]

---

49 Pamela Colman Smith Collection, Special Collections Department, Bryn Mawr College Library. https://archives.tricolib.brynmawr.edu/resources/bmc-m47

Everything in these letters, the books she reads and the plays she writes, the girls she obsesses over, sets the stage for what would come. Smith was embedded in a queer milieu of artists: later intimately connected to the actress Ellen Terry's daughter Edith Craig, who would go on to live in holy throupledom with two butches, Christopher St. John and Tony Atwood. Pixie then lived with a spiritualist named Nora Lake for decades, and left Lake everything in her will when she died. Another excitable letter I would read from, written January 5, 1898 from Brooklyn Heights, showed her childlike appreciation for folklore and fairy tales, deeply informative to her style of illustration:

> Dearest Bobby--
> Well! I was going to write yesterday! you see I have such a lot of scrummy! things to tell you about so if I am a little late don't mind! First here's a health to you and your family may things &c. &c. and a happy New Year! &c—Santa claus was very good to me! I got a lovely gold watch and a chain with little green balls on it! And a travelling clock in a red leather case— and a fountain pen that I am now using!
>
> And quite a lot of books! "A Legend of Camelot" by [George] DuMaurier — and "Mother Goose in Prose" illustrated by Maxfield Parrish! And "The Golden Egg" by Kenneth Graham from Haskie— Daddy gave me Camelot and "Stories of Famous Songs" and the Ogdins "Mother Goose"— Aunt Ellie gave me a silk petticoat and Granny "Old Carrol Days" illustrated by Albert Herter.

Reading through the letters of Pamela Colman Smith, thrumming with poetry and doodles and the endless rituals and pageantry of theater, was one of my earliest initiations into an alternative occult history, one that lies adjacent to the list of names I had first been given in my job interview. In this lineage, mysticism and gnosis went hand in hand with freaky, non-traditional family structures and friendships, gender-bending in art and life, and passionate romantic entanglements outside of marriage. In holding and transcribing these letters carefully, I was beginning to initiate myself into my own family tree as a queer person who practiced witchcraft. After years of dedicated work in archives, bringing my whole self and spirituality to the table was yielding results. I was happy to share them with all who asked, to embellish my own friendships with tales of Pamela Colman Smith and her intensely lived life.

Celebrating Pixie's birthday strengthened my relationship with her spirit as it presides over my Tarot card readings and began to bring me into my queer and trans lineage of witches, from the illustrator of the cards to the teachers I found who taught me to read them. As for Treadwell's, I witnessed how the tradition of celebrating the birthday worked another very distinct magical reward. After years of paying tribute to Pixie's life and legacy, I got a call from The Witch Queen one night saying: "I have found the hearth from Pamela Colman Smith's home in the Lizard, Cornwall on eBay. I am arranging to have it delivered to Treadwell's."

After World War I, Smith moved to Cornwall, a place popular with artists (some of them queer: Marlow Moss, Ithell Colquhoun, Gluck), and rented a house on the Lizard Peninsula where she lived with Nora Lake and also ran a holiday home for Catholic priests. This fireplace was, according to its owner and some follow-up research, from the home she had lived in with Lake.

What were the chances that, in the twenty-first century, someone living in the far reaches of the United Kingdom would take to eBay to offer a structural aspect of their home that they didn't need: an entire stone fireplace? The cost was merely its collection and delivery across nearly three hundred miles, and with some difficulty, it was arranged. Now, when you descend the basement of Treadwell's, you can sit and meditate with the fireplace, light a candle, leave an offering. There are photos of Pixie and Tarot cards left there, there are often flowers, and every February, there is a grand and theatrical place to gather around and sing happy birthday.

SEVENTY-EIGHT DEGREES OF WISDOM (1980)

Does it work? Is it accurate? Is it gonna tell me I'm gonna die? Does it really work? How does it work?

An important source of income for Treadwell's was Tarot card readings, and scheduling sessions with our regular readers was part of my job: half hour, £30; one hour, £60. Many of these walk-ins and first-time callers wanted to know: Does it work? My short answer was: Yes. My long answer was: the iconography found in Tarot is thousands of years old, and humans have been making and interpreting meaning from it that whole time. There is rich collective wisdom and consciousness embedded in this centuries-old tool. Divination with cards—like stargazing, like working with your hands in the soil—is a form of witchcraft that connects us to something deep and abiding about our humanity. A Tarot card reading will have one hundred percent accuracy as an act of self-evaluation and meaning-making. Our shop readers were all very experienced-the minimum number of readings one had to have done to be considered for the job was 10,000. It only doesn't work if you're totally shut down to it. And it won't tell you you're going to die—the Death card is about transformation, rebirth. Aleister Crowley said of the card: "Die daily," as in, every day is an opportunity to begin again and appreciate life anew.

> If any device will provide meaning, why Tarot? The answer is, any system will tell us something, but the quality of that something depends on the

> values contained in the system. The Tarot contains a philosophy, an outline of how human consciousness evolves, and a vast compendium of human experience. Shuffling the cards brings all these values into play with each other . . . The Tarot is objective because it bypasses conscious decision, but it is not impartial. On the contrary, it attempts to push us in certain directions: optimism, spirituality, a belief in the necessity and value of change.[50]

Tarot divination is a popular form of magic most people have encountered: anyone can read Tarot. As a teenager I had been expressly forbidden, the cards taken away from me. My interests led me elsewhere: hermeticism, alchemy, folklore. As a young adult I had been reawakened to them (Death) by my best friend, a Double-Scorpio with a heart of gold. One folk belief is that your first Tarot deck should be a gift, not bought. While I bought my first deck as a gift to myself, for me the real gift was receiving understanding and appreciation for the Tarot from my best friend, who'd been a Witch Baby Genius since childhood. Witch Baby Genius had set up as a "fortune teller" with their Tarot cards one day at school, maybe around fourth grade, and had read their teacher's cards so accurately she cried. The summer the Tarot bug really bit me, me and Witch Baby Genius were living together, and I was just starting to date women. It felt perfect to consult the Tarot to help navigate the world of dyke drama I'd been immediately thrown into: *She shames you for not being gay enough but lied about living with her ex-boyfriend. Her ex-boyfriend keeps threatening to beat you up, and she encourages it. Here's The Hanged Man: wisdom through suffering. You know you need to leave this toxic dynamic but you only will when you learn how to stand up for yourself and walk away calmly.*

50 Rachel Pollack, *Seventy-Eight Degrees of Wisdom: A Book of Tarot* (London: Element, 1997) 273.

Living in London, with Witch Baby Genius far away in New York, a gift I could give myself was to really dive deep into studying the seventy-eight cards of the Major and Minor Arcana. It would be a way to honor how much I missed my friend, to connect with the lifechanging experience of having their friendship to begin with; it would be another language we'd speak together. It would also be a way to help me keep grounded in the present—checked into myself—and an important tool for talking, processing, gossiping with the new friends I was making. After an afternoon wandering around Soho, Covent Garden, Seven Dials, I ended up in the Astrology shop and bought a pack of cards—the Visconti-Sforza Tarot-and a copy of Rachel Pollack's *Seventy-Eight Degrees ofWisdom*. I went with the Visconti-Sforza because they're the oldest known cards, commissioned in the middle of the fifteenth century, and the book because the title sounded the coolest. I mean, my intuition drew me to that book. When I got home, I read it in nearly a single sitting, so transfixed and compelled by the writing, the balance between its accessible interpretations and deep penetration into layer after layer of human consciousness. Looking up the author-of course she was an established sci-fi and fantasy writer, and a trans woman. The book became initiatory in more ways than one, leading me down a path of understanding the inextricable tangle of my body, my lifetime of gender non-conformity, and my spiritual path. It makes sense to me that in the witch panic my parents had over their teenager abandoning a bigoted religion to surrender to a faith based on the sanctity of everyday life—household spices and talismans made from quotidian kitsch—I was forbidden one of the queerest arts of all in divination through cards.

> The meanings for the cards given in this book leave a good deal of room for interpretation by the reader. In fact, they require it. This is because the practiced reader brings far more to her or his work than a detailed

> knowledge of the cards and their traditional meanings. Just as important is sensitivity—both to the pictures and to the person sitting there nervously and excitedly staring at the cards. A good reader does not simply repeat traditional fixed meanings. Rather, he or she will find new meanings and interpretations, will extend the patterns.[51]

There were four incredible Tarot readers at the shop, and they each had a regular shift, distinct vibe, and clientele. One was a high priestess who lived by the sea, her life structured by goddess worship; one was a gay French artist who read Tarot to fund his one-man cabaret; one was a mercurial magus whose magical name and address kept changing (exes would visit the shop from time to time looking out for him); and one was very reserved, polite, and totally unassuming, with a true psychic gift that produced uncannily specific readings. As staff members, we were entitled to a free reading every three months, and also received readings when new readers applied to work with us. But job openings weren't frequent. Our shop had the best rates in town, a 60/40 split to use the space, with the majority going to the reader—at other places it was reversed, and in some cases 70/30. What these readers paid us for was renting a cozy, private room to read in, and for logistics: we handled the scheduling.

Scheduling Tarot readings was more work than it sounds like; it was like being a psychic bouncer. The chief rule of Tarot at our shop was our version of the Rule of Threes: you could only get one reading every three months. We kept a careful spreadsheet of querent names, deleting records older than three months as time passed. This was an ethical consideration of the wise Witch Queen, with one foot planted firmly on the ground: she knew our readers were very good, and she knew that tarot was cheaper than therapy, but no substitute. People

51 Pollack, *Seventy-Eight Degrees of Wisdom*, 273.

could and did get addicted to receiving readings. They'd leave their session and want to book again immediately or book with a different reader for a different opinion. "The Tarot doesn't work like that," she would say: "You must be kind but firm with these people: if they need to change their lives they have to do it themselves. If they need support they have to find it, if they need to dump their boyfriend the Tarot isn't going to do it for them." The Rule of Three Months had to be actively enforced—the spreadsheet of tarot querents had to be up on a tab at all times to consult at short notice, because people called or visited the shop all the time to try to Get Answers. They'd beg and plead: *It'll just be this once, I'm going through a lot.* Or: *I just had a few follow up questions about my reading.* Or: *Something just happened to me and I think it will change the reading completely.* Occasionally someone would get a relative to book under their name to try and trick us, or give us a fake name, but for the most part we caught that when they came to the shop. The Witch Queen would stress that turning these people down was crucial not only for their own sake, but also to show our confidence in our readers: "We stand by the talent and experience of our Tarot readers, whatever they have told you in your reading is reliable. Integrate what you have learned from the reading into your life for at least three months."

Divination by Tarot was a booming business, with most of our readers fully booked and barely any room for walk-ins, but the section of Tarot books in the shop was small. Partially this was due to our place in the wider magical ecosystem in London: within about a half hour's walk, you could visit many different types of esoteric shops, and there were others that really "did" Tarot, with huge selections of decks and books. We didn't have the space for that. Our strengths were Wicca, folklore, histories and anthropologies of magic and esoteric orders, and a lot of academic publications that we vetted for accessibility. But every good bookshop's stock is shaped by the passions and niche specialisms of its booksellers. It was important for me to make sure I had copies of *Seventy-Eight Degrees of Wisdom* in stock at all times, to enthusiastically put into people's hands. I loved talking to people about Tarot, before and after their readings.I loved fielding their questions about whether it worked, and much of my thinking on why and how it *worked* came from my own experiences, my obsession with Renaissance iconography, and from reading Rachel Pollack. I must have sold hundreds of copies!

This was also a book I felt comfortable recommending to people who seemed inconsolable in their compulsion to seek out readings. I'd have them look at a copy and recommend, "You can take pictures of the pages if you need to, but when I've felt lost I've kept this book close to hand and meditated on one card per day." Unlike other book recommendations I made, this was a book that brought many back to the shop to tell me about how much they loved it, how they'd given it to a friend, how it opened a door they'd walked through into someplace new. This was the first book that unlocked a super power I have as a bookseller: I really can recommend books that change people's lives, sometimes that made me new friends, and sometimes it was uncomfortable.

It's hard to underestimate Rachel Pollack's influence on modern Tarot, an influence I watched unfold and expand even further in my years at the shop. The weight of that influence feels as impossible to ignore or quantify as the art of Pamela "Pixie" Colman Smith herself, in its exemplifications of, and deviations from, the direction of A. E. Waite and the Golden Dawn.

> If the Rider Minor cards serve us primarily as a commentary on ordinary life, they do not ignore or cut us off from deeper perceptions. On the contrary, the philosophical bias of the cards leads us always in the direction of "hidden forces" giving shape and meaning to ordinary experience. A truly realistic view of the

> world (as opposed to the narrow materialist ideology commonly thought of as "realism") will recognize the spiritual energy always present within the constantly shifting patterns of the world . . . But the Rider pack does more than teach us this awareness. Certain cards, taken in the right way, can help produce it . . . I call these cards Gates, because of the way they open a path from the ordinary world to the inner level of archetypal experiences. Each suit contains at least one of these cards, the Pentacles containing the most. They all share certain characteristics: complex, often contradictory meanings, and a myth-like Strangeness which no allegorical interpretation can completely penetrate.[52]

This concept of Gate cards could be said of the book itself: a portal of entry into deeper meanings, a sturdy companion to revisit and gain different insights from, a book that straddles the active and contemplative aspects of Tarot—at times meeting you where you're at, at times pushing you further than you might have gotten alone. I moved from *Seventy-Eight Degrees of Wisdom* to, among other writings, Pollack's essay, "Abandonment to the Body's Desire," a companion text in understanding my own transsexuality as an emotional as well as a spiritual imperative—a desire that I must place before all things if I am to live, a desire to which all other relationships and concerns in my life must submit to or be damned:

> Desire leads us to revelations, such as the very knowledge of ourselves in our true gender. What else but desire would lead us to do what we do? We take strong drugs to alter the shape and function of our bodies. We face the contempt and ridicule of society, friends, and even family. We take risks of imprisonment, enforced hospitalization, and torture in the form of

52 Pollack, *Seventy-Eight Degrees of Wisdom*, 159.

> electric shock and other kinds of "therapy." We run the danger of being beaten or even murdered if discovered at the wrong time by the wrong person. And finally, we undergo, we seek out, surgery on our genitals. Think of the power of a desire which can lead us to do such things. Most of us have experienced this as desperation. As long as we see only the desperation, as long as we cling to it for the dubious permission it gives us, we remain victims. When we start to recognize the driving force as passion, we allow ourselves the possibility of our own truth, of a life based on joy rather rather pity.[53]

I'd taken this and *Seventy-Eight Degrees of Wisdom* with me from place to place, revelation to revelation. When Rachel Pollack died in upstate New York, April 2023 I deeply mourned a teacher and boon companion I'd never met. I keep a candle for her on my altar and my well-read, dog-eared copy *Seventy-Eight Degrees of Wisdom* close to hand.

---

53 Rachel Pollack, "Abandonment to the Body's Desire," in *Balancing on the Mechitza: Transgender in the Jewish Community*, edited by Noach Dzmura (Berkeley: North Atlantic Books, 2010) 5.

INVOKING WISDOM

One day a lesbian-feminist High Priestess visited the shop and tapped me to take part in a ritual she was concocting. I'd heard about her in hushed, awed tones from The Witch Queen, who loved and admired her. She was old-school, participating in Dianic and goddess-driven witchcraft, as well as magical groups working more in the tradition of the Golden Dawn of the early twentieth century. Magically speaking, she'd seen it all. For her, crafting ritual was a deeply intuitive but highly scripted process that took months of research and preparation. She worked from scripts, some of them decades old if not older, carefully scouting individuals to take part in certain roles. In the lead up to whatever ritual she was holding (it usually had some astrological significance), she would hold several meetings and meditations to prepare participants. This sometimes posed a challenge to newer initiates in the craft: millennials and younger generations could be flakey when it came to months of dedication, commitment to dates and meetings, no cancellations or excuses. I was thrilled and flattered to even be noticed by her and ready to change anything in my schedule to be available. The allure of this precise kind of secretive and mysterious happening in the dead of night was a huge part of why I wanted the job to begin with.

But I was shocked and a little embarrassed that the part she was tapping me for was, literally, an incarnation of *Wisdom*. Me? Wise? Really? I had never been such a mess, felt like such a fool, a walking, talking, leaking open wound. I felt totally lost,

I was counting my breaths up and down to get by minute by minute. And I was supposed to don golden robes and wear a fucking lunar headpiece to represent an incarnation of the goddess of Wisdom on earth? It felt like a crazy proposal. I'd be a total sham. My homework to prepare was to read and try to memorize parts of *Thunder, Perfect Mind*, a Coptic text rediscovered in 1945:

> For I am knowledge and ignorance.
> I am shame and boldness.
> I am shameless; I am ashamed.
> I am strength and I am fear.
> I am war and peace.
> Give heed to me.[54]

So, okay, *Thunder, Perfect Mind* is an ancient text of contradictions. I guess I break through to Wisdom since I was certainly a fool, bold because I was certainly ashamed, strong because I was definitely afraid, calm and peaceful since my brain was definitely at war with itself. But could I do this in three months? My love of mystery and gossip, my desire to please, would have to pull me through. I had no real self-confidence, but I was already obsessed with this High Priestess and dying to know more about her, about the rituals she did. My curiosity won out, pushed me to accept the invitation.

She had done the ritual before: this was a revival, decades later. One day she came to the shop to give me the script of the ritual as she'd done it the first time around, the script she was adapting for this version. The humble documents of magic and ritual always fascinate me. So much of it is DIY, and therefore beholden to whatever the most accessible technology of its time happens to be. Typeset, stereotyped, mimeographed,

54 "The Thunder, Perfect Mind," translated by George W. MacRae, *The Gnostic Society Library*, http://gnosis.org/naghamm/thunder.html.

typewritten, photocopied, printed on a home printer, risographed—there's a lot of different textures to different magical writings over time. Ye Olde Manuscripts in beautiful handwriting and scripts made by typewriter look, aesthetically, the prettiest, but if you stick to aesthetics you'll miss out on a whole lot worth knowing. Some of the rarest books of the late twentieth century are self-published and very badly designed with the desktop publishing and clipart of their time. I couldn't be a snob—Angelfire websites and Geocities.com had been a huge part of my magical education. This particular script was spiral bound like a janky cook book and printed at home. In pencil, next to each role, she'd written the name of the person who performed the first time around—some of them incredibly well-known in the magical world, heavy-hitting adepts who'd written bestselling books on our shelves. I would be entering into a kind of communion with them.

My role was fairly simple: sit behind a screen in an elaborate costume for most of the ritual as each participant chants and makes their offering to invoke the goddess of Wisdom. At the end of a group conjuring, appear from behind the screen—a surprise to most participants—and recite whatever I could remember in the moment from *Thunder, Perfect Mind,* words thought to be copied down from the lips of the goddess of Wisdom herself. Afterward we would all have a little feast of thanksgiving together. My role—hidden apart from everyone, a dramatic reveal—shaped my experience of the ritual. Mostly I just experienced a trial of awkwardness, peeking through a break in the screen to see what was happening in the candlelight without me, listening to the chant, watching as candles and incense were lit, feeling the floor shake as one witch offered a dance to the goddess. I was nervous about my timing, and about getting my lines right, reciting parts of *Thunder, Perfect Mind* to myself over and over while each of the participants read their words, made offerings of dance and song, incense and herbs, to the goddess.

I am the silence that is incomprehensible
and the idea whose remembrance is frequent.
I am the voice whose sound is manifold
and the word whose appearance is multiple.
I am the utterance of my name.

I was constrained to the ritual preparation, rather than the the ritual itself, to encounter the goddess on my own terms, and I did. The main revelation came from the High Priestess herself, watching her in action, her method. One day she visited me at the shop and we'd gotten in new statues of Minerva, the goddess of wisdom. She looked over the new stock carefully. *You know, she said, decades ago some women and I met in a cottage and worked together to call back the influence of Minerva into England. It was during the Thatcher years, so we really needed it—there was so much hatred and cruelty parading as fiscal conservatism, it was a time of false wisdom and fear mongering. We met one weekend and performed a series of rituals—I'd done research to pick a place in Britain near known Roman settlements, and I'd looked into adapting Latin and Greek sources to work with Minerva and Pallas Athena alike. And would you believe it: a few months later, after we'd come and gone, they excavated statues and owls of Minerva not far away from that place.*

This was earth-shattering to me. It's hard to describe earth shattering moments that aren't, like, a marriage proposal or a pregnancy scare or a death sentence, but this was a moment of major impact that restructured how I thought of my spirituality. Under the exfoliating influence of my Saturn return I was scrubbed raw. The offhand and vague story told by the High Priestess was rich with possibility for me: hadn't I been researching my whole life, plumbing the depths of history for its heretics, its queers and outlaws, chasing down the objects of worship that propelled their blazing, visionary lives and outpourings? And couldn't I channel this knowledge in the same way?

I'd thought of it as my calling, my vocation, and had worked hard to shape that vocation into something that could get me a job. It was my begrudging capitulation to the world I lived in, one in which I needed to fend for myself to survive. That's why I'd gotten deep into academia: living scholarship to scholarship was the only financial picture I understood. But I'd gotten distracted by it; in being "bad with money" and "not concerned with material things" I'd fallen into an opposite extremity, so stupid that now money issues were ruling my life. From blissful ignorance to self-destructive ignorance. It only took a few years and a divorce to do it. I couldn't let my depressing situation take me away from what I actually loved, and this was the way to get back to it: I would use years of deep archival research to craft new rituals, new conjurings to bring new forces into my life. I had felt so adrift. I could root myself to the world through connecting with these sources I'd love so dearly. My archival rites would take what I'd learned and call them into my spiritual life. At the end of her visit, the High Priestess invited me over for tea the next evening.

I'd been told her flat was Something Else. I'd been told it was A Very Magical Place. She was a High Priestess in two senses: she'd had a long life of magical practice, and she had the kind of authority that only comes from taking no shortcuts. Some things just take time, and you have to claim that time yourself. But she was a High Priestess in the sense of the Tarot card: shy, withdrawn from much of society, a person who kept her life quiet in order to watch and listen carefully for the manifestations of the goddess in everyday life. When you say "no" to a party invitation or forego the pressure to be at every art opening, you're making time and space to stretch your awareness and potential in other ways. At least, she was.

Her *sanctum sanctorum*, a one-bedroom flat at the top of a hill, was insight into the riches of her spirit. It was crammed with an improbable amount of books and magical artifacts: statues of deities from around the world, images from holy cards, woodcut etchings, paintings of aspects of the divine, fine candlesticks, incense burners, an array of fabrics for altar clothes, veils, robes. Each room of the flat had its presiding deities: goddesses of wisdom, learning, communication, hearth, and home in the living room; goddesses of flora and fauna, magical potions and herbal knowledge in the kitchen; goddesses of love and spirituality and visions and dreaming in the bedroom; goddesses of the sea and the river, water sprites and nymphs and mermaids in the bathroom. I would accept every offer of a cup of tea in that flat just to give myself more time to stare at everything, it was to me a domestic ideal, *let every surface be an altar.* An artist in her own right, many of the artifacts had been made by the High Priestess herself—facsimiles of engravings and relics, magical finds from archaeological digs. She'd made her own versions to draw into her ritual, conduits for her veneration of the many spirits that live around us.

I was starved for this concrete vision of a life well lived. The warmth and coziness of the High Priestess's homemade sanctuary was an initiation into a calm, attainable magic. If I felt like I was living moment by moment to survive my panicked feeling, I realized I could also choose to live moment by moment to craft a worthwhile life. There was bounty everywhere, I had to redirect my focus to it, and I couldn't beat myself up for my lapses. So much about society was engineered to do just that, and I was only human. But to do it I needed some of that High Priestess energy: to retreat a little from the overstimulation of the world around me, to use what I had to make my magic. In the magical life she'd made for herself—a place so pulsing and thrumming with otherworldly potential I felt myself holding back delirious, nervous laughter; to think it was all sitting behind an unassuming door in an unassuming apartment building!—I could find instructions about what to do next, how to live. The historical materials I'd been working with for years now—rough, scruffy little mystical and political pamphlets from the seventeenth century, made by people imprisoned and outcast for their beliefs—taught me I, too, was the kind of person who could make trash into treasure, a miracle of surviving into thriving. The weird thing about having Saturn in your first house is that, after so much life-changing upheaval, my Saturn return would end with the planet entering my second house: material possessions, sense of value, and money. I could use my historic interests to inform rituals to conjure the historical artifacts I cared about. I would also figure out a way to make money doing it. I would become the ultimate bargain witch.

WHERE HALF-GODS GO (1922)

Bookshops are weird places in general; you never know who or what you're going to find there. An even weirder magnitude of bookshop is the kind that sells used books. The books people throw away, or resell, or die and have scattered, create a vast churning vortex of ink and paper that you step into when you look to buy a book secondhand. Or third hand, or fourth hand, or fifth hand—the older the books, the more hands. The weirdest magnitude of bookshop that sells used books is the niche kind: pick a field of knowledge you love and there will be a specialist somewhere in the world who sells it in secondhand and rare or out-of-print editions. I'm biased: the weirdest upon weirdest influx of secondhand books came to me when I worked at the occult bookshop. The titles you'd get from buying secondhand stock en bloc was just beyond what I'd ever heard, some of it impossible to find online (*Things I Wish My Magus Had Told Me*), some of it steamy (*The Fleshpots of Antiquity*) some of it transformed by context into an eldritch tome of surreal lore (*Moby-Dick*).

The people who deal in the secondhand economy of books are my people. It just feels philosophically gratifying and like the most harmlessly enjoyable scam of all time, to be able to convert hours browsing for books into a job, to find a book in the bargain bin for one dollar that is actually worth twenty. A book is only worth twenty dollars if you know who will pay that for it, so you have to know exactly who has been looking to add to their collection. Maybe you happen to know it's a first edition, it's the first book to employ a certain word or concept, it's the first journal to feature the first version of an article by an author you love. The interests and tastes you have sculpted around the things you love can make you a bit of money. Do it repeatedly and it can make you enough money to fund a gentle subsistence.

A stunning breadth of people do this kind of work. It's not unlike selling vintage clothes; the books often have a lived-in and well-worn feeling. You gently gather them up in your arms, dust them off and shepherd them along to the next person—or, to mix metaphors, you play matchmaker. If you sell directly to customers, you're a bookseller. If you sell to other booksellers who then find the customers, you're a book scout. Mostly you switch between the two modes, but there are some diehard scouts out there. Scouting, since it's not a forward-facing retail job per se, is the mercurial, psychopomp of bookselling that attracts the wildest characters, often men who fancy themselves unemployable for reasons that range from awesome (anti-capitalist) to awful (misogynist creep). But all kinds of people have done it: Patti Smith has written about buying a fifty cent book from the Strand's outdoor carts, and reselling it back to their secondhand department for a couple bucks all in one day. That's primo scouting, reselling someone their own merchandise for a profit. There's a reality to the romance of bookselling and scouting—intelligent, charismatic outlaws who question the conspiracy that capitalism is inevitable—and then there's its inverse, like, the kind of men who like to "play devil's advocate" and "do their own research" and despite a lifetime of reading books, buy into bigoted conspiracy theories that have aggregated into QAnon.

Then there's the reputation you get from *selling* secondhand books—once it's known, people come in off the street to sell you theirs: students, teachers, junkies, artists, widows, widowers, heirs. I've done that throughout my life, parted with books I loved, traded in for cash in hand. Secondhand books inhabit a mysterious and haphazard scale of value that makes you question the whole damn system. When my apartment was robbed and ransacked, the books on the shelves remained untouched. I started hiding valuable things in them—my passport, some emergency cash—and then had to sell some of the others to pay to replace the laptop that had been stolen. There's no accounting for taste; someone's trash is another's treasure. People make money from the most heinous commodities, valued at prices plucked outta thin air, all of the time. Used booksellers are just more honest about the scam: *This book is expensive not only because I love it, but because you do too. Or, you will.* Because the best booksellers are people whose instincts you trust. They know how to sell you what you didn't know you were dying to read.

One of the regular supplies of secondhand books at the occult bookshop was a man literally named Igor, a very shy person who'd arrive without warning at odd hours with boxes of books in an old truck painted black. These were cheap paperbacks we'd buy for a £1 each and sell for £4 or £5. If they didn't sell within a few months, they'd be marked back down to £1 and sold that way. There was a distinct clientele who only bought books from our £1 table, often £10 or £20 worth at a time.

Then there was an antiquarian bookseller who would come in monthly to visit and sell slightly rarer, older books about magic, mysticism, both Eastern and western Esoteric traditions, that he had found—*scouted*—mostly outside of London, at estate sales, flea markets, and provincial used book stores. Since I knew about rare books—had worked odd jobs dealing in printing from the fifteenth to the eighteen century, had gotten a degree in the materiality of texts—it was my job to schedule that meeting, select and record books from his stock, and pay him. Early twentieth century classics of folklore like *The Candle of Vision* and *Visions and Beliefs in the West of Ireland*; lurid collectible 1970s paperbacks, far-out histories like *Lost*

Continents, *The Templars' Secret Island*; New Age explorations like *The Book of Concealed Mystery* and *The Clairvoyant Theory of Perception*. Books on Tantra and Kabbalah, mental health and Hindu philosophy, sacred geometry and ley lines. Ideas to take seriously, but not necessarily literally. Ideas that say more about their cultural context than reality as we know it. Books that let folklore remain folklore (good), books that turn folklore into pseudoscience (bad). Ecclesiastes 12:12: *And further, by these, my son, be admonished: of making many books there is no end; and much study is a weariness of the flesh*. The original algorithm is a bibliography: books are always talking to and listing their references to one another. Fall down the slippery slope of citation and you can get trapped in a toxic trajectory of thinking and feeling. There are so many books, you can spend your whole life reading through one field of them, through only one lens.

This bookseller, Roland, would come in with his humble rucksack filled with mostly wonderful oddities of publishing history, the books that time and Amazon forgot. One day, instead of beginning with his usual rough sales pitch for titles like *Astrology and the Ductless Glands* (1936) or *Bird Gods* (1898) or *The Astral Body* (1930), he had a different opening, barely making eye contact: "I found a book that made me think of you. It's . . . uhm . . . it's an odd little volume that I found in an old house I was clearing. I've uh never seen it before, never heard of it, can't find any other copies on the market. Have a look and tell me what you think, but uh I think you might be interested. Here it is, it's by a suffragette, her name was Withall. Laetitia Withall. I couldn't find anything more about her other than a hunger strike medal with her name on it. Anyway, for you, I'd sell it for £30."

His lack of confidence was unusual and unnerving: Is Roland being awkward because he's trying to talk to me About My Sexuality? I wondered. The book was a gray paperback. Not white, not cream, a dull green-gray, its pages fragile in their binding and dust-wrapper. On the grainy paper dust-wrapper, in blue ink, was a line drawing of a shoreline at sunrise or sunset, a flock of birds flying into the horizon, the title: *When Half-Gods Go*, by Laetitia Withall. It was published in 1922 by the Theosophical Publishing House Ltd. and weirdly printed on the island of Guernsey. My fingers were tingling, a rare feeling of *Fingerspitzengefühl*, an archaic military idea given new meaning in the world of books, revived by lifelong same-sex partners and antiquarian booksellers Leona Rostenberg and Madeleine Stern to describe their "tingling of the fingertips [that] becomes an electrical current of suspense, excitement, recognition," when coming across an artifact. They use the term *Fingerspitzengefühl* to describe their intense lifelong collaboration, love and electricity being words they used for one another while rejecting the word lesbian. Using that phrase, seeking that feeling, I was already taking part in a queer process, and I hadn't even read the book. The dedication: "TO MY HEALER TEACHER FRIEND." The book describes itself as "a glimpse into other lives of two women, who (having looked for each other throughout the years) met—only to be parted again after a brief space of time." Yep, Roland was acting shy because he was trying to sell a dyke book to a big dyke.

> This book has grown up between the two of us, but just which parts are written by which it is impossible to say . . . it is a little loom on which we have both plied the shuttle.[55]

The book takes the form of a diary beginning November 12th:

> So there is to be another letter-writing phase in the story of our love, is there, Kathleen Alannah? It's the

55 Laetitia Withall, *When Half-Gods Go* (London: Theosophical Publishing House Ltd, 1922) 1.

> pen and the paper once more and the word-for-wording of thoughts, instead of the broken sentence, the quick look of comprehension, the scarce-spoken thought; the knowledge before speech; the fusion of mind with mind; the lightning-quick exchange...You are saying: "Nothing is over. I am alive. You are alive. Our love, our beautiful, star-crowned, God-made love is alive, warm, beating, and strong.

The work ends nearly a year later, on October 23rd, the anniversary of Kathleen's death:

> Night fell . . . and we were together.
> Dawn broke . . . and we were together.
> The day is here . . . and we are together.
> Together . . . so close together, so heart-to-heart and cheek-to-cheek that I tremble with the ecstasy of her nearness, the exaltation of her presence.

An April 1924 review of the book in the *Occult Review* praised the narrator's approach, in terms akin to what we might call autofiction: "the author may be congratulated on having breathed into it an ardour and a sincerity which give to the experiences described every semblance of reality. If it is not fiction but fact, one appreciates these qualities no less, while feeling, perhaps a faint surprise at the frankness which unveils so personal a story of love and loss in the cold light of print." The reviewer continued to applaud the portrayal of "country life" in the work. The narrator seems to live in a world populated only by female friends: Clemency, St. George, Tissa, Elma, and Joanna all work alongside her, wandering through forests to gather fruit and firewood, keeping "the Hut" in the Cotswolds where they live well-stocked and self-sufficient. The role of the landscape in nourishing these gender outlaws and lovers is strong—a character in and of itself—in a way that, in my mind, lends the book to a folk horror adaptation, a lesbian *Penda's Fen* perhaps. Uncharacteristically for the history of same-sex relationships in print, the narrator describes no shame in her desire, or in the relationship between the two, only coming to terms with its loss. Even the depths of her despair is tempered by her ecstatic spiritual connection with her dead lover.

What little information survives about Laetitia Withall provides a stark contrast from much of what has become known as the "sapphic modernism" of the time. The most striking object to survive bearing her name is the 1913 Hunger Strike medal Roland had mentioned, awarded by the Women's Social and Political Union "in recognition of a gallant action whereby through endurance to the last extremity of hunger and hardship, a great principle of political justice was vindicated." A portrait of Withall remains to be rediscovered: in 1924, Sarah Fanny Hockey, Benjamin Britten's eccentric aunt best known for her 1922 miniature of him, exhibited six paintings as a member of the Ipswich Art Club, including "Miss Letitia Withall." Although her date of death is unknown, the last published writing by Withall comes from a 1949 contribution to an issue of *The Vegetarian*, an article on "Ethical Aspects of Vegetarianism."

Only one other copy of *When Half-Gods Go* was listed on OCLC, the vast, global database of databases, aggregating across all public and institutional library collections-although, that doesn't mean more copies haven't survived. Rarity on OCLC is a significant, invisible feature of printed matter, especially when copies are lacking in the collections of American universities, who have big budgets for new acquisitions and persnickety guidelines for spending them. If something doesn't exist on OCLC, it's a major selling point; one copy (at the British Library), is the next best thing. At the time it could not be found online, and there was no Wikipedia article for Laetitia Withall, both of which have changed. Finding things in the world that have no digital footprint gets me hot (just like giving things a digital footprint gets other people hot). I like to find the things that elude the post-"enlightenment" desire to name and catalog the whole world, pretending to be god—and not any of the fun gods, just the controlling Christian one. I don't care about OCLC as a late example of colonial projects of naming things in a hierarchy to possess them, but I will bend OCLC to suit my financial needs, the sad reality that I have to make a quick buck to pay to survive. I'm just part of the ecosystem, like Igor and Roland, a temporary custodian. I bought the book and read all one hundred and seventy-five pages in one sitting, then a year later resold it to a university in the middle of Pennsylvania for $300. It's such a good book, it honestly should have been $3,000. The $300 was deposited into my bank account just in time to pay my credit card bill. I lit candles at my altar and said a prayer of thanksgiving to Laetitia Withall. I am always open and calling out to queer spirits to enter my life in the form of unassuming old books and ephemera, and I'm always up front that my ways of loving them include a) reading them carefully b) finding them a home where they can be best appreciated by the maximum number of people and given the best conservation and care, and c) charging money for this so that I can live to tell the tale.

QUEENS OF THE NIGHT

When I'm in the right place at the right time, I know right away without asking, I'm just fully present to it, a beautiful feeling. For the fiftieth anniversary of the Stonewall Rebellion in New York, I wanted to show up early, which ended up being right on time. The moment I arrived, I crossed paths with a witch who set me on a path to new revelations.

There was a witch in Christopher Park. It was four days before the fiftieth anniversary of the rebellion and tourists were swarming. I happened to be passing through town and thought: why not? I was sitting in Christopher Street Park just as she entered, activating the little green triangle of power that comprises the park. She was tall, maybe six-foot-two or six-foot-three, dressed in flowing black robes that wrapped up and around her head, shaping her face and crowning it with a widow's peak like the Evil Queen in Disney's *Snow White* (1937). She was made taller by a classic, pointy, broad-brimmed witch's hat. It was ninety degrees in the high humid heat of the afternoon, but she didn't seem to break a sweat.

There was a tourist, and he had a huge, nine-inch long-lens camera. He was trying to take photos of George Segal's ill-advised white statues that comprise the *Gay Liberation Monument* (1980). It's getting harder to tell these days, but nothing about this tourist read as particularly gay. And he was fumbling. He couldn't get a clear shot of the pasty statutes because the witch kept backing up her ass toward him, miming that she was about to sit on his camera lens. Her face was so serious as she did it, again and again. Each time, she barely acknowledged the person holding the lens as she backed up to rub her ass against it. The confused tourist could only laugh awkwardly and pull away the expensive lens each time. And of course, because this is New York, everyone around was acting like it wasn't happening. His reality denied, he had no choice but to get up and leave. The witch had a large speaker and immediately took up the bench the tourist had given up. She put on opera, loud. I recognized the *Queen of the Night* aria: *Hell's vengeance boils in my heart,/ Death and despair blaze about me*! I'm actually kindof an opera queen myself. In spite of the still heat, I feel a light breeze kick up. We look at each other. She blows a kiss, I feel myself blush and smile. I realize for a few moments in time, the park is empty, it's just us. We breathe and hold each other's gaze. By the time the breeze dies down the park is invaded by the next onslaught of tourists.

I'm so inspired by this witch's buggery pantomime, used to prevent photographing bad art (a public service). I have to do something!! I have to take this high holy hilarity and go into the Stonewall Inn. I have to tell the spirits there what I just saw, *immediately*. I'm not sure what I'm going to do exactly but I trust I'll know when I get there. Magic is contagious, I'm caught in her spell, or, as I have been taught well by my boss back at the bookshop: in ritual there is no audience, only participants. Responsibility comes with witnessing.

The bar isn't very full. It's a Monday. They're out of a lot—it was a busy weekend, the bartender tells me, *obviously*. I order a cold bottle of beer and sit at the bar to collect my thoughts. In my bag I always have: a compass, a pocketknife, some stray pieces of quartz and amethyst and obsidian. I can play music on my phone and I vaguely remember a detail from reading an interview with Joe Caldiero, who was sixteen-years-old the night everything kicked off:

> The jukebox was playing "In the Year 2525" in the front room and they turned it off. We put it back on again and they unplugged it. As the cops passed by us, they would punch us on the side of the stomach when they thought no one was looking. The police were such bullies and whispered threats to us and tried to scare us. They did a good job of that, we were scared to death. Some of the older queens tried to comfort us by telling us things would be OK and to just be quiet. But that is not the way it would happen that night for us, for any of us.[56]

Perfect incantation material, "In the Year 2525" is such a silly song. It doesn't age well, and that's also exactly what I want, something topical, its mock-profundity perfect to set the scene. I get up to go to the bathroom with my beer and my bag. No big deal—I'm alone, so of course I'd take all my stuff with me.

The bathroom is lit by a red light, like a darkroom to develop photography. I wash my hands, throw water on my face and the back of my neck, a quick cleanse. The compass orients me so I can call the corners, East, South, West, and North. I find the song "In the Year 2525" by Zager and Evans on my phone and put it on repeat. It's too corny to distract me. I can play music out loud, the music in the bar itself drowns me out I'm sure. I look into the mirror, pour an offering of beer into the sink and into the toilet bowl, then sprinkle some on the mirror and draw a circle with my finger in the drops of beer. I look inside the circle and chant:

Mirror Mirror on the wall,
Spirits Spirits one and all,
I honor you, your guts and gall,
Listen listen to my call.

---

56 Interviewed by Michael G. Lloyd in *Bull of Heaven: The Mythic Life of Eddie Buczynski and the Rise of the New York Pagan* (Hubbardston, MA: Asphodel Press, 2012), 72-73.

I'm improvising! And the witch looked like the evil queen from Snow White, right? You don't have to rhyme when working spells, but if you can do that with language it feels more magical somehow. Sometimes it comes to me that way, or a scrap of nursery rhyme or folk wisdom sets me off. I raise my hands, palms outward, and take a deep breath. I don't know how much time passes but I feel the hair on the back of my neck stand up. I speak with a little more confidence.

Mirror Mirror on the wall,
Spirits Spirits one and all,
I honor you, your guts and gall,
Listen listen to my call.

Hello, hello, honored spirits of the Stonewall!!!! I love you, spirits of the Stonewall. It's nearly fifty years since you unleashed something explosive, something that has contributed a part of me to myself. I will never know who I am without you, and for that I am grateful. Because of that we'll always be together. It happened that night, but it began before it, our inextricable link, our shared path. You are my forebears and I am your heir. By the earth, by the fire, by the water, by the air, hear me now, I have only come to sing your praises and speak of your legacy.

We who are you, are all witches now, there are witches all around us. We, the enchanted, feel your presence and carry you with us. We, the enchanted, frolic and fuck and fight, as you have. We frolic and fuck and fight for ourselves and for you.

A lot of my ritual work is just opening up a space to talk to the dead. At the beginning it can be weird, ancient, rhyming, formal, but then I basically talk myself into intimacy with whomever shows up, much like I do with the embodied world.

The only difference is how quickly and frequently I talk about love to these spirits.

> *I just saw it happen, and I thought you'd all laugh and love to see it: a sisterwitch on Christopher Street using dance, using sex, using faggotry to push a straight man off our turf. It worked, for a few moments in time. The place was altered forever after she camped it up. She looked amazing: the evil queen in Snow White meets the Wicked Witch of the West, head to toe black, her face framed with a wicked widow's peak. And then she played Mozart. For you, for us.*

I felt my heart race faster as I thought about how the witch had used and referenced only items that would have been known to the girls of the Stonewall Inn: a 1937 Disney film, THE iconically gay film of 1939 that launched Judy Garland's career, an eighteenth-century opera. *That witch knew what she was doing,* and I believed it: *she knows what I'm doing now.*

I put on "Der Hölle Rache kocht in meinem Herzen" from *The Magic Flute*, the Queen of the Night aria played in the park.

> *She played a song for herself and a song for you—my glorious dead queens of the night. I love you. She loves you. The streets of New York are filled with people who love you. Many more people remain to learn about you and the minute they do they'll love you too. You are exactly who we have always longed to love.*
>
> *Let these songs be an offering to you whom I love, and whose memory I carry with me through all the world, in my frolicking, fucking, and fighting.*
>
> *Grant me your blessings, speak to me in my dreams, come find me whenever you need me, and I will give you my love and devotion. I am your acolyte, and grant that I may find ever more of your spirit on this earth, let me find more of*

you in this world, here and now. We need outpourings upon outpourings upon outpourings of you here now.

From here I poured out the rest of the beer in the sink, slammed a stray penny in my pocket onto the ledge, closed down the ritual, flushed the toilet, and went back out into the harsh light of day, feeling a little dazed and unnerved and weak in the knees, the way that I always feel after stepping outside of a circle of magic, blessed and blissed out and excited about the consequences I will face, most of them mysterious. In circles of magic, I have surrendered again and again to the unknown. Even when I get exactly what you want, it brings with it the unknown. All of the best moments of my life had begun with this surrender; and now through the gift of working at the bookshop, I'd made it almost daily practice. My sense of awareness was sharp, and my powers were heightened.

Doreen Valiente writes about scrying in terms of its different technologies, different kinds of mirrors. What you scry in is called a *speculum*, she says, with no mention of gynecology and the more chilling popular use of the word. A black bowl filled with water is her quick and dirty preference for scrying, easily assembled and easily dispatched. Crystal-gazing is one way, but not very common outside of the homes of elite ceremonial magicians who could afford them, and, historically, who could afford to be seen to own them without endangering their reputations. Valiente gathers together examples of the finest polished stones for crystal-gazing—green or blue beryl, jet or obsidian—the idea being that clear, colorless glass is a more recent tradition. For a long time, glass was an expensive luxury, not a common household feature—windows were covered up with paper or cloth. So: witches were said to use water in a bowl, or repurpose polished stones, or fisherman's glass floats, or old bottles filled with water, like the one made of blue glass the nineteenth-century Irish healer, Biddy Early was said to have used.

Valiente's recipe for making your own scrying mirror is a good one: take a round piece of glass, like one from an old round picture frame or the glass from an old clock. If it is slightly bowl-shaped or bent, choose the convex or upward-curving side, and paint it three coats of black paint. You must do this during the increase of the moon, while allowing each of the three coats of paint to dry completely before applying the next one. Valiente suggests framing the mirror somehow. Then, finding a nice box to store it in that can be closed to keep the speculum in darkness, wrapped in a black silk or velvet cloth. No magic mirror should be exposed to direct sunlight, she warns, or bright light in general, since this can ruin the charge of the object and its ability to work for you. Moonlight is the best for it and can charge the mirror with power. The best time to consecrate the object for use is during the full moon. I would add the suggestion that the moon be full in a water sign, to promote emotional connection and intuition.

Here is how to scry according to Valiente: sit in dim light, candlelight, keeping that light behind you. Then relax and look "intently but naturally" into the mirror. "There is no need to gaze in a strained, unwinking manner . . . The art of scrying needs concentration and practice" in order to see things in the mirror that will appear to mist over as you focus upon it, sometimes yielding symbols for you to interpret like you would in any system of divination, sometimes yielding more literal visions.[57] Valiente gives two examples of scrying with the mirror she consecrated while in a magic circle. The first was symbolic: she asked about her correspondence with an estranged friend, did the letter she just sent reach them? In the mirror she saw the symbol of an X-shaped cross and got the strong impression

57 Doreen Valiente, *An ABC of Witchcraft Past and Present*, (London: Robert Hale, 1986 reprinted from 1973) 302.

that their letters had crossed paths; sure enough, with the arrival of the mail, she had gotten a letter from the long silent friend who'd been moved to write, and their letters had crossed in the mail. In the other example, she saw a rugged scene of a desolate valley with large standing stones, a place she'd never been before, but not long after, was surprised to see firsthand when she visited Cornwall for the first time.

Scrying isn't a tradition I've participated in much; I'm of the *Bloody Mary* generation. I don't mean I was one of the Protestants murdered when Henry VIII's daughter Mary I ascended the throne of England in 1553 and tried to force Catholicism back on its people. I mean that from roughly sixth through eighth grade, at a handful of sleepovers, I was dared to chant Bloody Mary anywhere between three and thirteen times in the bathroom with the lights off and the door closed while staring into the mirror. I never saw anything, so figured it wasn't for me. Then I read about mirror scrying in general and found that a lot of the folklore concerns women looking in a mirror in order to see either 1) a glimpse of their future husband 2) a skull symbolizing that they'd die before marriage. I was a very "death before marriage" kind of kid and I didn't need a mirror to tell me that.

But I'd always had an attraction to old mirrors. After begging, *begging*, my parents to take me to the Philadelphia Museum of Art for the first time to see a Salvador Daliexhibition in 2005, I had my first experience with one. After taking in a glut of art by one of the weirdest people I had access to at age seventeen, I will never forget the real star of my visit, found while wandering into the European galleries. I was drawn to a mirror in a simply carved wooden frame from the fifteenth century. Something about looking into it made me feel crazy—like I was walking along and suddenly there I was framed by something so old. I felt captivated as in captured. It was just the next thing on the wall, hung without fanfare and without much comment, like it was no big deal, a casual survival of over five hundred years. I swooned calculating its age: *How many people have looked into this mirror?* I looked in and probably because I was a champion disassociator I felt like I could see some of them, eyes and facial expression from totally different times, changing, flickering qualities of light. Something moved me to say: *Hello!* I felt stupid but it just felt right, like, *Hello in there!* But feeling silly was always the usual sign I was onto something spiritual. I picked up the habit of speaking into mirrors then, I don't know why. But only when I got a strong sense that *this mirror has seen some real freaky shit!*

Over a decade later, the feeling of deep movement and connection across time hit me again at Preston Park Manor, just outside of Brighton, where Doreen Valiente lived—this time, in front of a mirror on the wall nestled in a wooden frame carved in the shape of a witch's friendly face, pointy hat and all. The mirror had belonged to Valiente herself—like much of her magical collection, she had thrifted it from Snooper's Paradise in the Brighton Arcades. As I tried to focus on speaking to Valiente through the mirror and thanking her, modern mother of the Craft, my girlfriend came up behind me and took our photo together. We looked great in that photo, smitten. Like maybe Doreen Valiente had given her blessing? We rode our bikes to Snooper's Paradise to see what magical kitsch we could find for our own. My refrain to mirrors remained: *Hello! Whatever is left of you who have looked here, show yourself to me. Come out into the open where I can see you.* But I'd never really felt myself to have gotten a response other than an honest sense of awe that, for a long time, people have sought to capture their own reflections. As someone who'd mostly avoided my own, it fascinated me. Looking for other people in the mirror made it easier to see myself, or, coming up with a weird reason to look into old mirrors helped me to justify why mirrors had always seemed *eerie.*

My scrying at the Stonewall had a more literal result than I would have imagined when, eight months later, the spirits of the Stonewall contacted me through an eBay listing. It takes time to materialize from beyond the grave and beyond the mirror—I'm not talking about the cheesecloth spiritualists swallowed and threw up at seances and claimed to be ectoplasm. I'm talking objects with heft: bound books, paper, ink, photographs, typescripts. I found the materialization I was looking for by what I perceived, in my limited human mind, as chance. It simply occurred to me to look on ebay one night, because I hadn't in awhile, on leap day, 2020.

Scrolling late at night I came upon an item for sale described as: "1950s LGBT GAY Trans Scrapbook Jewel Box Revue, Photos, Autographs, Jackie Maye." The scrapbook wasn't well photographed in the listing, blurry images of it, a plain green binding with the word "Photographs" stamped in gold on the cover. The opening pages featured photos cut out from magazines and headshots of James Dean, Lucille Ball, and a famous female impersonator of the time, Jackie Maye aka John Rushmore Crandall. The Jewel Box Revue I had heard of. Founded in Miami in 1939 by two lovers, Doc Benner and Danny Brown, it was the earliest known traveling show to be racially integrated, and that was dangerously radical at the time and in the decades following. The revue famously advertised having "25 Men and 1 Woman;" could audience members guess who was the "real" woman? It was Stormé DeLarverie, a male impersonator and emcee of the show. DeLarverie was also at the Stonewall Inn on June 28, 1969, resisting arrest, standing up to cops, standing with the queens throwing a shower of pennies in self-defense. I had spoken my intentions clearly into the mirror of the Stonewall Inn. Now, here was my response.

The seller had found the album in a storage locker whose contents they'd successfully bid on in Arizona. They were still based in the USA, so I had it shipped to a friend in Brooklyn, and then, because my girlfriend was going there for work, she picked it up and brought it back to London. There were over two hundred photographs, some beginning in the late fifties, the majority of them dated from the early sixties: 1962, 1963. There were also a few programs from Jewel Box Revue performances, one of which had been cut up and used for scrapbooking purposes alongside some newspaper clippings.

Page six was the threshold page; moving from headshots and press photos to the creator's own photographs. The woman who had made the album was named Nancy DeLisle, sometimes Nancy Terry, and from some receipts kept in the album, it's clear she had worked as a photographer in Toledo, Ohio. There was a handwritten inscription on page six that read: "For those under "21," or folks who don't appreciate "Show Business" — For the rest of the Album there is..." This is over a black and white photograph of a drag queen named Chunga—that is, Chunga Ochoa, choreographer and premiere dancer of the Jewel Box Revue—pointing to a sign reading "POSITIVELY NO ADMITTANCE." On either side of the photograph there were pasted cut-outs of cartoon pin-up girls and: "DANGER CURVES AHEAD."

Turn the page and we're launched into the world of the Jewel Box Revue girls: singing and dancing on stage, beating their faces backstage in sweaty, smoky photos, and living their lives offstage. There are photographs of Jackie Maye out of drag with his lover Eddie Fisher, probably a sailor, definitely a hunk, posing shirtless in the sun and showing off the swallow tattoos on his chest. There is a photograph of Jackie ("Jacks") as an infant. There are photographs of Maye and Fisher on a trip to Old Faithful, at a post office in Wyoming, opposite photos of Maye getting ready for a show in her dressing room. More than a fan or audience member, the intimacy and variety of these photographs show that Nancy had built true friendships with performers in the Revue: Jackie Maye, Ralph Albert, Laurie Knight, Gita Gilmore, and Chunga. About twenty pages in there's a photograph of the photographer herself, labelled, "Chunga and Me," the queen in full beat, perched daintily on Nancy's lap. She's holding up a cocktail, toasting the photographer and now me, the glass obscures part of her chin but her look is unmistakable in its bravado. She's wearing a suit and her hair is done up so as to look short, her other arm around Chunga and her hand firmly grabbing Chunga's thigh.

In the same spread of photographs, we see Stormé DeLarverie for the first time in blurry black and white photographs, dressed in a turban, performing from the "Arabian Nights" number of the Revue, a radiant smile on her face. On the next page there's a sequence of ten photographs showing DeLarverie in a double-breasted mauve suit, alone, in a spotlight before a microphone singing, gesticulating like any crooner of the time. On the next page, tucked behind a headshot of DeLarverie in a white tuxedo, there's a letter. At this point I'm shaking from the experience of encountering this photo album, everything it had survived to remain so crisp and clean, in such pristine condition, and now a letter, written in big butch boxed capital letters on paper decorated with pinstripes:

WED

Hi—

Was sitting in the Dressing Room - and talking to Bob. So thought this would be a fine time to thank you for the pictures. They were real fine. Thank you very much.

How's every thing by you—hope this finds you well + having a wonderful time. Say Hello to everyone for Me.

I know this isn't much of a letter. Will try to do better next time.

Nancy I wonder if you would send me the negatives to these pictures. So I could have 5x7's made. I sent the

pictures so you would know which one's I wanted —
Thanks Baby—Take care of Yourself + Be Sweet.

My Best,
Stormé

P.S. Hello from Joyce

I was lightheaded. I was riveted to my seat. The clarity of the letter hit me physically. I pictured Stormé DeLarverie sitting in her dressing room on a Wednesday night. ("Bob" is a common name backstage at the Revue, so it's hard to know who she's talking to: Bobby Lake? Bobby Snyder? A few pages later in the album, there's Bobby Synder posing in various costumes, then with a lover named "Joe," then hugging an older woman with a caption in Nancy's hand: "Finally! At Last! Bobby's Mom, Selma Snyder")

The letter is my favorite kind of revelation: a quiet moment, a remnant of long distance friendship and easy intimacy, writing to Nancy to thank her for photos and ask for a favor—basically a work-based letter with flashes of intimacy: "Thanks Baby," "Be Sweet," "Hello from Joyce." My girlfriend is looking at the album with me, we both have tears in our eyes and take a moment to hold hands over the photo album. "It's just about friendship," she says. And she's right; we can't truly reconstruct the chaos of what happened the nights that DeLarverie would describe as a Rebellion, not a Riot, a few years later at Stonewall in 1969, but we can glimpse the fragments and friendships that create the momentum and add up to a meaningful life, a world worth fighting for.

From here on in the album, Stormé DeLarverie comes and goes among other emerging friendships: a drag queen called Little Joe doing a striptease, photographs and a letter from Sandy Howard, including a photo of her dressed as a bride with a line of six other people, all cross-dressing, with Nancy herself in a man's suit. There's a photo of a butch lesbian leaning on a car labelled "Smitty." There are photos of a Halloween costume competition, with "Don Beverly as Sophia LOREN."

Finally, tucked into the back of the album is a three-page typescript dated "1954," earlier than any of the photographs themselves, with an anonymous, disarming confession:

> The most eligible looking fellows . . . the ones who dress neat and clean and look like a walking Hat advertisement are just not to be had. They're either already taken or they are living with another man. A girl couldn't get to more than polite words with them. But don't waste your time . . . they're man-made and theres no two ways about it.
>
> Still I won't give up hoping for the Right fellow. This disgust for people is only temporary, I hope. I say people because I am including women in with all those crazy men. You see—not liking men doesn't mean you like women only. When I say it . . . it means . . . I don't like women, too. This decision puts me totally in the middle between Men, Women, and It's. So after much deliberation I conclude that I am by my own preference disengaging myself from all three sexes and throwing myself wholeheartedly into the abyss of compromise; Merely another spectator of human events counting the days until something or someone changes my mental attitude toward being a part of God's world.

And:

> Each day seems like it may be the last one I'll ever see. Can't seem to picture any kind of a future. And all for one reason . . . All because I'm hanging on to a thread of hope that I can find happiness in a friendship without sex.

The ambivalence and despair here seem related to the album itself—talking about sexuality, homosexuality, bisexuality, asexuality—and yet the album's contents literally picture the future this writer made for herself, a future of friendship and partying and travel and crossdressing. And unmistakably, happiness and love. The album survives a counter-argument to this unsigned, private reflection—significant enough to its owner to be typed up in a fair, crisp copy. Whoever Nancy was, she had the capacity for happiness, and she found it at least for the moments in time documented here.

I remained the custodian of Nancy's Photo Album for one year, but it was a pandemic year, so it felt much longer. The time I spent poring over its pages with reverence for my own friendships was charged with a new kind of desperation. I wrote letters to my friends near and far, late at night, leaning on the album to rub off its friendly energy onto my notes, telling people I loved them and I missed them and I wished them good health. I printed talismans carved into linoleum in thick inks to ward off the latest plague and sent them out into the world with my letters, a spell of multiplication. I lit candles and spoke to the spirits captured in the photographs. I posted pictures online and wrote a few articles about the book, spreading its contents as a kind of gospel. Spreading them to give people a break from the relentlessness of the collapse we were living through.

By the end of the year, a curator I knew at Harvard had seen an essay I'd written about the album and contacted me: would I be interested in selling it? He was working on an exhibition about American Drag; he could promise the album would be well cared for, living among photographs from the same time period—kindred spirits. It would be digitized and freely available, used in teaching classes.

The money I made selling the album to him—it cost $1,000 on eBay, and however priceless it seemed, I asked $5,000 for it—was a huge amount of money for me, I'd never made such a profit reselling a book.

I disturbed myself: I'd worked in libraries or bookshops my whole adult life leading up to the occult bookshop, and the gentle economy of it hadn't really bothered me before. Bookselling was an old, old profession that felt wholesome. Booksellers flatter themselves they're doing a net positive for "culture" and "the arts and humanities" and by and large it's true, I flattered myself in that way. It's not arms dealing. It's not big pharma. It's nowhere close to the prices of the art world. And then my specialism in rare and secondhand books—much less harmful to the trees!

Years earlier, I worked for a firm in London that had specialized in books printed from the 1450s until the turn of the eighteenth century—rarer, fancier, much higher end books whose retail prices occasionally soared into five figures. But that hadn't phased me, because it was someone else's money, someone else's books. I counted myself as lucky to have handled the rarities and gems of western print history: works by Kepler and Copernicus on the heavens, Vesalius on the human body, Gesner's weird history of *Foure-footed Beastes* and other natural histories. And of course, works on witchcraft and magic: Reginald Scot's *Discoverie of Witchcraft* and similar condemnations of the witch hunts written by Johannes Weyer. Weyer's teacher Heinrich Agrippa's *Three Books of Occult Philosophy,* and then books advocating for the arrest and execution of witches by Nicholas Rémy and Jean Bodin. Centuries old, the high values placed upon these volumes felt so abstract to me. And as I was scandalously underpaid at this job, I didn't really experience any benefit from the profit I was making for the company by researching and selling them.

The trade in rare books and archival materials related to queer and trans history had, over the course of my time in the book trade, exploded. Suddenly every bigot who'd dissed me both to my face and *behind my back* was selling books, photo albums, archives labelled "Of LGBT Interest." People who'd said they didn't think *people like me should be married.* Or looked at my suits and asked, *So do you really think you're a man?*, Booksellers who'd never hired a queer and never intended to were issuing "Pride Month" catalogues asking tens of thousands of dollars for books by Oscar Wilde. And here I was, using magic to find these rare materials that old colleagues wanted to buy. When I'd gotten my first job in the trade in 2010 I'd been the only out out out dyke. The few gay men there were hit or miss, subject to internalized homophobia and externalized misogyny. And there weren't any trans people at the antiquarian bookfairs or in the trade associations. What did it mean to use my training as a historian and instincts as a bookseller, to set up on my own, trucking in queer and trans heritage—like this photo album I barely wanted to part with?

Well, rich people got help all the time: inherited wealth to underwrite unpaid internships, introductions and references, careers without even applying for a job, money for a down payment on an apartment. I had seen the good that did a person, the stability it gave them. But I was mystified as to how I was going to get by without all that *help*. And then I walked into the Stonewall giddy with excitement over a funny story I wanted to share with some ghosts and walked out on a path to an inheritance that would change my life. The $4,000 profit was exactly the windfall I'd needed to sign up with an online service called GenderGP that would give me my diagnosis for gender dysphoria and then give me a shady Romanian prescription for hormones—the best that was possible in a healthcare system with an eight-year waiting list to get a consultation at the gender identity clinic. I had prayed, and my prayers had been answered. So, I can honestly claim: chanting into a mirror, conjuring up a couple hundred photos of drag performers, and Harvard University, paid for the start of my sex change.

CODA: SLOW MAGIC

There are spells I've done with immediate results—for instance, offering candles, roses, and poundcake to St. Expeditus for a top surgery date which worked almost too quickly to keep up with—and then there are spells I've performed and come away from feeling sweaty and faint and trusted to have worked, only to find their consequences tap into something much bigger than instant gratification. This has been true for the magic I have brought about through writing, printing zines, and scattering them at astrologically timed intervals. And it is especially true for the magic involved in writing this book, which is a culmination of the sum of my experiences as a witch in search of spiritual fulfillment, artistic expression, and cosmic love.

Here's the slower than slow magic: it's a Saturday morning in October 2019. I'm tabling at a bookfair in the basement of the Barbican, a brutalist concrete ziggurat in the heart of London with performance spaces and little flats that sell for a million pounds. It's been a year of striking out on my own from Treadwell's as an artist and bookseller, although I'm still a regular at the shop. I've done administrative work in exchange for a free table at the bookfair portion of a feminist festival held at the Barbican, and like all free things, it's the worst table on offer. No natural lighting, barely any artificial light, around the corner from most of the other booksellers. At least I'll have a good time, because who should be tabling next to me but my old boss at the bookshop, The Witch Queen herself! However much we see one another I miss her, it's hard to go from the daily intimacy of working toward a shared vision, to turning off to take up a new path. She's family now, and always will be, the day won't be a waste of time because now we'll have seven hours to catch up.

I've set up my table with charged crystals and letterpress posters I produced on an old printing press as part of a ritual engagement with queer history. I'm really doing it! I have some zines to sell that I made, some prints, and other printed goods on behalf of friends, some medium-rare books on offer. I'm still broke, selling books I love from my own library, hoping they'll go to good homes: like first edition, signed copies of Marge Piercy's *A Woman on the Edge of Time* and my favorite Daphne Du Maurier novel, *The House on the Strand.* It's fairly quiet: most of the exhibitors are bigger publishers with new books, it's not really a zine fair so I'm something of an anomaly. It's a long day, fairly slow, my badly positioned table doing me no favors. Most people who find me say, *Oh wow, I had no idea you were back here.* The book fair is part of a larger day of programming, there are lectures and workshops to keep people occupied.

Off in the distance of the large hall, I see the backs of two women walking toward the exit, and one stops abruptly and turns around to look at me. I had just been staring off into middle-distance but when it happened—what stuck with me was how from that distance it looked like she'd been jerked around and forced to look. She watches me for a few second and then goes outside with the others to take a picture together. She returns inside and makes a beeline for me. I recognize her as the writer Michelle Tea. How amazing: I love her writing, it had influenced me deeply and opened up new ideas about the kind of shenanigans I could get up to, new daydreams about the kind of girls I could love who might love me back. Books like *Valencia* and *Black Wave* had given me companionship in dark and confusing times.

"So is this some kind of community bookshop?" she asks.

"Well, kind of, it's me and my prints, zines by my friends, and rare and used books by authors I love, but it's just a traveling bookshop for now. Someday it will be a real place I think, that's the big dream at least." Ugh, telling Michelle Tea about my "dreams," so boring. I felt myself getting very nervous, very unlike me.

"That's cool."

"Here, have a print, I made it as a keepsake for today."

It's a small letterpress print that I'd made from wood and lead, my girlfriend had illustrated it with stamps of suns in red, yellow, orange. It read: THERE'S NOTHING NEW UNDER THE SUN / BUT THERE ARE NEW SUNS. / -OCTAVIA BUTLER. It was one of my favorite poems, and it was also the text that had given the bookfair and festival its name. I'd printed sixty-six copies of them on the sun's day beginning at the sun's hour, wearing my gold robes and chewing on sunflower and marigold petals.

"Thanks!"

I feel shaky, my palms sweating, I really didn't know what to say. It was bizarre, my nerves felt disproportionate to the encounter. I moved into host mode as a kind of autopilot, insisting she meet The Witch Queen, so Treadwell's would stock the book about Tarot she'd just published. This was all a cover to give me time to think and feel: *Something important is happening!!* my body was telling me. It was one of very few times in my life where my internal voice sounded like a voice I didn't know, certainly not my own: *Pay Attention, Pay Attention, Pay Attention.* But I didn't know what it was or what it meant. I was just getting momentous vibes, like, this uncanny sense that I was meeting someone I was meant to know. My girlfriend and another friend, Sim, had been hanging around and were staring at me. "Wow," said Sim, "What was that about?"

I wasn't sure, which meant I wasn't sure if I'd blown it or not. I followed @michelleteaz online and as the months gave way to the outbreak of a global pandemic, I didn't think about it much. *Maybe we'll cross paths again at some point? Maybe we're meant to be friends?* In my voracious pandemic reading I kept buying books that thanked Michelle Tea: Brontez Purnell, Cooper Lee Bombardier, Bett Williams. *Maybe she's meant to be some kind of writing mentor?* And then she started a podcast about Magic. *Maybe I'm meant to go into podcasting about magic?* But that didn't feel right either, I was a printer. At one point I started to draft an email: *Hi, you probably don't remember me, but if you ever wanted to do a zine or book versions of your podcast, I could help design and print them.* I deleted the draft.

I was getting frustrated by the nagging feeling, an interior voice that kept saying: Pay attention! I didn't know what to look for, I felt obsessive and a little frantic but I didn't quite know about what. I kept hearing: *Keep Watching Keep Watching.* I kept revisiting the encounter: was there anything that I had overlooked?

One day, March 10th, Michelle Tea posted about a book that had just been published called: *Make Your Art No Matter What*, by Beth Pickens. I made a mental note to order the book. I forgot the mental note, it was overwhelmed by too much time on social media where the constraints of posting level the meaning of everything by obliterating it altogether. Then on April 8th Michelle Tea posted about the book again. I ordered the book then and there so I wouldn't forget: *Make Your Art No Matter What.* On the one hand I'd never read a self-help book, on the other hand, I had barely read anything that hadn't thanked Michelle Tea in the acknowledgements. And I was having trouble getting my life together I didn't really have any "adults" giving me support or encouragement or mentorship of any kind. How could I be an artist? All of the artists I knew had older people who cared about their work. All of the artists I knew had gone to one of two art schools in London and kept very closed ranks when it came to sharing opportunities. Even at this festival that brought together artists, I was treated purely like staff. I wanted structure and a sense of direction, and in its absence, I did what I'd always done in the absence of adult supervision: I found a book to help me out.

Something clicked when the book arrived, and I devoured it in a sitting. *I have to find out more about this author.* There she was in her author photo, wow, a real babe, image credit to Amos Mac, what a small world, I loved his *Original Plumbing,* it had been a lifeline. Anything can be a sign, everything felt like a sign. I availed myself of the laziest version of following that little voice again: I found Beth Pickens online. It was one of many things I didn't realize were all part of the slow magic that was years in the making: carving a space in the world for myself as an artist, acting on the increasingly dangerous unease in my own body by seeking out healthcare and hormones, taking seriously how ready I was to return to the USA, how exhausted I'd been trying to make a living in London, the OG hostile austere metropolis of empire with a huge and corrupt financial services industry.

That summer I inoculated a book with oyster mushrooms, an open-ended, freestyle spell: I wanted to cook up and eat a book I loved, I wanted to cook up and eat a book that had the kind of personality I needed more of in my life. In the Book of Revelation, St. John consults an angel and asks for a scroll. The angel gives him the scroll and says: *Take it, and eat it up; and it shall make thy belly bitter, but it shall be in thy mouth sweet as honey.* This was my own riff on revelation: take and cook up and eat a book that would help me figure out how to move my life back to the USA. I wanted to pick a book that really got me and one that I had read several times, so I choose my well-loved copy of Francesca Lia Block's *Weetzie Bat.* It took weeks for the spores to weave themselves into a mycelium and produce fruiting bodies. I sautéed the mushrooms in butter and rosemary and ate them on toast, wondering how eating *Weetzie Bat* would alter my reality.

A month later I saw Beth Pickens post on social media about a kind of accountability group she facilitated to help artists. Turned out, she was based in LA, Weetzie Bat's world. I joined the group.

The first time I saw Beth Pickens in October and heard her speak I was struck by a thought in another voice like lightning: *This is why you ran into Michelle Tea. This is the next step. This person is going to be in your life.* I wasn't articulate, or able to actually translate into language the jolt I'd experienced in my body which I now know meant: *This person is the absolute love of your life in every lifetime you've lived and will live. This person is who you have taught yourself to find through years of listening carefully to yourself.* I didn't even believe in past lives at that point, it was a cosmology I respected for other people, not me. I guess it makes sense to me that bodies can feel momentousness, but minds are overburdened with so much baggage they can get incapable of registering it with much precision. I hate metaphors, but one that comes to mind is a broken Geiger counter. Still, the moment I saw her I knew I'd made progress even if I didn't quite understand the extent of it. And from practice, I knew I had to stick with a feeling that was both familiar—intuition—and novel, leading me somewhere I'd never been.

The same month Michelle Tea's Magical Podcast announced they were starting a bookclub. A-HA! I knew from experience what book clubs could do for me, so I joined. *Maybe we're meant to be in a book club together? Maybe this was the next step?* I was high on the brain chemicals of feeling like I'd made progress and hungry for more positive reinforcement. I was also impatient, I wanted something big to happen in my life, I kept praying every night before bed: *I'm ready I'm ready I'm ready for something big*. I kept it vague, I didn't know what, I just wanted change.

The inaugural bookclub would happen in Sagittarius Season. My whole self was ready, and it was time to fully petition the gods for insight—who better than Mercury, the swift messenger? Given the eight-hour time difference I would stay up late into the evening to tune into this online book club. I set up my laptop in a circle of eight orange candles into which I had carved the sigil of Mercury and written COMMUNIC8 MY F8. Using an online planetary hours calculator, at each hour of Mercury I lit the candles, burned lavender incense, drew out and burned the magic square of Mercury, and chanted the orphic hymn to Hermes eight times before petitioning the god: "COMMUNICATE MY FATE." Given the time difference, the book club would coincide with the last hour of Mercury before sunrise. I'd stay up all night working in the studio and printing so that the candles would burn all the way down. I needed to know if my internal voice—the one I'd been listening to—was an angel or a demon. The book club happened, I was too tired and spacey to really participate. I tried not to smile too crazily with my video on but my sound muted as I felt myself surrounded by candles and billowing incense that the little people boxed on my computer screen couldn't see. I don't believe in doing magic on people without their consent, but doing magic surrounded by oblivious online participants felt fine somehow. Was I crossing a line? I closed my laptop and recited the Orphic hymn to Hermes a final eight times, feeling totally spent, burnt out as the candles burned down.

> *Dire weapon of the tongue, which men revere, be present, Hermes, and thy suppliant hear;*
> *Assist my works, conclude my life with peace, give graceful speech, and me memory's increase.*

I went outside to the river to watch the sun rise, then home to rest an hour or two. Nothing happened beyond the crazy feeling of missing a night's sleep, there would be no instant gratification for whatever was going on in my life. You never know when you'll be faced with Hermes the trickster rather than Hermes the messenger, you just have to trust that whomever you meet gives you the lesson you need. I thought the spell didn't work.

It would take another two years of fairly ignorant decision-making to meet Beth Pickens in person and become aware, for the first time in this lifetime, of love as both deep memory and endless potential. There were major steps to take to prepare myself: I had to get sober, I had to get hormones, I had to continue to get quiet long enough to listen to myself. Once I'd made these big decisions, I had to follow them to their conclusions in the small ways they crept up in my daily life. I had to choose loving myself in the smallest and biggest, most dramatic ways at once, in order to redirect my life and my loyalties toward myself. I had to learn the lessons of Saturn once again, but this time, during my Jupiter return, a time of expansion and benevolence. It didn't occur to me that in returning to the essence of myself—a transsexual—in ways sometimes selfish, sometimes cruel, sometimes messy, sometimes desperate, but always doing the best I could with what I knew to be true at the time—I was preparing for something more heightened. My fifth house of sex and creativity was starting to light up with Jupiter's movement through it, my Jupiter return, and through its conjunction with the north node. Then, a month after I met Beth and knew I'd have to change my entire life to be closer to her in LA, I received an email on the day of the Aries eclipse from Michelle Tea: *Do you want to to write a book about witchcraft for my imprint?* After a lifetime of devotion to books, and years of involvement in countercultures of their publication and circulation, I still could not have imagined how sweet this culmination would be.

My moments of snatching agency and awareness from growing mushrooms, anointing candles, casting circles, chanting hymns, and ultimately cultivating an interior voice to trust, were coordinates on a map much larger than I could comprehend at any time in their unfolding. As I write this, the spell is still unfurling, and as slow as it must go, I know I have surrendered to the swift current of a witchcraft much more vast than I can grasp. It was only when sitting down to write this book and comb over my memories of working at Treadwell's that I realized the dream that first signaled my deeper initiation has come to its fullest expression: the doors of the bookshop *have* opened out into a desert where I now live, yet could have never imagined living at the time.

Between Saturn's return and Jupiter's return, I found a deeper love for myself and for the world. I write my books with Michelle Tea sitting across from me, we throw parties and sing songs on a karaoke machine in the living room. I live my life with Beth Pickens among the Joshua Trees, creosote, and cactus in a desert of hulking, living rock formations, hundreds of millions of years old. Our lives have joined together in ecstatic communion and we're planning our next moves, casting our latest spells, and thanking our lucky stars.

ACKNOWLEDGEMENTS

Nothing is written in a vacuum, and *Bargain Witch* is filled with books not only to invoke the feeling of working in a bookshop but also as an act of devotion to the authors that have given my life meaning and made me dare to write. I thank all of the writers quoted in this book and all of the writers whose books I have yet to read and love! When my best friend Alvin, read a draft of this book, they said it made them want to write, and I hope this book makes you want to write too. I can't wait to meet the weirdos *Bargain Witch* brings into my life!

There are many whose love has contributed to this book in some way over the years:

RIP Lisa Jardine, Rudolph Slobins, Johnny McQuillan, who brought magic, friendship, and learning into my life that continues beyond death.

Thanks to the Witches of Treadwell's: Martin Bladh, Michelle Chaso, Coco Corr, Suzanne Corbie, Phil Hine, Carl Holmes, Sim Grey Ritson, Fleur Shearman, Marco Visconti.

Thanks to my Gay's the Word witches, Uli Lenart, Jim McSweeney, Erica Gillingham.

Thanks to the UK Witches I hold dear: Louisa Bailey, Jamie Bauermeister, Joyce Cronin, Simon Goode, Lauren J. Joseph, Bones Tan Jones, Hudda Khaireh, Heiba Lamara, Esther McManus, Marlowe Mortimer, Rose Nordin, Morgan M. Page, Sophie Pau, Ames Pennington, Richard Porter, John Raimo, Gemma Rolls-Bentley, Paul Sammut, E-J Scott, Jordan Taylor, Gregory Vass, Kaiya Waerea, Sam Whetton, Danielle

Wilde, Ira Yonemura. Thanks to Jason Atomic and the Satanic Fleamarket for facilitating occulture. Thanks to Rosie Cooper and Wysing Arts Centre, and Chloe Page and Hannah Wallis who brought me there to be an artist-in-residence the summer of 2022, where I finally had time to rest and dream of this book in a field of sunflowers.

Thanks to the Witches of the East Coast, my oldest friends: DIY or Die goddess Grace Ambrose, Dirtbag Medievalist Megan Cook, God's gift Charlie Frohne, True Wizard Jesse Harding, Leatherdaddy Supremo Gerard Leone, Sister of the Moon Lauren Mancuso, Ethereal Fairy Shelley Marlow, Michael Tom Vassallo who first made me watch *The Craft*, Bibliomancer Dreamboat Thomas Ward, Loyal Witch and Beloved Angel Bilge Uz.

Thanks to the Witches of the West Coast, who initiated me into California: Amelia Ada, Sydney Baloue, Lucky Benson, Vera Blossom, Seth Bogart, Jibz Cameron, Sam Cohen, Cal Dobbs, Sam Early, Amanda Yates Garcia, Clement Goldberg, Amanda Faye Jimenez, Hedi el Kholti, Amos Mac, Karla Nielson, Carolyn Pennypacker Riggs, Stacy Wood. Thanks to Susan Stryker for *everything*. Thanks to Vishnu Dass for the Steven Arnold photo. Thanks and blessed be to the QVC. Thanks to the Huntington Library and Botanical Gardens, where I was a writer-in-residence the autumn of 2023, and could start writing this book in the desert garden. Quotes from pre-1800 works on witchcraft come from books I consulted there, with special thanks to Sandra Brooke-Gordon, Susan Jester, Sarah Francis, Pamela Garrison, Chris Lutz, Jazmin Rue-Pinchem, and everyone at reader services for making me feel so welcome.

Thanks to my beloved writing group: Marie Condron, Emilia Richeson-Valiente, Anya Ventura, I would not have finished this book without your consistent generosity, and all of the feedback you gave me with my best interests at heart. You Make Writing Fun (sung to the tune of "You Make Loving

Fun" by Fleetwood Mac). New writer friends who came into my life and brought distinct magic and genius and accountability: Patricia Zabellos, Kirk Read, Sara Greenberger Rafferty, Erin Markey, Kaelen Medeiros, Amanda Verwey.

Profound gratitude to my trusted early readers, whose deep care and perspectives carried me over the finish line: dreamy Pisces poet James La Marre and Witch Baby Genius BFFAAF Alvin Frohne.

Thank you Christina Oakley-Harrington, The Witch Queen, for so many years and counting of friendship anchored in spiritual pursuits and good humor.

Thank you visionary Michelle Tea who is the most generous writer and reader, there is no better witch to publish with! I feel so lucky I get to make the kind of book I have always wanted to see more of in the world: a book that thanks you in its acknowledgements for your support and hype!

Thank you Frankie, the wild beast who saved me, and Sammy, the baby sealpig.

Thank you Beth Pickens, my perfect one, you make me the richest person alive and I love you more every day.

Photo by Amos Mac

Brooke Palmieri is a writer and artist working at the intersection of memory, history, and transsexual alternate realities. His writing spans hundreds of years of queer and trans history; the magic, mystery and deep emotion of working in archives; and the past as a supernatural encounter. Brooke has trained as a historian at the University of Pennsylvania and Oxford, and in 2017 completed a PhD in radical 17th century printing history at University College London. In 2018, Brooke founded CAMP BOOKS to promote access to queer and trans history through rare archival materials, cheap zines, and sculptural installations. Born and raised in Philadelphia, he spent fourteen years in London and now lives in the Mojave Desert. http://bspalmieri.com

Publisher contact:
The MIT Press
Massachusetts Institute of Technology
77 Massachusetts Avenue, Cambridge, MA 02139
mitpress.mit.edu

EU Authorised Representative:
Easy Access System Europe, Mustamäe tee 50,
10621 Tallinn, Estonia
gpsr.requests@easproject.com

Printed by Integrated Books International,
United States of America